General Editor: M. Rolf Olsen

Tavistock Library of
Social Work Practice

Behaviour Modification

Behaviour Modification

Theory, practice, and philosophy

BRIAN SHELDON

TAVISTOCK PUBLICATIONS
London and New York

First published in 1982 by
Tavistock Publications Ltd
11 New Fetter Lane, London EC4P 4EE
Published in the USA by
Tavistock Publications
in association with Methuen, Inc.
733 Third Avenue, New York, NY 10017

© 1982 Brian Sheldon
General editor's foreword © 1982 M. Rolf Olsen

Photoset by
Nene Phototypesetters Ltd, Northampton
and printed in Great Britain at the
University Press, Cambridge

All rights reserved. No part of this book may be reprinted or reproduced or utilized in any form or by any electronic, mechanical or other means, now known or hereafter invented, including photocopying and recording, or in any information storage or retrieval system, without permission in writing from the publishers.

British Library Cataloguing in Publication Data

Sheldon, Brian
Behaviour Modification. – (Tavistock
library of social work practice)
1. Behaviour modification
I. Title
153.8'5   BF637.B4
ISBN 0–422–77060–4
ISBN 0–422–77070–1 Pbk

Library of Congress Cataloging in Publication Data

Sheldon, Brian.
Behaviour modification.
(Tavistock library of social work practice)
Bibliography: p.
Includes index.
1. Social case work – Great Britain.
2. Social case work – Great Britain – Moral and ethical aspects. 3. Behavior modification.
4. Behaviorism (Psychology)   I. Title.
II. Series.
HV245.S47   361.3'01'9   81–23313
ISBN 0–422–77060–4   AACR2
ISBN 0–422–77070–1 (pbk.)

Contents

General editor's foreword vii
Acknowledgements ix
Preface xi

1 The disciplinary context *1*
2 The philosophical implications of behaviourism *23*
3 Theories of learning *38*
4 Emotional reactions *92*
5 Assessment and evaluation *98*
6 Stimulus control (contingency management) techniques *142*
7 Response control techniques *180*
8 Ethical considerations *222*
 Appendix: Checking baseline/outcome differences by simple statistical measurement *246*

References 251
Name index 264
Subject index 267

General editor's foreword

Tavistock Library of Social Work Practice is a new series of books primarily written for practitioners and students of social work and the personal social services, but also for those who work in the allied fields of health, education, and other public services. The series represents the collaborative effort of social work academics, practitioners, and managers. In addition to considering the theoretical and philosophical debate surrounding the topics under consideration, the texts are firmly rooted in practice issues and the problems associated with the organization of the services. Therefore the series will be of particular value to undergraduate and post-graduate students of social work and social administration.

The series was prompted by the growth and increasing importance of the social services in our society. Until recently there has been a general approbation of social work, reflected in a benedictory increase in manpower and resources, which has led to an unprecedented expansion of the personal social services, a proliferation of the statutory duties placed upon them, and major reorganization. The result has been the emergence of a profession faced with the immense responsibility of promoting individual and social betterment, and bearing a primary responsibility to advocate on behalf of individuals and groups who do not always fulfil or respect normal social expectations of behaviour. In spite of the growth in services these tasks are often carried out with inadequate resources, an uncertain knowledge base, and as yet unresolved difficulties associated with the reorganization of the personal social services in 1970. In recent years these difficulties have been compounded by a level of criticism unprecedented since the Poor Law. The anti-social work critique has fostered some improbable alliances between groups of social administrators, sociologists, doctors, and the media, united in their belief that social work has failed in its general obligation to 'provide services to the people', and in its particular duty to socialize the delinquent, restrain parents who abuse their children, prevent old people from dying alone, and provide a satisfactory level of community care for the sick, the chronically handicapped, and the mentally disabled.

These developments highlight three major issues that deserve particular attention. First, is the need to construct a methodology for analysing social and personal situations and prescribing action; second, is the necessity to apply techniques that measure the performance of the individual worker and the profession as a whole in meeting stated objectives; third, and outstanding, is the requirement to develop a knowledge base against which the needs of clients are understood and decisions about their care are taken. Overall, the volumes in this series make explicit and clarify these issues; contribute to the search for the distinctive knowledge base of social work; increase our understanding of the aetiology and care of personal, familial, and social problems; describe and explore new techniques and practice skills; aim to raise our commitment towards low status groups which suffer public, political, and professional neglect; and to promote the enactment of comprehensive and socially just policies. Above all, these volumes aim to promote an understanding which interprets the needs of individuals, groups, and communities in terms of the synthesis between inner needs and the social realities that impinge upon them, and which aspire to develop informed and skilled practice.

M. ROLF OLSEN
Birmingham University
1981

Acknowledgements

I would like to take this opportunity to thank the following people for helping with the production of this book: Valerie Matthews for her patient help in preparing the manuscript; Rolf Olsen for discharging his editorial duties so painlessly; and Barbara Hudson, Peter Baird, John Cypher, and Donald Charlton for their general encouragement.

For Rita, Sally,
and Kate, with love

Preface

I have tried to keep the following objectives in view while writing this book. First, I wanted to fill a gap in the literature with a text on behavioural psychology and its applications which, though accessible to social workers with all their other legitimate interests, would yet reflect the latest research trends, some of which are quite complex. This raised questions as to the proper balance between the need to understand theory in detail, and the need for straightforward practical suggestions about how to apply its principles. The reader must be the final judge of whether the correct balance has been achieved. The task has not been an easy one because of the sheer volume of new writing and research in this field.

Second, I wanted to write a book which took British, local authority, social work as its reference point when the application of techniques was discussed. Behaviour modification is a specialized discipline, but it is too important to be left entirely to specialists, who always run the risk of looking at social problems in a blinkered way. I have tried to reflect this concern in my choice of case examples, each of which is authentic, and the result of either my own practice, work done in collaboration with students, or the work of colleagues participating in my research project.

Third, I have tried to analyse, and to come to some conclusions about, the present ills of social work – with particular reference to the research literature on casework effectiveness. My view is that a number of our present problems could be alleviated if social workers were to shrug off the debilitating influence of half-baked psychodynamic concepts and look instead to the empirical tradition in psychology for useful ideas about what makes people tick, and how best to go about helping them when they are in trouble. In this regard I consider it far more important for social workers to be broadly 'empirical' (both in what they are prepared to accept as a valid theoretical proposition and in what they subsequently do on the basis of this) rather than 'behavioural'. Often this amounts to the same thing, but where it does not, the former stance is the correct one, and the book tries to reflect this view.

I hope this book will be useful to students looking for a thorough grounding in behavioural principles and practice; to their fieldwork supervisors, who may have taken courses which provided only an appreciation of behavioural methods, rather than any detailed understanding of what is involved; and to field and residential workers who would like to do something about improving the effectiveness of those parts of their work where applied psychology can make a contribution. I have not written a 'cook book', for I am against such an approach to personal problems. That, however, is quite a different thing from saying that I think social workers should be left entirely to 'do their own thing'. Some very nasty concoctions indeed can result from this!

The book contains chapters on philosophy and on the ethical issues raised by the use of behavioural methods, since I am concerned that readers give at least as much consideration to these 'why' questions as to the 'how' questions raised in the technical sections. However, it must be remembered that an important ethical obligation on the provider of any service, is to check that they are delivering the goods as ordered, and indeed, as paid for – particularly where the cost of the goods is high, and where potentially, they could do much to enhance the individual's chance of a better life.

As to the level of this text: it takes the reader through some basic principles, and then building on these, introduces him to some rather more complex material on the variables influencing behaviour (including cognitive factors) and on how these can be harnessed for therapeutic purposes. I think the title is probably the best guide to the book's scope, and a concern that social work should provide tangible evidence of effectiveness is its overall theme.

BRIAN SHELDON
November, 1981.

1
The disciplinary context

I would like to attempt three things in this opening chapter. First, to look at the historical relationship (some would say lack of relationship) between social work and behavioural science. Second, to examine some of the ills of present-day social work, for which behaviourism may well have some remedies. Third, to try to identify the likely scope of behavioural methods in the hands of social workers, and to review some of the special difficulties that they are likely to encounter in using them.

I include this discussion here in support of the belief that choosing an approach to another individual's problems ought, as far as possible, to be a rational act. Social work has suffered rather more than the other helping professions from what can only be described as 'fads and fancies'. These sweep through the profession periodically with the force of minor epidemics. In the prosperous 1960s and early 1970s these fads tended to be optimistic, outgoing, and soft-hearted. In these days of economic recession, people tend to favour hard-headed notions, such as accountability, efficiency, and effectiveness. This is for good reasons: our discipline is not in good shape, and our profession does not stand as high as it should in public esteem. But although this state of affairs can give a superficial attractiveness to the use of behavioural methods, there are better reasons for embarking upon a study of such approaches than that they are a fad that happens to capture the spirit of the times.

Contrary to popular belief in the profession, there are adequately objective criteria that can be applied to the various competing explanations of how people get into social difficulties, and what can be

2 Behaviour Modification

done to help them (Sheldon 1978a). Standards exist, such as the specificity and testability of theories; whether techniques derived from them have anything more than a metaphorical relationship to the original research (and indeed whether there has *been* any original research); and whether it is possible to evaluate the relative successes and failures of attempts to apply the theories' lessons in practice. These scientific standards of theoretical and methodological adequacy, used quite successfully in other disciplines at least as complex as our own, can no longer be ignored by social workers. Sir Frederick Seebohm put the point well:

> 'The personal social services are large scale experiments in helping those in need. It is both wasteful and irresponsible to set experiments in motion and to omit to record and analyse what happens. It makes no sense in terms of administrative efficiency, and *however little intended*, indicates a careless attitude towards human welfare.'
>
> (Seebohm Report 1968 : 142, my emphasis)

My point here, is that it is important to look carefully at what behavioural methods have to offer, not just because they are 'new', or attractively tough-sounding at a time when this is very much in fashion, but because they are based on a steady accumulation of reliable knowledge which suggests that they are both wide in scope and effective in application. The decision to use them should not be a question of belief, or affiliation to a new movement, but an empirical one. On the evidence we have at present, they are, quite simply, the most sophisticated and reliable methods available.

There are other important factors of course, such as ethical questions, problems arising from the intrusiveness of certain methods as compared to others, and problems of labour intensity and cost. Each of these considerations will be dealt with as it arises in subsequent discussions. For now, the question is whether we can afford to continue to respond to canvassing by the proponents of largely untested therapeutic methods, unsupported by any convincing research. Many of these approaches acquire a quasi-religious status, and are difficult to challenge effectively because of the almost mystical aura that surrounds them. It might be said that this can also apply to behaviourists; however, as I have suggested, the grounds for the acceptance or rejection of behaviour therapy are quite different from those that apparently suffice for most other therapeutic methods. To begin with, behavioural theories are falsifiable (Popper 1963). That is, it is possible to conceive of practical tests for them which they may well not survive, and the results of which could not easily be dismissed even by their active proponents. This is not true of very many other popular social work affiliations. Second, behavioural methods are *tangible*. You can watch someone doing behaviour modification without causing its effects to evaporate; disturbing its subtle dynamics so that ('just this once') it fails to work, and also without needing to suspend your critical faculties.

The volume of empirical research testifying to the efficacy of behaviour modification procedures in problems likely to be encountered by social workers is now very large indeed. Herbert (1979) has suggested that the time has now come to ask the question very forcibly: 'why *not* behavioural social work?'

Behaviourism and social work – mislaid plans

Arguably, the most surprising thing about behaviour modification is that it is still not part of everyday social work in this country. The knowledge has been around for long enough. Texts relating learning theory specifically to social problems, and encouraging just such a development were published in the mid-1960s (Jehu 1967). Suddenly, at what seems to some of the party faithful a rather late stage, there is a renewal of interest. Demand for training courses is now proving hard to satisfy, a new UK-based journal has been launched *(I.J.B.S.W.)*, and a special interest group has been set up (B.S.W.G.).

Why should this be happening now? Part of the answer must be that the profession is beginning to draw breath after the Seebohm reorganization. This very mixed blessing diverted the attention of a generation of social workers away from technical and disciplinary issues to the task of trying to discern a coherent shape in a profession expanding in several different directions at once.

Social workers in Britain now appear to be responsible for anything that does not fall directly into the ambit of the police, the medical profession, or the fire service. Hence the reappearance throughout the literature of this period of the 'what *is* social work? (discuss)' debate. This is a question that the public might reasonably expect that we would have well behind us after seventy-five or so years. Hence also the recent interest in what some American writers insist on calling 'holistic conceptualisations of social work practice'.

4 Behaviour Modification

That is, with models and conceptual frameworks that try to encompass social work's many different aspects and relate them to each other (Pincus and Minahan 1973). By and large these have served a useful function. Arguably however, having learned what we can from them, the time has come to return to some of the older 'how to do it' issues, which these models do not address in any detail (Sheldon 1978b).

These developments are of importance, since they will continue to pose problems to the acceptance of behavioural methods in social work. As Alice said: 'With a name like yours, you might be any shape, almost.' Depending on which of the many kinds of social work you do, your perspective on the whole, and your sense of priorities, are different. People who do community work often see Social Services casework as an irrelevance. Social Services staff look askance at what they see as the mollycoddling working conditions enjoyed in Child Guidance. In the professional literature (to paraphrase Shaw) it is impossible for one social worker to open his mouth (or pick up his pen) without making another social worker despise him. This search for the 'one true essence' of something that is really a series of different, interrelated jobs, is a mistaken quest and a serious drain on available energies. It makes anyone with anything at all definite or specific to say think twice, and add on a string of qualifications – usually rendering the whole thing into a characteristic mixture of abstraction and pretentiousness beloved of leader-writers on slow news days. The following quotation should give the flavour of what I mean.

> 'Qualified social workers would see themselves as having professional skills in linking individuals, families or groups with the available and appropriate resources, services and opportunities, while at the same time promoting effective and humane operation of such facilities. Social workers are also concerned to enhance the capacities of the particular client(s) to solve problems and to deal appropriately and effectively with situations.'
>
> (Birch Report 1976 : 69)

I hope the reader will agree that the major portion of the above quotation applies equally well to telephonists as to social workers. In trying to encompass everything, and appeal to everyone, statements of this kind become meaningless, and appeal to no one.

Because of this unwholesome tradition, my *bête noire* takes the form of an imaginary Glaswegian social worker, who I envisage snapping shut this book in disgust, because it has so little to do with the plight of alienated youth in the inner city. He would be right too, and neither have I written much that is specific to group work or intermediate treatment – although a reader already familiar with these fields might well find something of value to apply. My point is, that the present tendency to try to apply universal criteria to specific contributions, or to texts on specific methods, though understandable, is wrong-headed. In writing about behaviour modification I do not imply that this is more important than, say, fighting youth unemployment, giving financial advice, or caring for the elderly. Nor am I suggesting, by implication, that we should abandon community work projects in favour of trying to change the behaviour of individuals directly. The method chosen must depend on some assessment of the nature of the problem – I would hope one emphasizing empirical data rather than pure ideology – and on some decision about how much influence the social workers can expect to have, and where best to apply it. It seems to me just as silly for social workers to concern themselves exclusively with changing individuals, as it does for them to spend all their time changing 'circumstances' (which usually means the behaviour of *other* people), on behalf of individuals. The question, then, is not whether behaviour modification should be chosen, but when, for what types of problem, and with what effect in mind. For all its other faults, the medical profession solved this problem of the 'one true faith' some time ago. They have heart surgeons *and* public health specialists. Occasionally the latter claim that the former have a disproportionate share of available resources, or that drains rather than scalpels are the key to good health. But by and large, they accept the principle that the term 'medical practitioner' covers all sorts of related functions in the health field. What is more, they do not try to write books, or attempt definitions, that cover both the repair of mitral valves and the repair of hospital sewage systems.

This point out of the way, I am free to suggest that behavioural methods can best be applied in therapeutic social work, where they can provide an objectively superior psychological basis for social casework. Beyond this, the literature is full of useful examples of small group work (Rose and Marshall 1975) and of its application in residential settings (Gambrill 1977). Behaviourist theories can also be quite revealing when applied to the problems of organizations (Luthans and Kreitner 1975) and to community projects (Sheldon

6 Behaviour Modification

1978b), but caution is necessary if the principles are not to be overstretched in such settings.

The current revival of interest in behavioural methods in this country represents a welcome return of technical and disciplinary concerns about how to help people more effectively through the provision of a personal service. It seems to be part of a desire – particularly among recently trained workers – to put flesh on some of those skeleton frameworks, abstract models, and practice 'outlines', left lying around the theoretical deserts of social work during the past decade.

The ills of professional social work

The change in the fortunes of social work has happened by stages. It began with questions about its general value, prompted by romantic, pre-industrial notions that caring communities should look after their own. These were easily countered with a few historical facts and the odd contemporary quote. The next stage of slow deterioration in relations with the public (from the late 1960s to the mid-1970s) resulted from the perception that apparently there were thousands of social workers (3127 qualifications were awarded in 1976) who not only appeared incapable of preventing parents from killing their children, but stubbornly refused to accept the blame for these tragedies, *or* to define exactly what it was that they *could* do well.

The third stage in social worker/public relations promises to be much more clear cut. The press, and the opponents of social work (see Brewer and Lait 1980) have got hold of the crude figures from research into social work effectiveness; the same figures that various academic Cassandras (myself included) have been going on about, to little avail, for quite some time (Sheldon 1979b). These critics are giving the benefit of no doubts, and making the worst possible interpretations of the evidence. Even allowing for this, results from the first main thrust of research into the question of whether social workers make any difference to the course of social problems are very disappointing. There is a case here that the profession has to try to answer.

Here is the conclusion of one eminent author after an extensive review of the research conducted between 1949 and 1972:

'The available controlled research strongly suggests that at present lack of evidence of the effectiveness of professional casework is the

rule rather than the exception. A technical research corollary to this conclusion and a comment frequently appearing in the social work literature, is that we also lack good scientific proof of ineffectiveness. This assertion, however, taken alone, would appear to be rather insubstantial grounds on which to support a profession.'
(Fischer 1973:19)

Or, if you would like a second opinion, there is this conclusion from a rather more optimistically-slanted review of research findings from roughly the same period: 'The researchers, for many reasons, were rarely able to conclude that a programme had even modest success in achieving its major goals' (Mullen and Dumpson 1972:251). This research requires more interpretation than it usually gets. However, we would be foolish to try to explain away its findings for purely defensive reasons. Until recently the reaction in social work was rather ostrich-like – which has meant that instead of responding critically and constructively to the results of individual studies, we have tended to wait for the publication of large-scale reviews before reacting. Even then, most of the discussion has centred on questions such as, whether social work is the kind of activity which *can* be looked into scientifically; or whether the researchers were investigating what we, personally, would call *real* social work. What follows is an attempt to decide what the proper balance between discomfort and optimism should rationally be. Certainly, these research findings will not just go away, and knowledge of them is increasing among our critics as is the tendency to apply them indiscriminately to suit their own case.

THE VALIDITY OF THE RESEARCH-INDICATORS USED

A common reaction to the kind of depressing conclusion cited above, is that the research procedures used are in themselves 'unfair' to social work. The studies investigated in the two major reviews quoted are of the relatively large-scale, matched-control variety. That is, half of a matched sample of regular clients receive social work (the independent variable) and half do not (the control). At the end of the study a comparison is made against pre-decided measures or *indicators* of positive outcome. These indicators of success and failure are usually of the 'hard' kind: that is, they are as far as possible unequivocal measures of progress, or lack of it, such as the possession of new behaviours and skills; attendance records; improved school grades;

improved work output; reduced reconviction rates, or fewer readmissions to hospital. As such, they represent a severe test for a profession which has generally been reluctant to define its goals in this sort of tangible and public way. Is there any evidence that the social work carried out was distorted by the application of these indicators? That there is some, is part of social work folk lore, but I can find no convincing information on this. Most of the studies are distinguished by the way in which the social workers were encouraged to participate in the selection of evaluation criteria. Most often, the workers were being assessed on their own views of what would constitute a reasonable test of their powers, although some of them may have seen the achievement of these targets as a superficial representation of the complex tasks they were really attempting to carry out.

The view, still common in social work, that the results of intervention are impossible to measure in this way, is quite wrong in my view. The profession must be able to demonstrate a tangible impact on social problems. Other, qualitative, bonus-effects, such as a client's reported 'greater peace of mind' or increased sense of 'self esteem', should be brought into research much more than they have been, but these reports of altered states of mind will surely not do *instead* of demonstrable, quantifiable change. People who have more confidence, or are less disparaging of their own abilities, *behave* differently from those who do not, or are not. This is the only generally acceptable view of evaluation: that, if the exercise is to be worthwhile, changes inside the heads of clients (particularly where they are expensive to produce) must be matched by logically connected changes in what people do, and do not do; the extent to which they show up in criminal statistics, absenteeism records, and on hospital rolls – when compared with other similar people who have not been 'helped' professionally. The indicators used in this research are not 'unfair', just necessarily tough.

CONTROL GROUP EFFECTS

However, the trouble with group-controlled studies is that they average out individual results. It may be that a range of different talents in the workers being investigated will mean that whereas some clients will be helped profoundly, others may actually be harmed by the process. Truax and Carkhuff (1967) report convincingly on such variations in outcome. (It is not at all unknown for an experimental group to *deteriorate* in comparison with controls in this way.) Caution is needed before jumping to this conclusion about individual differences however, because it does imply a rather large measure of coincidence; that is, that the averaging-out effects always come to zero or minus, when one would expect them occasionally to show positive results, reflecting a particular cluster of useful talent in an agency. Often the material on individual successes and failures is not available. Its absence reflects the mistaken view that we are investigating a uniform process – the therapist uniformity myth.

In view of these 'cancelling-out' effects several authors have argued that before launching a new series of controlled studies, social work should first experiment with more detailed small-scale methods of case evaluation (Bloom 1975; Sheldon and Baird 1978). An account of these procedures can be found in Chapter Five.

THE APPLICABILITY OF AMERICAN FINDINGS

Most of the available research on social work effectiveness is of American origin and its results cannot simply be transferred to the British context. Apart from cultural differences, and an entirely different pattern of social service provision, the methods used by social workers are likely to be rather different. There are several factors requiring discussion here. First, the targets set by social workers in some of these studies (see Meyer, Borgatta, and Jones 1965) look, to many here, rather optimistic. Pretty dramatic alterations to existing habits and practices are expected, often against a background of general social deprivation, and lack of cooperation from clients and/or their families. Second, the methods used in pursuit of these goals look rather suspect. By and large, this first phase of effectiveness research is an evaluation of casework based on the Freudian and neo-Freudian principles that took American social work by storm in the 1920s and that are still a much greater feature of training there than here. In many cases it comes as no surprise that there is no tangible effect and that people end up more confused than previously. Here is the reaction of a British client to this approach:

> 'My husband's gambling was driving me round the bend, and I thought maybe the welfare lady could help me do something about it. But all the lady wanted to do was talk – "what was he like when he gambled", "did we quarrel" and silly things like that. She was trying to help and it made me feel good knowing someone cared.

But you can't solve a problem by *talking* about it. Something's got to be done!'   (Mayer and Timms 1970:1)

We also have evidence from empirical research testifying to the failure of these methods to produce demonstrable change (Eysenck 1976; but see also Sloane *et al.* 1975).

We are left then with three questions: (i) to what extent are casework methods *per se* still employed? (ii) do psychodynamic theories still play a large part in everyday social work — particularly in this country? (iii) are the objectives of social work in Britain more realistic? Each of these points will now be taken in turn.

Most social workers in Britain are wary of admitting that they do something called casework. This reticence is due to several factors, not least, the pounding such approaches have received in the professional literature recently. In addition to this, the radical left takes a dim view of helping people through psychological procedures when their 'real' difficulties, it is said, result exclusively from economic and structural factors. In fact, recent surveys show that there has been something of a flight from theory altogether (Stevenson and Parsloe 1978). This does not mean, however, that social workers no longer use theories — their own and other people's — just that they no longer wear the appropriate lapel badges. Such a reaction is understandable, if regrettable. Trenchant criticism and out-of-hand condemnation, of the kind seen recently in both the national and professional press, are forms of punishment. They are intended to discourage bad practice, but often have a more generalized effect, and end up discouraging all sorts of risk taking — of which theorizing is one kind. As the reader will see later, punishment acts as a general suppressant of behaviour. Because of this, social workers are no longer sure what it is safe to own up to using. But this means that the theories and hypotheses that they cannot *avoid* using, become implicit rather than explicit, and so are not readily available for discussion and criticism. My own experience of ninety students per year, plus many visits to fieldwork agencies, is that social workers still spend a lot of time doing casework in one form or another. That is:

(a) time and energy is devoted to providing friendly, supportive, and confidential relationships with clients, in which context personal problems can be discussed freely, and where an attempt is made to understand behaviour — whatever its shortcomings in the eyes of the community at large;

(b) an attempt is made to analyse problems and their antecedents,

and clients are encouraged to reflect on possible lessons and solutions – the medium of change is verbal influence;
(c) there is an intention that an individual's attitudes and behaviour will change as a result of this process, and that he or she will feel better and more able to cope as a result of it;
(d) implicitly or explicitly some use will be made of psychological concepts, both to provide explanations of problems, and to guide the social worker's actions in trying to overcome them.

This is my definition of social casework, and this is a style of work I see going on in agencies all around me. It is true that practical services are (rightly) taken more seriously these days, as are the various things that are done on *behalf* of clients rather than *to* them. Contact is briefer, more task centred (Reid and Shyne 1968) and happily the therapeutic relationship is seen more clearly as just the medium of help rather than its message. Nevertheless, my contention is that given the type of problems they face, social workers cannot avoid doing something like casework – however unfashionable it may be at the moment. Therefore, following effectiveness research, and other psychological research (Fischer 1976; Marmor 1962), social workers need to think very seriously about the extent to which they rely purely on verbal influence in this regard.

My impression is that talking with clients about problems in order to promote a greater understanding of these is, not surprisingly, still the dominant method in social work. But if there is one clear, unequivocal message from casework and psychotherapy research conducted over the last three decades it is that understanding and 'insight' need to be heavily supplemented by an active, or 'doing' element – what Bandura (1977) calls a 'performance component'. The client must *practise* alternative ways of behaving, or changes must be made on his or her behalf of the circumstances that can be shown to influence present behaviour, or which prevent the emergence of more adaptive alternatives. Understanding one's problems is certainly a facilitative condition of change, but there is no evidence that it is, generally, a sufficient condition. There are not many clients who simply lack information about what to do. To rely on talking and giving insight, is to grossly underestimate the power of habit; reinforcement provided by the status quo; the controlling power of environment; and the effects of deficits in problem-solving skills.

The clients (so prevalent in accredited casework texts) who respond eagerly to discussions of their problem with variants of: 'Gee

Miss Ponobscott, I never saw it *that* way before!' are almost entirely fictional in my view. Think for a moment of your own reserves of insight, and then about the problems of actually translating them into behavioural change. To argue, as certain psychodynamic writers do, that this cannot therefore be *real* insight, is nonsense, and renders the concept that they seek to defend completely redundant. The same goes for the pursuit of changes in attitude, as a necessary precursor of behavioural change:

> 'Attitude changes resulting from persuasive influences are relatively unstable and will disappear unless the corresponding overt behaviour is sustained by adequate consequences. This view assumes that attitudes produce temporary performance changes: however, when environmental contingencies do not support the new activities, individuals revert to their old behaviour and the newly established attitudes are similarly altered to coincide with the actions.' (Festinger 1964 : 138)

This point about reliance on verbal influence procedures seems to me more important than worries over the extent to which psychodynamic theories are employed by a small therapeutic 'underground movement' in British social work (Baird 1981). Psychodynamic theory is responsible for two distracting ideas which are still taken far too seriously by social workers. The first is, that behavioural problems are symptomatic of psychological tangles that not even the client need be conscious of having. This means that clients' protests (should they be bold enough to make them) that the social worker is on the wrong track need not be taken seriously. The scope for miscommunication here is very great (see Mayer and Timms 1970). Second, there is the suggestion that interior, or developmental factors, such as personality types and particular 'fixations', are responsible for the difficulties that people get into. This diverts attention from factors in the here-and-now, and from exterior pressures in the clients' nearby environment.

Turning now to the point about over-ambitious and vaguely defined goals: this is still a very serious problem, and a good reason for not dismissing the American effectiveness research out of hand. Remember, the goals being investigated were largely the *social workers'* goals. The only difference being, that hard indicators were assigned to them to prevent extended negotiation about whether they had been achieved or not (a discussion of goal-setting and its problems can be found in Chapter Five). It is only necessary here to make the point that loose phrasing such as: 'the aim of this project is to promote a better degree of integration between residents and members of the local community', is almost impossible to evaluate, unless clear descriptions are given of what tangible events or classes of events must occur before it can be reasonably claimed that the project has been successful (an example might be increased attendance by local residents at hostel meetings). The most serious indictment of social work contained in the American research, is not that it shows clearly that ineffective methods were being used, but that these had been in use for many years *without anyone being able to tell that this was so* (Sheldon 1977).

BRITISH RESEARCH

The first thing that must be acknowledged is that, given the size and cost of the enterprise, research into social work effectiveness in Britain is woefully inadequate both in quality and extent. When it is carried out at all, the tendency is to evaluate projects separately, and to a level of methodological adequacy capable of supplying only suggestive evidence. Though inadequate for academic purposes, mimeographed research reports of this kind are often sufficient to satisfy managers and local policy makers. While this method of evaluation provides quick and relatively cheap information on social work programmes, the findings are rarely acceptable to a wider audience, though they may provide some useful feedback to those actually doing the work.

There have been more sophisticated attempts to investigate the wider role of the social worker, as advocate, and provider of day care, fostering services, and so on, and some of these results are quite encouraging. See, for example, the regular bulletins of the University of Birmingham Clearing House for Social Services Research. However, with one or two recent exceptions (NACRO 1980; Cooper *et al.* 1975; Shaw 1974; Rose and Marshall 1974) the results of British research, where differences directly attributable to contact with a social worker provide the point of evaluation, are equally disappointing. To this conclusion must be added the strong impression that some of the methods employed by the workers in these studies match those of their American counterparts in their 'fuzziness' and have the same aura of breezy optimism about how easy it is to change people. The

IMPACT study (Folkard 1975) is typical. Here, a widely drawn sample of probation clients were randomly divided into experimental and control groups. The Probation Officers in the experimental group had their caseloads drastically reduced and were encouraged to engage in intensive casework with their clients. It was expected that this extra concentration of time and effort would produce superior results. The control group were seen as usual, the availability of the officer being dictated by the pressure of his (unreduced) caseload.

Checks on the frequency and content of interviews revealed that the experimental group did in fact receive a more intensive service. Unfortunately, when outcome comparisons were made against a range of indicators connected with recidivism, there were no measurable differences between the two groups. Subsequent attempts to remould this result by suggesting, for example, that probation is at least a cheaper alternative than prison, and has fewer side effects (Folkard 1980), though true, are only a partial answer to the basic problem. We would attempt to improve the input, rather than retrospectively devaluing the outcome measures employed. To the question, popular in probation circles these days, 'Whoever expected Probation Officers to be able to affect recidivism rates?' the answer is probably: 'About 90 per cent of the population'.

RECENT RESEARCH – HOPEFUL TRENDS

There is heartening evidence to be found in effectiveness research conducted after 1973 (see Cooper *et al.* 1975; NACRO 1981). The increased use of task-centred approaches and behaviour modification is producing more positive results (Reid 1980). The programmes under scrutiny also impress more by being better planned, having clearly specified goals, and by depending upon more direct and better focused approaches (see Stein and Gambrill 1976). However, there are no grounds for complacency here. It should be remembered that it is research *trends*, rather than the results of isolated studies, that should govern our thinking about what we do. Also, we should remember that the onus is on us, the providers of these expensive services, to demonstrate that they make a worthwhile difference.

PROCESS OR OUTCOME?

Finally, there is the idea that it is the *process* of work with clients that we should be concentrating on, rather than trying to establish outcome. This view, expressed unequivocally in the quotation that follows, is deeply ingrained in social work training and in patterns of work supervision, and is one reason why we lack experience of outcome measurement:

> 'The outcome of professional practice, when it can be measured at all, although of considerable interest in other connections is of little value in the assessment of competence. . . . Since outcomes are obviously a questionable basis for defining and assessing social work . . . a more hopeful alternative is required. . . . Its essential component must be what goes into social work practice, not what comes out as a result.' (Levy 1974 : 337)

More recent contributions, of an overtly political kind, drawing on marxist sociology, rather than on psychology, also embody this conclusion (Corrigan and Leonard 1978). This view suggests two things at an implicit level: (i) that the outcome will look after itself if the *process* of social work is properly handled; (ii) that the *medium* of change is all important and that as Fats Waller once put it: 'It ain't what you do, it's the way that you do it, that's what gets results.' Given our research track record, the first assumption is patently unreliable (see also Davies 1979), the second raises more complex issues, such as, the impact of the social worker's 'personality' on the problems he or she is handling.

THERAPIST VARIABLES

It is a common mistake to regard therapist variables and 'placebo' factors (that is, unintentional influences) as magically indeterminate and undefinable. Considerable research is now being done to investigate these factors, and the work of Truax and Carkhuff (1967) though troubled with problems of construct validity, is exemplary in this regard. It contains some very tough-minded empirical measurements of how different therapist behaviours affect clients. In their research, these authors have identified three major therapist variables and a battery of other significant influences. The three main items are: *warmth*, *genuineness*, and *accurate empathy*, and the important point is that Truax and Carkhuff have so refined these concepts that they are identifiable on video tape and can be scaled to a high degree of reliability. Let us now look at each of these in a little more detail.

Non-possessive warmth consists of: (i) getting across to clients feelings of respect, liking, caring, acceptance, and concern; (ii) managing to do this in a non-threatening way, so that there is no question of the client feeling managed or taken over, and no question that his or her standing in the eyes of the therapist depends on the production of 'approved of' responses to questions. Such a contingency is similar to Rogers' (1951) 'unconditional positive regard'. This obviously poses problems for behaviourists – indeed for any therapist. The first problem is that it may be that few of us can live up to it. This may be especially true of behaviourists, because of our interest in deliberately produced and manifest change. A key principle of behaviour modification is that behaviourists expect change to occur through the rewarding contingencies they produce. However, the approval and the disapproval of the therapist must be counted as a significant shaping influence – whether the therapist is aware of the process, or not. The literature is full of evidence of the unwanted shaping of clients by therapists of all persuasions (Heine 1953). Presumably these findings apply to behaviour therapists too. Perhaps Truax and Carkhuff are warning us of the dangers of the deliberate and easily visible presentation and withdrawal of approval – in a highly mechanical way? There is evidence to suggest that to the degree that clients feel coerced and manipulated, they will feel free to abandon discussions made in this context whenever the going gets rough (Festinger 1957). But this poses ethical problems, because does it not suggest that effective shaping equals covert shaping? (See Chapter Eight.)

The second problem is that even if we could do it, it may not be a good idea. Here are Bandura's forthright views on the matter:

> 'Even if unconditional social approval and acceptance were possible, it would be no more meaningful as a precondition for change than non-contingent reinforcement in modifying any form of behaviour. If this principle were applied in child rearing, parents would respond approvingly and affectionately when their children appeared with stolen goods, behaved unmanageably in school, physically injured their siblings and peers, refused to follow any household routines etc. "Unconditional love" would make children directionless, impossible and completely unpredictable.'
> (Bandura 1969 : 79)

The traditional solution to this difference is to argue for the possibility of 'loving the sinner and hating the sin' – a very powerful set of contingencies but not easy to manage! The idea of separating off 'the behaviour' from 'the person' is a difficult one for a discipline that has always argued that 'the person *is* the behaviour'. My own solution is to argue that first, a recognition of the power of external forces on behaviour and second, recognition of the enormous potential for change that exists in human beings, helps considerably with the development of that other prerequisite for good therapists – a liking for people of all shapes and sizes. Further assistance comes from the idea of a behaviour modification *programme* – note the word. To succeed, behavioural schemes have to be 'packaged' in some way. In my view they are best used as a special therapeutic device within a broader therapeutic relationship. Therefore it is possible to conceive of applying Truax and Carkhuff's principle overall, partly as an ethical stance, partly as a supportive device; but within this context there should also exist an agreed course of action wherein different behaviours will produce different consequences. Failure to meet these special therapeutic contingencies will not and should not threaten the status of the client as a person of worth, but differential reinforcement of responses has to occur at certain points in the interests of producing worthwhile change. This suggestion is similar to that found in Hollis (1964) who argues for a distinction between 'sustaining procedures' and 'procedures of direct influence' in social casework. The implication is that, in complex cases, behaviour therapy *per se* would exist as a 'module' within a less distinctively technical approach based on relationship-maintaining attributes. Moving from one set of concerns to the other would then involve a noticeable 'change of gear' signalling to the client that now there are more closely prescribed tasks to be attempted.

Genuineness. Truax and Carkhuff (1967) have given us the best definition of this therapist attribute by telling us what it is not. To be 'genuine' in this sense is not to be 'phoney', not to hide behind a professional facade or 'image', not to be defensive in the face of criticism or challenge, and not to be unpredictable in the type of responses made to the client. Genuineness is to do with confidence, being yourself, not acting a part, appearing relaxed and at ease with yourself. The only (extra) problem here for behaviour therapists stems from the somewhat technical nature of our discipline. Many social workers and some clients reject behavioural approaches because of this aura of 'treating people like machines' – the 'Clockwork Orange' type of imagery that surrounds it. It is no good just dismissing this as ignorance; better to think of ways of presenting behaviour therapy in such a way that it does not sound so artificial and does not put up a barrier between client and helper. Behaviour therapy contains rather more 'headwork' than other, more gushing approaches, and this can be problematic if it produces an excessively businesslike 'Mr Fix It' style: 'What have we got here? Tantrums, eh? Right, do this three times a day for a week and . . .'. There is no necessity for a mechanical approach to behavioural methods. Indeed, the Sloane *et al.* study (1975) found that clients rated the behavioural workers higher than other groups on friendliness and empathy.

Accurate empathy is also a particular category of *behaviour* shown by the therapist. Positive feelings that the therapist has inside are of little practical use unless their presence is communicated to the client. Similarly, any detailed knowledge that the therapist achieves of the client's problem is likely to affect the client only to the extent that it can be accurately communicated to him. There are three key elements in this behaviour: (i) accuracy of understanding – letting the client know that you have a pointed grasp of his problems and dilemmas; (ii) showing the client that you are really trying to see things from *his* vantage point; (iii) letting the client see that your own mood and feelings are in tune with his. This ability is at least as much an attribute as a skill capable of being taught. It is the ability to imagine just how it must be to stand in the shoes of another person and to be able to experience feelings similar to those of the other person, and to demonstrate, in a tentative way, that this is the case.

Resource implications of behaviour modification approaches

Most field social workers in Britain are able to spend about 30 per cent of their official working week in face-to-face contact with clients. Assuming an average caseload of about forty, this allows for a potential weekly visit per client lasting about eighteen minutes. This is hardly a good basis for detailed therapeutic work whatever the theories subscribed to. Although pretty bad, the real position is not quite like this. Many clients can be best helped by the social worker being in the office making telephone calls and writing letters on their behalf. Some come in for interviews, others need seeing less often than once a week. But the fact remains that for much of the time, social workers will be the planners, instigators, and supervisors of behavioural schemes rather than the people who administer their daily operation. Experience teaches us that there are some ways around these problems.

(a) The demands for really close contact tend to come at the beginning of a case, during the assessment phase, and in the first stage of operation – when changes and reappraisals sometimes need to be made. Budget then for lengthier periods of contact at the beginning, and shorter supervisory visits once the scheme is established.

(b) Although it is essential that there is a responsible 'key worker', sometimes the more routine work of programme supervision can be shared between colleagues so that the chances of someone being in the area, or available at short notice, are greater. This kind of teamwork demands three things: (i) a background familiarity with a range of cases; (ii) clear, regularly summarized case recording; (iii) a willingness to pursue existing policy rather than suggest impressive new departures 'off the cuff'. Very detailed or intensive work can also be carried out by case-sharing, so that a family might get to know two or three workers who have agreed on a therapeutic policy and then visit frequently on a rota basis.

THE USE OF MEDIATORS

Mediators are people who are willing to supervise the day-to-day operation of a behaviour modification scheme. On such people, whether drawn from the family and friends of the client, or from colleagues in other professions (community nurses, health visitors, and so on), depends the success of a great many of the schemes described in this book. Sometimes the choice of mediators is circumscribed by the setting the client happens to be in; for example, it usually makes sense to use the family of a child client, the teachers of a person having difficulties at school, and residential care staff for a person living in a hostel. But not *always*, since clients sometimes see these people as part of the problem rather than part of the solution. It is better to begin by looking objectively at the likely tasks of the mediator.

(a) Obviously the mediator must be someone who is likely to be around when the target behaviour is being performed. Therefore, many fieldwork programmes require a group of such people:

parents to monitor the behaviour at home; a cooperative Youth Club leader to watch for variants of it during the evenings; teachers doing the same during the day. This range may not cover the whole day, but it will yield representative examples of behaviour in different types of setting.

(b) Mediators must be able to grasp the simple principles on which the programme is formulated. Time spent taking up possible objections and likely problems of implementation, is time well spent. Consistency is all, and mediators need to understand the reasons for this. Training can sometimes be given, and the main points to concentrate on are: (i) discrimination, distinguishing the target behaviour from other actions a bit like it; (ii) focusing on *behaviour*, not interpreting what supposedly lies behind it; (iii) prompting as necessary.

(c) The mediator must not only be someone who can apply positive and negative consequences appropriately, he or she must be generally acceptable to the client in this role. This is not to say that all mediators must be well-liked. There is some evidence that clients change their opinions of people who regularly reward them, and sometimes this is the main intention of the programme. But where a potential mediator is *actively* disliked, then obviously it is wiser to use someone else.

(d) There are certain situations in which it is hard to use mediators, for example with certain behaviours in children that occur mainly in peer group settings. Some behavioural work has been done by youth workers who have attached themselves to gangs and gradually brought them into youth centres, but this is very difficult territory. The principle of using high-status mediators holds good, but for many children 'adult' equals 'low status'.

The use of mediators poses some problems of consistency and training, but where these can be overcome, there are many advantages to their involvement. Often they have a long-standing relationship with the client and know his or her moods and the subtleties of his or her behaviour better than the social worker can ever hope to. Tharp and Wetzel (1969) see the use of mediators in behaviour modification as a useful corrective to the present over-reliance on 'experts' in the helping professions:

'If the full potential of society is to be mobilized for the help of its less fortunate members, then the helping enterprises must be despecialized. The hyper-professionalisation of the mental health professions militates against the use of society's greatest resources; the clients' natural relationships with their extraordinary potential power for generating behaviour change....'

(Tharp and Wetzel 1969:1)

Conclusion

Some of the American research material reviewed in this chapter undoubtedly applies to what British social workers do today. In some of the studies, the workers were both well trained, had relatively small caseloads, and clients who were not severely disadvantaged or uncooperative. This body of research, when combined with British findings and with similar material from psychotherapy and psychiatry (Clare 1976) marks the end of half a century of optimism about the ease with which behavioural changes can be induced by verbal counselling methods. Later research is more encouraging, particularly when added to the mass of independent evidence testifying to the effectiveness of behavioural methods. The picture is no longer one of unrelieved gloom; we now have some positive trends which can be reinforced.

I said at the beginning of this chapter, that behavioural methods might well be able to supply a remedy for some of the problems that have now been outlined. Perhaps the most encouraging thing is that these methods have characteristics which are almost the exact opposite of those patterns of service investigated in the research referred to above. In behavioural work a close specification of goals is seen, not just because it is a good general idea, but because it is a working necessity. Evaluation methods are part of the approach; they are built in to the process. There is a concentration on *doing*, on practising new modes of behaviour, rather than exclusively on talking.

Behaviour therapists make it their business to find out what environmental influences are at work in the problem. The main focus is on factors in the here and now, on the problems that the client complains of, and on factors that work to *maintain* his or her problems in force. At the very least, the widespread application and concurrent evaluation of these methods in social work will be a useful and dramatic experiment.

It should be said, finally, that in carrying out this experiment, social workers will meet obstacles and receive setbacks which are not well-reported on in the behavioural literature. The target problems dealt with by social workers are likely to be less clearly differentiated than elsewhere in the helping professions, so particular attention will need to be given to questions of problem-definition and goal-specification. Moreover, problems are more likely to come in 'clumps'; to have many different interacting elements; and to have been already looked into, and advised upon, by a range of other professionals. I have suggested elsewhere (Sheldon 1980) that the song about Liza and the leaky bucket is the best available formulation of the kinds of problems dealt with by social workers: each obvious solution is blocked by some other feature of the problem. The success of behavioural methods in our hands will depend therefore on a willingness to be rigorous about the way in which we adapt them to our special purposes, and on our ability to extract key problems from a range of other difficulties and deal with these intensively. Using behavioural procedures in settings far removed from the psychological laboratory and the specialist clinic is likely to be a less clear-cut and predictable business than some of the behavioural literature implies and due weight will be given to these considerations in the rest of this text.

2
The philosophical implications of behaviourism

In this chapter I shall review some of the philosophical issues arising from the use of behaviour modification techniques. Although the greater part of this book is necessarily devoted to technical matters, it is not my intention to try to persuade social workers to become just technicians. Given the controversial nature of many of the problems confronting them, it is vital that they should be able to think for themselves and make clear judgements about what their actions – even apparently commonsense and non-theoretical actions – assume about the person needing their help, and about the best way of providing such help. Therefore, they cannot afford to be philosophically naive.

The first set of questions concerns the processes by which behaviour is instigated, influenced, and controlled.

Mind and body

The commonly held view of behaviour in our culture is that it is a surface manifestation of a much more complex and interesting process going on somewhere inside our heads. Further, that (except in the case of a few bodily reflexes), a non-material, non-detectable 'something', obeying none of the known physical laws, nevertheless manages to control, via its host organ, the brain, the sum total of our behaviour. I refer, of course, to the concept of mind. So much is obvious, you might think. But however commonplace and taken-for-granted this concept, there are many logical problems associated with it. How, for example, *can* a non-physical, quasi-spiritual entity give rise to anything so concrete and tangible as behaviour? Speaking metaphorically: what kind of cerebral 'clutch-mechanism' connects and disconnects mental activity and physical activity? How can an event of any kind, even a thought, arise *spontaneously* out of nothing – as an *uncaused* happening? Certainly such things are not within our everyday experience of the rest of the material world. Nor are they known to science. So why do we suppose that we are not bound by the same laws that appear to forbid this elsewhere? Part of the answer is, that given the anticipated complexity of having to account scientifically, that is materially, for something so enormously divergent as human behaviour, there is an almost irresistible temptation to assign the whole question of causality to the action of some magical 'black box' phenomenon within, thereby short-circuiting the whole vexing issue, or at least moving the discussion to a metaphysical plane. This done, we are left to contemplate only whether 'the mind' is a unity, or how it is different from 'the soul'; whether it has 'compartments' and 'faculties' or an unconscious bit; how it can get 'diseased' or 'unbalanced' and so forth. In the same way, it is easier to explain the origins and development of life by inventing another supreme being, a marvellous version of ourselves, who fortunately views us as His favourite creation. Then we can assign to Him the responsibility for everything. Similarly, many of us prefer to account for our daily fortunes by the movements of the stars and planets. We do it because, despite appearances, it is easier. The alternative would be to try to work out the complex inter-relationship between our actions and the forces of the environment to which we respond – and which responds to us.

The notion of man as a physical shell, piloted from within by another kind of influence, is amusingly caricatured in the children's comic strip opposite. The trick is to try to imagine what these homunculi have inside *their* heads, controlling *their* actions.

An early advocate of this idea of man as some kind of complicated machine, driven from within, was the seventeenth-century philosopher René Descartes. In trying to make his interest in materialism and natural science compatible with his orthodox Roman Catholic beliefs, he invented the doctrine of dualism. Here is the first half of it:

'I desire, I say, that you consider that these functions (respiration, sight, hearing, ideas) occur naturally in this machine solely by the

Philosophical implications 25

Figure 2(1) The Numskulls

Source: Reproduced from *The Beezer Book* 1980. © D. C. Thomson & Co. Ltd.

disposition of its organs, not less than the movements of a clock.'
(Descartes 1664)

As to the other half of this duality which so mysteriously influences 'the clockwork' at every click and turn, no knowledge was claimed of it beyond the certainty of its existence. Descartes saw thinking as the main evidence for it, and a surer guide to his own existence than the inferred sensations of his physical body. He expressed this view in his famous dictum: *cogito ergo sum* – 'I think, therefore I am'.

Descartes made his analogy with the most complex machine available to him – the clock. Today behaviour is more likely to be seen as resulting from the operation of some cerebral computer – the most complex machine available to us. But even in this contemporary version, 'the computer' is usually said to be controlled from within by the magic of mind, by a 'ghost in the machine' (Ryle 1949).

Gilbert Ryle has argued with great clarity that this problem of the mind–body relationship is less a scientific conundrum than a philosophical one. It is an error of attribution, or in his terms a 'category mistake' and a 'philosopher's myth'. He offers the following illustration of this view:

> 'A foreigner visiting Oxford for the first time is shown a number of colleges, libraries, playing fields, museums, scientific departments and administrative offices. He then asks "But where is the University? I have seen where the members of the colleges live, where the Registrar works, where the scientists experiment and the rest. But I have not yet seen the University in which reside and work the members of your University." It has then to be explained to him that the University is just another collateral institution, some ulterior counterpart to the colleges, laboratories and offices which he has seen. The University is just the way in which all that he has already seen is organized. . . . He was mistakenly allocating the University to the same category as that to which the other institutions belong.'
> (Ryle 1949:17)

Accepting that attempts to define 'mind' as an independent entity, with self-generating causative properties, have fallen into this 'category mistake', it is possible to see how much more logical it is to infer 'mind' from observable behaviour. This is the view of Behaviourism – which can best be thought of as the philosophy of the emerging science of human behaviour (Skinner 1974).

Behaviourism further suggests that since behaviour occurs as a phenomenon within the physical universe it must be part of its processes and therefore, must obey the same laws of cause and effect. Behaviour is seen in this philosophy, as an organic adaptation to an ambivalent physical and social environment. In turn, man's behaviour acts upon this environment, changes it, and so provides a source of stimulation for others and of feedback for himself. In this sense, we may speak of the 'natural selection' of behaviour by the pressure of environment, which rewards some actions and discourages others. Behaviourism also proposes that, contrary to the established view, the cognitive processes which we call consciousness, are an interesting by-product of this relationship between body and environment. *Ago ergo sum* – I act, therefore I am.

The experience that we have learned to categorize as 'mind' is the experience of our brains at work, processing sensory stimuli, and, through the use of language, encoding, classifying, manipulating, and storing in symbolic form, information about the contingencies of our environment and the likely effects of our future behaviour upon these. Given that this organ has ten thousand million nerve cells, we really have no need to resort to 'ghosts in machines'. A 'machine' of this incredible complexity is likely to have some pretty ghostly properties of its own:

> 'Each cubic inch of the cerebral cortex probably contains more than ten thousand miles of nerve fibres, connecting the cells together. If the cells and fibres in one human brain were all stretched out end to end they would certainly reach to the moon and back. Yet the fact that they are *not* arranged end to end enabled man to go there himself. The astonishing tangle within our heads makes us what we are. Every cell in the cortex receives on its surface an average of several thousand terminals from the fibres of other cells. The richness of interconnection makes each neuron a Cartesian soul.' (Blakemore 1976:85)

Popper and Eccles (1977) (a philosopher collaborating with a neurologist) have described the effects of the almost unimaginably complex development hinted at here as 'materialism transcending itself'. Their view seems to be, that a quantitative extention of function to this seemingly near-infinite degree results 'without any violating of the laws of physics' in *qualitatively* different effects.

Behaviourism does not seek to deny the importance of consciousness, rather to challenge views of this phenomenon which represent it as some sort of disconnected entity, impervious, when it chooses, to environmental influence. Now, while I can have direct access to my own conscious processes, I cannot have access to yours. What you may tell me about the goings on inside your head is subject to all sorts of internal and external pressures and distortions before it reaches me. A genuinely scientific account of the relationship between thinking and doing must therefore concentrate, as fully as it can, on the doing part of the equation. When reference to possible interior goings-on seems to help the investigation along – as perhaps with the concept of 'attitude', the level of inference should always be kept at the lowest possible level. This position on what counts as evidence in the assessment of human behaviour gives findings in this field their relatively greater certainty and replicability.

Free will versus environmental control

All new heresies which suggest that man (or in this case, the experience of 'inner man') may not necessarily be the centre of the universe, give rise to uncomfortable feelings. Furthermore, they appear to deny commonsense. I *know* that the world revolves around me, and that I spontaneously cause things to happen in it, just as I know that the sun revolves around the earth and that the earth is flat. I see these things every day. Similarly, I know that my will is free and that if I wanted to, '*really* wanted to I mean', I could leave this writing table now and go and sit outside in the sunshine instead. The fact that I forego this opportunity and continue to write, is because I *want* to. Clear enough? It shouldn't be. As an explanation of my present actions it is pure tautology. It says nothing about causes, and does little to advance the reader's knowledge of the factors leading to my present behaviour. A more complicated explanation of my extraordinary behaviour, is that in the past I have had pleasant experiences (experiences that I have learned to connect with comfort or excitement, feelings of satisfaction, control over my circumstances, and so on) as a result of doing things like this at the expense of other, perhaps more immediately pleasurable activities. So, again, because of my learning history, as I sit here I have emotions that arouse images of similar future events: handing over the manuscript with a sigh of relief; holding a bound copy one day; a favourable review perhaps; the approval of colleagues (well, some of them at least); the image of an interested reader, and so on. This is the reason why my present behaviour continues. In addition, there is the anticipation of aversive consequences lying in wait for me, should I do anything else: sitting in the sun, but as a *wastrel*; some unpleasantness about royalties already advanced, and so forth. My behaviour is following a pattern, as does all behaviour, though it is not always an easy task to identify the controlling factors, especially not from the outside, where in the present case, it might look as if I were just sitting at a table scribbling away. Were one of these controlling factors to change, or a new one to emerge – the noise from outside my window of a low flying aircraft, or the news that the deadline for this book had been extended, then my behaviour would change markedly, and fall under the control of a new set of variables. Does this mean that I am a robot? I certainly don't *feel* like a robot, nor do I experience the behaviour of other people as robotic, and it may be that this is the important thing about free will and determinism. We have the experience of free choice, though we do not choose our choices.

Skinner (1974) argues that the absolute prediction of human behaviour from its causes would be a task similar in complexity to that facing a physicist trying to predict the individual trajectories of all the droplets in a rainstorm (in my view a gross underestimation of the problem). But the fact that it cannot be done does not mean that such trajectories do not exist or that they are not the result of known forces. Nor does it mean that we should not try to identify general trends or to 'split off' bits of the problem to see what we can find out about it – using this information to frame hypotheses about more complex events.

Rather than fretting over the issue of 'free will' or questions of self-determination, the concern of the behaviourist should be to widen the range of possible responses the individual can make to his or her environment – including responses which seek to change it.

In response to such a discussion Dr Johnson once said 'we *know* our will is free and *there's* an end on't!' (Boswell 1740). With due deference, given what we have learned in the behavioural sciences in the last sixty years, it would be more reasonable to argue that our 'will' is an inference from our behaviour – which is *not* free. However, given the enormous complexity of this interaction of stimulus and response, we *feel* that it is (and there's an end of it?). As before, a quantitative change from one single, simple reflex to a multiplicity of stimulus–response connections, produces a qualitative change in appearance, and behaviour turns into a *process* in the same way that a series of film stills is turned into movement and drama by the rapid motion of the movie projector. The stills are there all the time and are the invisible components that give rise to the perception of behaviour on the screen. Action and interaction become a *flow* of behaviour, or a *stream* of events. However, we need to remember that even streams have their component parts, right down to the individual molecules of hydrogen and oxygen that are their building blocks. The view of interaction taken here, is that discrete elements in this process of influence by the environment, and re-influence by the individual, are blurred by the speed and complexity of events. Such a view acknowledges multiple causation and recognizes that what is often regarded as the cause of something, is merely the last of, or the most conspicuous part of, a great many pre-conditions necessary to its occurrence (Verworn 1916). In this way it can be said that operating the switch *caused* the light bulb to illuminate, but in fact, many other complex factors were at work to bring this about.

The 'medical' model of behaviour and its alternatives

I have proposed an alternative conception of the relationship between consciousness and behaviour: that contrary to the established view, consciousness flows from behaviour, rather than the reverse. However, the by now traditional Cartesian version of this relationship, that behaviour is merely symptomatic, still holds most of the ground in psychiatry, social work, and to a lesser extent, in psychology. It also has its clinical counterparts in conceptualizations of abnormal behaviour in these disciplines. The dominant model here is the medical, or disease-entity model. This suggests that disturbance or unusualness, whether in the form of behavioural deficits, excesses of behaviour, or out-of-context behaviour, results from underlying conditions in the same way that excessive coughing (symptom) may be the result of a germ-infested larynx (cause). Similarly, excessive cleanliness (symptom) is often said to be the result of a 'guilt complex' (cause), and delusional talk (symptom) to be the outward expression of 'schizophrenia'. There is a heavy element of tautology here. In the last case, the existence of the 'schizophrenia' is inferred from the symptom, which is the only evidence of its existence. Likewise, Mrs Brown's poor social functioning can be said to stem from 'an inadequate personality' or, if profound, from a personality *disorder*. Billy fails to thrive at school *because* he is retarded, and Mr Brown lacks assertiveness *because* he has 'an inferiority complex'. Historically, such views are an effect of the 'psychiatric deluge', when social work in particular caught a bad case of psychoanalysis, from which it has yet to fully recover.

Philosophical implications 31

Let us now review the basic assumptions of this medical model.
(a) People with behavioural problems are often 'sick', if not in a physical sense, then mentally 'sick'. This condition follows a similar pattern to that of physical illness and requires a similar approach, and similar training, to deal with it effectively. This model also extends to certain categories of social problems. (Reiner and Kaufman (1959) link law breaking and industrial unrest with 'bad mental hygiene', for example.)
(b) As a corollary to the above, these behavioural 'symptoms' fall into clusters, and from these patterns it is possible to determine the underlying process of causation.
(c) The process of diagnosing such disorders and syndromes can be almost as value-free as the process of diagnosis in physical disorder.
(d) Assessment decisions based on this model have an acceptable level of validity and reliability. Syndromes can be clearly identified, and this makes a difference to what is done to treat them, and to the outcome of such attempts.
(e) Direct intervention to deal specifically with 'symptoms' may occasionally have a palliative effect, but is more likely to result in their re-emergence – perhaps in a more pernicious form. This is the idea of symptom-substitution, which is supposed to be a limitation on the application of behavioural methods.
(f) The identification of these underlying, causal processes, and intervention with specific remedies to deal with these, requires a high level of professional expertise, and is not a process to be meddled in by relatives, 'para-professions', and 'laymen', although they may have a subsidiary part to play, if closely supervised (Brewer and Lait 1980).

Give or take an emphasis, this is how the proponents of the medical model view things. However, there are several problems associated with this formulation of abnormal behaviour, whether applied to psychiatric, psychological, or social ailments. I have already touched on the problem of tautology. Although it may seem, on the face of it, that we have accomplished something by classifying certain troublesome behaviour as indicative of, say, a neurosis or an 'inferiority complex', in fact, very little has been achieved unless we can establish testable hypotheses which can shed light on a relevant causal sequence. We also require a prognosis that is based on something other than our own self-fulfilling prophecies, or on our own ideas of the suitability of remedial action: for example, 'mothers with "inadequate personalities" make bad parents'; 'children with "authority problems" often get into trouble with the police'. To say that Mr A behaves as he does because of his inadequate personality, or that Mr B behaves in this or that way because he is retarded, adds nothing to our understanding of the behaviour of Mr A or Mr B. It simply means, that we have attached a polysyllabic label with scientific pretensions onto our client. We may as well say that Mr A behaves in an inadequate way because he is inadequate, or that Mr B behaves in a retarded fashion because of his retardation! Bandura (1969) indicts this process of circular reasoning about behavioural problems as having clogged up our thinking on such matters for decades. By thinking in this way, we are diverted from the investigation of factors that may initiate and maintain unwanted behaviour, or from thinking about the circumstances which prevent other, more adaptive behaviour from being learned. In our own field Smale (1977) has produced a useful analysis of this problem.

The idea that maladaptive and troublesome behaviours fall into neat groups needs also to be viewed with caution. As with all decision-making processes, selective-perception, and the necessary human tendency to impose patterns on discrete or even random events, can mislead us into thinking that we are applying objective criteria and merely describing or systematizing 'what is there'. Often we are guilty of looking for data to confirm our own implicitly held theories about what 'should' be there. This is a process, not of discovery, but of invention. The research of Heine (1953) demonstrates clearly that the factors accounting for change in psychotherapy clients, plus many of the details of each case record, could be acurately predicted just by knowing the theoretical leanings of the therapist. Studies of this kind have led many in the behavioural field to view insight-giving and other conversational approaches to what is essentially deviant *behaviour*, as having more to do with labelling, and social conversion (to the therapist's point of view) than they have to do with the resolving of deeply buried conflicts.

The philosopher, Karl Popper, has interesting things to say about this process of confirming our own theories. Where the theories are loosely-formulated they are also highly resistant to refutation as a result of disconfirming experience:

'I found that those of my friends who were admirers of Marx, Freud, and Adler, were impressed by a number of points common to those theories, and especially by their apparent *explanatory power*. These theories appeared to be able to explain practically everything that happened within the fields to which they referred. The study of any of them seemed to have the effect of an intellectual conversion or revelation, opening your eyes to a new truth hidden from those not yet initiated. Once your eyes were thus opened, you saw confirming instances everywhere: the world was full of *verifications* of the theory. Whatever happened always confirmed it. Thus its truth appeared manifest; and unbelievers were clearly people who did not want to see the manifest truth; who refused to see it, either because it was against their class interest, or because of their repressions which were still "un-analysed" and crying aloud for treatment.' (Popper 1963 : 54)

Now if committed Rogerians are almost bound to find inappropriate self-concepts, is it not also true that behaviourists are equally bound to find inappropriate reinforcement contingencies? There is no doubt that behaviourists can fall victim to the same distorting influences, but it is also true that the behavioural approach works against, rather than with, such tendencies. For example, the controlling conditions that behaviourists seek to investigate are amenable to systematic variation: consequently the relationship between reinforcement contingencies and behaviour is readily verifiable (Bandura 1969). In addition, the hypotheses used in behaviour therapy approach Karl Popper's ideal of 'riskiness' (Popper 1963). That is, it is quite possible to conceive of eventualities that would call them into question – such as the 're-emergence' of 'symptoms' following a behaviour modification programme. The fact that this does not occur, in the face of the potential vulnerability of the theory at this point, adds weight to its validity (Yates 1958).

In addition to questions of validity, there is the problem of the reliability of the various problem-classification schemes built upon the medical model. For example, do therapists, when confronted with the same, or very similar, case material, assign it to the same broad general category? Most of the available research on this topic has been done by psychologists using psychiatrists as their subjects (Ullman and Krasner 1969). However the findings are relevant too in social work. With our paucity of guidelines, it is not uncommon for practitioners to completely alter a previous diagnosis when placed in charge of a case.

Research into diagnostic reliability throughout the helping professions has yielded consistently disappointing results. The following results *(Table 2(1))* are typical, and show low levels of concordance between psychiatric observers – certainly nothing approaching the level of 80 per cent agreement, usually thought necessary in this kind of study.

Table 2(1) *Percentage of agreement among psychiatrists for twelve different categories*

Category	Number of calls	% Agreement
All categories	910	57
Schizophrenics	170	74
Mental deficiency	40	73
Personality disorder	205	66
Chronic brain syndrome	56	66
Psychoneurosis	223	56
Acute brain syndrome	40	46
Psychophysiologic reaction	25	40
Manic depressive	45	36
Involutional psychotic	59	26
Psychotic depressive	33	22
Psychotic reaction, other	4	17
Paranoid reaction	10	13

Source: Sandifer, Pettus, and Quale (1964). Copyright 1964 The Williams and Wilkins Co., Baltimore. Reproduced by permission.

Trying to assign objective labels for the purpose of predicting behaviour can be very self-deluding, even at the level of broad problem categories. Suppose we lower our sights still further. Is there any evidence to show that the presence or absence of the various syndromes said to be at work in deviant behaviour can be reliably ascertained? The answer is, 'not very much'. Two ingeniously constructed studies serve to illustrate the problems. The first, is the work of Rosenhan (1973). He and his confederates caused themselves to be admitted to an American mental hospital, by giving vague reports of well-known psychotic symptoms – such as passivity feelings. The important point though, is that following admission, they reverted to normal, everyday behaviour. Perhaps surprisingly, none of the medical, or nursing, staff noticed this. When written work associated with the study was carried out openly, this was seen as yet further evidence of 'illness' by the ward staff. The only group that recognized the fact of some sort of diagnostic anomaly, were the other patients!

The second study (Temerlin 1968) was based on tape recordings of actors conversing normally. When panels of volunteer psychiatrists and psychologists were asked to assign these people to one of the mental illness categories, they went merrily ahead. Inter-observer ratings were disappointingly low as usual, but, more seriously, only 7.6 per cent of the psychiatrists (N = 95) decided that there were no signs of pathology. Categorizations were strongly influenced by a prior suggestion of vaguely defined 'mental problems'. (The psychologists did a little better, but barely-trained psychology students did best of all!)

The debate is regularly raised in the helping professions, as to whether a high level of investment in reaching an 'accurate' diagnosis is worthwhile. This applies to both psychiatry and to social work. In our case we have spent huge sums on expensive assessment centres, capable of recommending very specific kinds of remedial placement for children. The only problem is that often these placements are not available, through lack of investment in treatment facilities. In the case of psychiatry, accurate diagnosis may do more for the practitioner than the patient. Having arrived at a decision, the prognosis is often very poor, and can be made worse by the patient and his or her family having knowledge of the gloomy pseudo-scientific label chosen. Second, because the treatment procedures applied to various conditions are not as differentiated as one might suppose, great effort is expended in trying to decide what patient Mr X is 'suffering from', when, broadly speaking, the specificity of the diagnosis cannot be matched by any parallel specificity in treatment.

There is good reason too, for treating all diagnostic procedures with great suspicion, whether they are our own loosely formulated categories in social work, or whether they are categories handed on to us by other professions. Fortunately, perhaps, social workers quickly acquire a healthy distrust of other people's labels; particularly those of the referral agent.

By limiting ourselves to good *descriptions* of behaviour, many of the problems of inter-observer reliability referred to above can be overcome. In behaviour modification we are concerned to discover what someone who is supposedly 'schizophrenic', or 'neurotic' *does*, does *not* do, or does in an unusual *setting*. By keeping inference to a minimum, limiting ourselves as far as possible to the directly observable, both our assessments of cases, and our findings during treatment, become more accurate and more transferable to others working in the same field. (These points are dealt with in more detail in Chapter Five.)

The danger with this position on diagnostic reliability, is that it can easily lead to a vague idea that 'everyone is normal *really*'; that all deviant behaviour is the result of the pessimistic and self-fulfilling prophecy of society's authoritarian labellers. Or, that it is explainable entirely in terms of crude and obvious environmental pressure – such as shortage of money, large families, or boring work conditions. We know, of course, that these can be very powerful effects, but then there are thousands of people who do *not* succumb to them. Further, using this kind of reasoning it is easy to slide into a position where 'undemocratic' influences such as genetics and physiology are ignored altogether (Eysenck 1964).

Next, let us consider in more detail the point about the dangers of symptom substitution, referred to above. Together with the association of behaviour modification with crude aversion therapy, this misconception accounts more than any other factor for the refusal of social workers to make use of behavioural methods. To use a term often directed against the activities of behaviourists, many potential users have been 'brainwashed' into believing that symptom-substitution is inevitable, and fail to see that this view depends entirely upon the dualistic disease-entity or mental cause/behavioural-effect models of behaviour reviewed above – which, paradoxically, many social workers disclaim any affiliation to. The anti-behaviourists would say that a problem re-emerges because 'the problem' is something inside the head of the client and is merely *giving rise* to problematic behaviour. If (on good evidence) we regard the behaviour *as* the problem, *per se*, then this notion of re-emergence evaporates. More tellingly, we can look at the scientific evidence *for* the concept of symptom-substitution. As far as I can discover, there is none, at least none of basically acceptable scientific quality. In fact, the most surprising thing about symptom-substitution is its prevalence and potency as an *idea* in the absence of any consistent descriptions of the phenomenon at work. Or perhaps this is not so surprising, since supporters of the theory have singularly failed to develop criteria by which genuinely re-emerging 'symptoms' could be distinguished either from other difficulties that have always been present (but are perhaps highlighted by the absence of the identified problem), or from problems that have developed in the period between the ending of treatment and the follow-up point.

There is however a wealth of information available to support the contrary view: that symptom-substitution is a clinical problem of very little importance (Yates 1958; Grossberg 1964; Bandura 1969). On the basis of these problems and shortcomings we have need of an approach to the assessment of problematic behaviour that scores highly on the following list of ideal characteristics.

(a) It should allow a high level of inter-observer reliability; that is, different observers of the same set of phenomena should be able to agree fairly easily about what is going on.

(b) The assessment should include a causal account of the problems under review. It is insufficient to infer condition A from 'symptom' B when the significance of B is inferred, in turn, from A.

(c) Concepts employed in defining the problem(s) under scrutiny must not be so loosely woven as to stretch easily over any discrepant data. The good assessment, like the good theory, is the one that forbids endless interpretation; that is, is the least negotiable (Popper 1963; Sheldon 1978a).

(d) The assessment hypotheses produced should be of such a character and quality as to be open to subsequent refutation or confirmation: this is needed as a basis for establishing the outcome of intervention as clearly as possible.

(e) There should be a substantive, logical, and theoretical link between assessment decisions and intervention procedures; that is, specific approaches for specifically identified problems.

(f) Any special terminology used to describe problematic behaviour and its controlling features should be as free as possible from excessively pessimistic connotations, likely to lead to negatively self-fulfilling effects.

This list summarizes many of the problems of the medical model discussed in the preceeding passages. The medical model does not score highly on *any* of the above characteristics (see Ullman and Krasner 1969). My purpose in presenting it is so that the reader can apply it to the behavioural model of assessment, which is presented as an alternative approach, in Chapter Five.

3
Theories of learning

This chapter seeks to outline the different theories of learning from which the techniques known collectively, if a little ungrammatically, as Behaviour Modification, are derived. Such an account is necessary for two reasons. First, so that the person applying the techniques will understand the reasons for what he or she is doing, rather than just dipping into a bag of therapeutic tricks and hoping to come up with the right approach. Second, so that a proper assessment of the client's problems can be made. In this field, there are no 'general purpose' procedures, and decisions about which techniques to use are based upon certain well-established theories of how behaviour, including problematic or deviant behaviour, is acquired in the first place.

Until quite recently, an exercise such as this would have been relatively straightforward, but as the reader will see, new research into the role of cognitive variables and their effects on overt behaviour (Michenbaum 1977) and recently formulated theories of social learning (Bandura 1977) are tugging this discipline out of its previously neat and tidy shape. While all this is very exciting, it makes the task of the newcomer more difficult. Let us apply a good behavioural principle to this problem and start off simply, moving on to the more difficult and speculative issues later on. Here is a list of behaviour modification's basic theoretical assumptions, which could perhaps be described as 'the orthodox version'.

(a) By far the greater portion of the behavioural repertoire with which individuals are equipped is the product of learning. This vast range of possible responses is acquired through a lengthy

interaction with an ambivalent physical and social environment.
(b) Genetic and other physiological factors also influence behaviour in a general sense, and there is an interaction between these and environment (Thomas, Chess, and Birch 1968; Tsuang and Vandermey 1980).
(c) Two broad processes of associative learning account for the acquisition and maintenance of motor, verbal, and emotional responses. These are: *classical* or *respondent* conditioning, based on the work of the great Russian physiologist I. P. Pavlov; and *operant* or *instrumental* conditioning, based on the work of the American psychologists, E. L. Thorndike (1898) and B. F. Skinner (1953).
(d) Behaviours that we judge to be 'maladaptive' or 'abnormal', are learned in exactly the same way as behaviours that we are disposed to call 'adaptive' or 'normal'. Any apparent differences between the two, apart from questions of degree, are a property of the attributive and evaluative judgements that we make about behaviour, rather than of the behaviour itself or its origin (Ullman and Krasner 1969).
(e) The behavioural therapies owe their existence to learning theory, which is itself underpinned by replicable scientific experimentation.
(f) Properly applied, these techniques have a direct and tangible effect on problematic behaviour and results obtained are not threatened by a re-emergence of 'symptoms' in some different form.
(g) The behaviourist is not greatly concerned with the thoughts and feelings *per se* of clients, since this kind of data is notoriously unreliable, and also we have no guaranteed evidence that such private events play a direct part in eliciting and maintaining behaviour. Their status, therefore, is that of interesting epiphenomena (Skinner 1974).

My aim in presenting this list of assumptions in this way, is to get the reader to respond to them critically from the start. Many of these points still hold good, but certain items are increasingly subject to qualification. Nevertheless, the list gives the flavour of the discipline, and will do to start with.

The next thing of which the reader needs to be made aware, is that there is not one master learning theory from which all these principles are derived, but many different, overlapping theories, which produce between them areas of broad theoretical consensus, and yet other areas riddled with dispute. However, before we can proceed to examine these differences, we need a general definition of learning. There are many such definitions available, but they tend to range from the general but vaguely unsatisfactory, to the meticulous but barely usable (Smith 1969). The common ground between them all is that the concept of learning applies to the processes whereby new and relatively durable responses are added to the individual's behavioural repertoire. For our present purposes, the following simple outline will do to work on. (For the interested reader an extended technical definition is available in Hillner (1979).)

> 'Learning may be defined as a relatively permanent change in behaviour that occurs as the result of prior experience.'
> (Hilgard, Atkinson, and Atkinson 1979:181)

Three qualifications are immediately necessary even to this short, formal definition. First, and contrary to the everyday meaning of the term, there need be no intention on anyone's part to impart learning for it to take place. Nor need there be any intention on the part of the learner to acquire new information or behaviour. Second, we must exclude from this definition all effects due to fatigue, demonstrable illness, or the influence of drugs. Third, the effects of learning may not be immediately apparent. A newly acquired potential for behaviour can be stored in memory until circumstances are propitious for its performance in some form.

The next question is, how do organisms learn? As I have indicated, arguments still rage over the precise nature of the process, but four related influences are usually cited.

(a) Classical conditioning: whereby the association of one stimulus with another – already capable of producing a certain response – leads eventually to responding to either stimulus alone.
(b) Operant conditioning: learning occurs as a result of our experience of the rewarding and punishing consequences of learned responses.
(c) Vicarious learning: new responses are required by observing the behaviour of others and the outcomes that their actions produce.
(d) Cognitive – mediational theories (including (c) above according to some writers): lays greater stress on the role of thought and the *interpretation* of stimuli, rather than on the direct relation-

ship between environmental stimulation and behavioural response.
Let us now examine each of these processes in more detail.

Classical conditioning

Classical conditioning is a term first applied by Hilgard (1948) to the work of Pavlov, to distinguish the principles from the newer *operant* model of learning (see page 51). The prefix 'classical' then, refers only to the venerability of the concept; an alternative label for this process is *respondent* conditioning. Pavlov's work dates from the turn of this century and his real achievement stems from his painstaking methodology and careful analysis of results; from the detail and the certainty of his findings rather than from their complete novelty. His experiments were designed to settle an argument over the nature of certain 'psychical' secretions from the salivary glands of animals. 'Psychical' here refers to secretions of saliva present *before* the presentation of any food – a reaction presumed to originate spontaneously from the mind of the animal (Pavlov 1897). Crossing into the psychological domain Pavlov soon found himself lacking a satisfactory means of investigating this phenomenon and so turned back to the methods of natural science:

> 'In our "psychical" experiments on the salivary glands, at first we honestly endeavoured to explain our results by fancying the subjective condition of the animal. But nothing came of it except unsuccessful controversies and individual, personal, uncoordinated opinion. We had no alternative but to place the investigation on a purely objective basis.' (Pavlov 1897:183)

Pavlov's procedure was as follows: A dog underwent a small operation to facilitate the collection of saliva directly from the cheek gland. The dog was then trained to stand quietly in a harness. The laboratory was soundproofed and the experimenters observed the proceedings through a one-way screen. Thus, there was no possibility of extraneous sounds or movements distracting the animal. The sequence of the experiment is as follows. A bell is rung – the animal reacts only slightly to the new noise. No salivary flow is recorded. Next, a quantity of meat powder is delivered to a food tray in front of the dog. He salivates and eats it. After a few pairings of the bell (or light, or range of other neutral stimuli) with the food, the dog begins to salivate to the sound of the bell (or light) alone. He continues to do this over many trials, even though no food is forthcoming. The dog has learned a new response.

Let us look at this process of associative learning schematically, to see what is involved *(Figure 3(1))*.

Figure 3(1) A diagram of classical conditioning

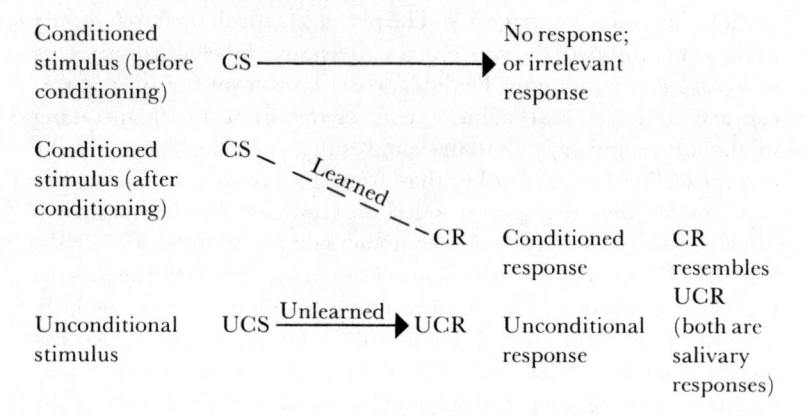

Conditioned stimulus (before conditioning)	CS ──────────────▶	No response; or irrelevant response	
Conditioned stimulus (after conditioning)	CS ╲ ╲ *Learned* ╲ ╲ ╲▶ CR	Conditioned response	CR resembles UCR
Unconditional stimulus	UCS ──*Unlearned*──▶ UCR	Unconditional response	(both are salivary responses)

The association between the unconditional stimulus and the unconditional response exists at the start of the experiment and does not have to be learned. The association between the conditioned stimulus and the conditioned response is a learned one. It arises through the pairing of the conditioned and unconditional stimuli followed by the unconditional response (i.e. reinforcement). The conditioned response resembles the unconditional one (though they need not be identical).

Source: Adapted from *Introduction to Psychology*, fourth edition by Ernest R. Hilgard and Richard C. Atkinson, copyright © 1967 by Harcourt Brace Jovanovich, Inc. Reprinted by permission of the publisher.

There is considerable misunderstanding about the role of animal experimentation and its relevance in advancing our knowledge of human behaviour. Much of the basic experimentation in the behavioural field has involved the use of animals. The function of these experiments is to investigate the truth of relatively simple propositions under better controlled conditions than would be possible with human subjects. Once this first stage in the research has been satisfactorily completed, then adaptations of the same procedures, now better understood, can be applied to human subjects to see how transferable the results are.

An example of this progression is to be found in the celebrated study of fear acquisition through classical conditioning, carried out by Watson and Rayner (1920). The subject of this experiment was a toddler known to history as 'little Albert' (partly in parody of Freud's elaborate analysis of a boy with a phobia of horses, called 'little Hans'). The procedure was as follows: A tame white rat (CS) was introduced into a playpen containing little Albert, and he began to play with it without fear. (Fear of small animals is not innate in man.) However during subsequent trials, whenever the rat was introduced, a metal bar suspended over the pen was struck vigorously to produce a loud noise (UCS). A fear reaction to sudden loud noises *is* innate in humans, and so this unconditionally produced a response (UCR). Soon little Albert became distressed just at the sight of the small animal, even when its presentation was *not* accompanied by a loud noise (CR). A new, conditioned response (fear of small furry animals) had been acquired. Classical conditioning is particularly important in the acquisition of new emotional responses (see Chapter Four).

However, in any field, the general direction of research findings is more important than the results of isolated studies. While in the field of conditioning there is plenty of evidence that new fear responses *can* be generated by simple contiguous association, it is an error of logic to assume that therefore *all* fear responses develop in this way. Recent research (see Davey 1981) suggests that conditioning is a much more complex phenomenon than originally envisaged by Pavlov. In this research there are three important trends to take note of.

(a) Some investigators have raised doubts as to the distinctness of classical learning procedures and have put forward single process theories (favouring an exclusively operant analysis of learning; see Williams and Williams (1969)). Later in this chapter the reader will see that the two models do overlap at certain points (see page 54). In this book the view that there are two distinct learning processes is retained, partly as a heuristic device and partly because, as yet, the research that threatens this position is insufficient to justify a radical reappraisal (see Gray 1975).

(b) If the Pavlovian concepts were universally true, then it should be possible to condition a fear reaction to anything. The fact that certain kinds of objects (CSs) can set up conditioned reactions much more easily than others, raises questions about the simple paired-association model. This idea of *preparedness* – that perhaps for reasons of natural selection and genetic inheritance, there are certain stimuli of which we are especially prone to learn to be afraid – is an interesting feature of contemporary research (Seligman 1971).

(c) Since it is possible for human subjects to have powerful fears of objects and animals which they have never seen and are unlikely to come across (e.g., snakes) it is more than likely that cognitive variables are involved in fear conditioning. Thus, in the absence of any real snakes we acquire a fear of an image, presented to the accompaniment of anxiety. Here perceived parental distress may be the UCS, the child's anxiety in the face of this the UCR, the snake image the CS, and the eventual fear reaction to the *idea* of snakes, the CR. Lazarus (1971) provides an interesting account, in cognitive terms, of how strong fears can develop without any apparent basis in the overt behavioural experience of the subject.

STIMULUS GENERALIZATION

To return to Watson and Rayner's work, the next stage in the experiment illustrates a clinically important phenomenon called stimulus generalization. Once the conditioned response was established, similar responses could be obtained to a variety of like stimuli, for example other small animals, parcels of furry material, a fur coat. This effect was noted also by Pavlov who found that having conditioned dogs to salivate to the sound of a bell, the same kind of response could then be induced by other noises of a broadly similar kind.

This phenomenon of generalization gives us a clue to the biological purpose of associative learning of this kind. It has great survival value to the organism, and anything that confers a biological advantage is likely to be selected for in the evolutionary process. Clearly, the conditioned reflex is a winner in this respect. Nature cannot 'foresee' all eventualities and therefore it can work only to a very limited extent through *specific* genetic endowment. Faced with the problem of changing, and highly variable environments, nature instead confers *conditionability*, or the ability to learn by association about the functional relations between objects and events in the environment. Thus, well before the food enters the dog's mouth, its upper digestive tract is prepared for it and is ready to break it down chemically for its nutritional value. The earlier this process begins, the better from a survival point of view, and if an animal can learn to respond to stimuli which come reliably in advance of the opportunity to feed, so much the better. Try it yourself: it is a crisp autumn morning, and standing in the garden you smell Sunday lunch cooking – roast lamb and mint sauce (vegetarians can substitute mushroom flan, or, if all else fails, imagine licking half a lemon). The response that will have taken place (saliva filling the mouth) is another example of classical conditioning. This particular response is established through the past pairing of actual food with images of food, and words that eventually come to represent and signal the likely presence of food.

Because stimuli tend to impinge in groups, it is biologically advantageous for those reliably associated with each other to have the same general effect. Once a new association has been formed, it can itself form the basis of new learning. Thus the process of classical conditioning 'strings together' stimulus-response connections.

We have seen that conditioned reflexes provide different forms of reliable early warning for the organism. They allow the body to gear itself up to cope with potentially advantageous or potentially threatening situations. Our state of constant readiness in this respect is governed by the autonomic nervous system, which acts mainly automatically through the glands and the smooth muscles, to help us to gain an *edge* over our potentially hostile environment. Thus we do not have to wait until the burglar we have interrupted downstairs actually hits us over the head, before we begin to react to the threat that he might pose. An unusual noise at night will set our pulses racing, our muscles will stiffen ready for action, our pores will open, sweating will begin so that we can cool our body efficiently if strenuous activity follows, our pupils will dilate so that we can make best use of what light there is, and so forth (see also pp. 93–4). Similarly, we do not have to wait to be told that since we have failed to prepare adequately for an important meeting, we have entered a sequence of events where we stand at risk of losing the esteem of our colleagues and our employers, possibly of losing our livelihood, of not being able to maintain our families, of being discredited socially, and so on. The chairman of the meeting need only look from the surprisingly well-stocked files of others, to the vacant table in front of us, and this is stimulus enough to trigger an emotional reaction, based on a

46 Behaviour Modification

long chain of associations, which stretches back to our basic concerns about survival. As far as our bodies are concerned, we could be getting ready to take on a small pterodactyl!

This physiological trigger-reaction is sometimes called the 'fight/flight mechanism', and we experience its effect as fear and various other less dramatic states of arousal. The fact that under modern social conditions, to run away from a threat, or to punch it in the eye, is seldom an adaptive response, is neither here nor there. Evolution has not yet caught up with this fact, and so human conditionability has its side effects. The following case illustration should demonstrate this point.

CASE ILLUSTRATION SHOWING THE ORIGINS AND DEVELOPMENT OF A PHOBIA

Mrs Wood, aged forty, was referred to the Social Services Department for 'support' by her somewhat exasperated family doctor. In his view Mrs Wood suffered from agoraphobia (fear of going out of doors), a 'dependent personality', and a number of unspecified 'psychiatric difficulties'. The doctor also had some worries about Mrs Wood's young son, because not only had Mrs Wood barely left the house in the previous three years, but also, very little had been seen of the child.

Background

During the first interview Mrs Wood was very wary of discussing her problems, and was still sulking a little about her doctor 'washing his hands' of her case and passing her on to the Out-Patient Department of the local mental hospital. She had subsequently been offered an out-patient's appointment at a clinic eighteen miles away from her home! During the second home visit Mrs Wood was more forthcoming, and the following pattern to her problem emerged.

- Mrs Wood had a lifelong fear of hospitals, stemming from her mother's confinement with her younger sister. Her mother had nearly died in childbirth.
- Mrs Wood became pregnant 'by accident', comparatively late in life. In order to persuade her to have the baby in hospital, the doctor had played up the dangers of a home confinement, raising her already high level of anxiety about the birth.

- One hot summer's day, when she was seven months pregnant, Mrs Wood had fainted while crossing a footbridge spanning a small river near to her home. 'I was sure I was going to fall in, and when I came round, people said an ambulance was on the way. I panicked. People were trying to hold me down, covering me with coats.'
- 'I knew I had to get away, I got very upset, and eventually I persuaded someone to take me home. When I got in I was shaking all over. I shut and bolted the doors, back and front. . . . I was sure that the ambulance was going to call at the house. . . . I hid out of sight of the windows . . . and eventually (it took about an hour) I calmed down, and sat waiting for my husband to come home from work.'
- Mrs Wood had her baby at home, against medical advice, but without serious complication. She tried to go out several times after that but never got further than the front garden, or, if at night, as far as the front gate.
- She reported the following feelings at each attempt: 'Shivering; awful feelings in the pit of my stomach; pounding heart; light headedness.' 'In the daytime everywhere seems very bright and stark. I feel conspicuous out in the open, almost as if I might be struck down any minute.' 'My breathing is loud in my ears all the time and my biggest fear is that I shall collapse again.' 'I have thought at times that I should die.'
- Mrs Wood eventually gave up these attempts and remained indoors for the next four years. For the first two of these she reported that she didn't really miss going out: 'the family were very good, they took the baby out, got the shopping, they are marvellous; so are the neighbours.' Later, however, Mrs Wood began to experience feelings of dissatisfaction and frustration with her confined existence.
- When Mrs Wood *had* to go out, for example to peg out washing, she reports making a quick dash out the back, hoping no one would see her or try to talk to her, and 'great relief when I get back in and close the door. I think there must be something seriously wrong with me . . . in my mind . . .'

If we examine this case in the light of classical conditioning theory, the following pattern emerges.

- Against a background of heightened anxiety about pregnancy,

dreading the thought of having to go into hospital, Mrs Wood experiences a traumatic incident (UCS) which arouses in her a very powerful fear reaction (UCR).
- This incident, when paired with the previously neutral stimulus of the footbridge and other stimuli associated with being out of doors, for example seeing other people (CS), produces eventually a conditioned response to these stimuli. Even after the incident itself has passed, and the pregnancy is over, she is perfectly well, and the crowd is no longer in sight (the eliciting stimuli), she still experienced a powerful fear reaction to the original context.
- Mrs Wood reports that her panic state was made worse by the attempts of would-be helpers to restrain her until the ambulance came. Escape behaviour was prevented, thus intensifying her fear.
- This conditioned fear response quickly generalizes to virtually all outdoor circumstances, even though objectively, they barely resemble the circumstances of her collapse. Furthermore, every time Mrs Wood tries to go out of doors at this stage she is punished for the attempt by her powerful fear reaction, even though she sees these feelings as irrational and illogical.
- Every time Mrs Wood manages to escape from the circumstances that elicit the conditioned fear response, her strongly aversive fears are terminated: this strengthens her avoidance behaviour, and makes future experiments less likely.
- Mrs Wood's family and friends reward her long-term maladaption to her phobia by relieving her of many of her responsibilities regarding her child and by reassuring her that they do not mind her staying behind rather than going on family outings.

It will not have escaped the reader's attention that as we move from laboratory to natural-environment examples of classical conditioning, it has become rather more difficult to specify the key stimuli with the same precision. Was it the already-learned fear of hospitals that became connected with particular outdoor circumstances? Or was it loss of consciousness and a fear of ending up in hospital? Or was it a fear of falling helplessly into the water? To what extent did fears for the unborn baby, or even embarrassment, play a part? To what extent did the unsympathetic words of a family doctor predispose Mrs Wood to what happened? It is likely that *all* these factors were influential in producing the unconditional fear and panic response. In the natural environment, stimuli tend to come in untidy bundles, as do responses, and it is often difficult to tease out their different effects. Mrs Wood remembers particularly the idea of being 'a prisoner of the crowd', the fear of hospitals, and the narrowness of the footbridge. She also has a vivid recollection of the brightness of the day. Her memories cover the key stimuli but we have no idea of their relative importance. The analysis is not as neat as the one provided by Pavlov in his carefully controlled experiments, but is made within the framework he painstakingly constructed, and dependent upon exactly the same general principles. Details of the treatment approach used in this case can be found on page 217.

Now we turn to some other dimensions of the classical conditioning process.

CLASSICAL EXTINCTION

If the bell in Pavlov's experiment is rung repeatedly, but without any food ever appearing, the conditioned salivary response (or any other classically conditioned response in animals or humans) eventually disappears. This too is biologically advantageous to the organism since there is no survival value in conditioning to respond forever to unreliable associations. The process is called *extinction*, and it is an important feature of operant conditioning too (see page 173). However, well-conditioned responses such as the phobia discussed above are very resistant to extinction; they take a considerable time to 'unlearn'. This may be because of a repeated pairing of key stimuli; because of one very dramatic conjugation; or because the new behaviour has pleasant consequences not immediately apparent to outside observers.

EXPERIMENTAL NEUROSIS

Following his work on classical conditioning, Pavlov and his co-workers conducted a series of experiments to investigate how animals cope with being conditioned to respond to contradictory or ambiguous stimuli. Such situations are fairly prevalent in the complex social environments of human beings, and so the findings have considerable relevance outside the field of animal behaviour.

The experimenters conditioned animals to anticipate food on the presentation of a particular visual stimulus. For example, the animal was taught to salivate to a circle of light but not to an ellipse

(Shenger-Krestovnika 1921). It was then made increasingly difficult for the animal to distinguish between these stimuli, by arranging for the circle to become narrowed at the sides, and for the ellipse to come increasingly to resemble a circle. Another variation of this experiment involved the random substitution of consequences – so that the animal was unable to predict whether food or pain would follow a given stimulus (Masserman 1943). The effects of these rather cruel studies were that the animals first became extremely agitated and their behaviour very uncharacteristic (hence the term 'experimental neurosis'). Later, the animals lost their ability to make even crude discriminations, and the experimenters began to use words such as 'depression' and 'catatonia' to describe their immobilized condition. In later experiments animals just accepted shocks rather than take an escape route because they had been unpredictably shocked in the past for so doing. This work has given rise to a wide range of experimentation aimed at investigating the parallels between the artificial environments of these animals, and those found in human society. Some of the most fruitful recent work is that of Seligman (1975) whose *Learned Helplessness* theory is of great interest to behaviour therapists. Seligman's view is that when an individual learns through experience that there is little or no reliable connection between stimuli, and that his behaviour has little effect in modifying stimuli (reducing painful effects and boosting pleasant ones), the individual's behaviour first becomes very erratic as he or she tries to re-establish some control. If this fails, then, just as in animal experiments, the individual gradually withdraws from the world, since the environment supports so few of his attempts to adapt to it positively. Neither conditioned emotional reactions, nor the anticipation of pleasure, nor the arousal states useful in combating threats, serve any useful purpose any longer, and so they die away, leaving the individual in a state of complete apathy.

Further work needs to be done on Seligman's proposals, but they are well grounded in basic laboratory research. They have a ring of truth to anyone familiar with the case histories of psychiatric patients admitted to hospital for neurotic depression or, at a less serious level, to anyone familiar with the backgrounds of clients labelled as 'inadequate personalities', 'problem families', and so on. Behavioural approaches help to combat such states to the extent that they are able to re-establish some order and predictability in the circumstances of clients, and to the extent that such approaches can equip the clients with new skills and teach them how to reassert some control over their environment.

Operant conditioning

The term *operant conditioning* (together with its synonym, *instrumental conditioning*) refers to the way in which organisms *operate* on their environment, which in turn selectively strengthens, or reinforces certain patterns of behaviour at the expense of others. This can happen either accidentally, or because the environment has been specifically programmed to support certain behaviours and discourage others, as in the workings of a large organization, or through the rules of the classroom.

The root principle of operant conditioning is that behaviour is a function of its consequences. Parents who respond favourably, first to the random gurglings of their infant, then to specific noises, then to approximations of words, are making use of this principle and helping along the acquisition of spoken language. Similarly, the school child who notices that an act of disruption produces a level of peer approval previously unknown, will be more likely to repeat the behaviour in future. The lecturer who tries to set his audience at ease by starting with a joke, but gets puzzled frowns rather than the good-humoured laughter he anticipated, will be unlikely to repeat the exercise for a while. He too is on the receiving end of an operant consequence, which will powerfully affect his future behaviour.

An operant, then, is a sequence of behaviour, not under the direct control of an experimenter, that produces an environmental consequence. A useful analogy here is that of sonar or radar. The individual manoeuvres himself through his physical and social environment according to the 'return signals' he receives from it as to the consequences of his behaviour. The more (or less) pleasurable the environmental feedback he receives, the more (or less) likely he is to engage in the behaviour again in similar circumstances.

The groundwork for this theory of behaviour was carried out by E. L. Thorndike (1898:1931). However, the extension and detailed investigation of the theory has been the life work of B. F. Skinner (1953). Skinner's contribution has been to investigate with great precision the large number of variables that influence the course of learning through experience of consequences; to formulate this into a comprehensive theory; and to apply the theory very successfully to human behaviour. A description of Skinner's basic animal experiments will be useful as a way of clarifying some basic principles.

A hungry pigeon, or rat (not both), is placed in a glass-sided box (now called a 'Skinner Box') which is equipped with a food dispenser which, once discovered, is capable of being operated automatically by means of a disc or a lever inside; *or* by the experimenter from outside. The advantage of this device, from the point of view of the experimenter, is that the ratio of the delivery of food, to the animals rate of correct responding (called the *schedule* (see page 62) is readily controllable. Therefore the experimenter has control over the main environmental contingencies that affect the behaviour of the animal. These can be systematically varied, and any resultant shifts in the pattern of responding accurately recorded.

TYPES OF REINFORCEMENT

There are two main types of reinforcement: *positive* and *negative*. Both processes *increase* the frequency, and/or magnitude, and/or speed of a response. Another way of putting it is to say that positive and negative reinforcers increase the probability of a response, or that they 'accelerate' behaviour.

Positive reinforcement

In Skinner's famous experiments, a rat or a pigeon was placed in a special box and left to its own devices. Eventually, through random exploratory activity (operant behaviour), the food release lever is accidentally nudged and a food pellet dropped into the tray. The release-operating behaviour then occurs more and more frequently, and is said to be positively reinforced by the food consequence. The term 'reinforced' simply means strengthened, and refers to the fact that, as a result of a certain consequence, the particular sequence of behaviour leading up to it is more likely to occur under similar circumstances in future. Therefore a reinforcer is a stimulus which, when paired with a response, increases the frequency of that response. In other words, a reinforcer is said to be positive when it strengthens the behaviour which it follows.

Reinforcers are therefore defined exclusively in terms of their effects. Pigeon corn is unlikely to strengthen the disc-pecking behaviour of a bloated pigeon, and so it is *not* a positive reinforcer in that instance. The everyday term 'reward' is too vague to describe this process since it is derived mainly from the intentions of the would-be-rewarder, or is used because the stimulus being delivered belongs to some general class of things or happenings *usually* experienced as pleasant by *most* people, or usually responded to predictably by an animal. In fact, there is no such thing as a universal reward. This has long been recognized in the old adage: 'One man's meat is another's poison.' Appetites also change dramatically over time and from setting to setting. The praise given by the elderly schoolmaster for a certain style of dress, although intended to reward the behaviour which produces this effect, can easily have the opposite effect. The policeman who ticks off an unruly football supporter in front of his pals is intending to punish, and thereby decrease, rowdy behaviour, but he may well positively reinforce it by this action, making it more likely to occur.

Negative reinforcement

Negative reinforcement is a clumsy term and in my experience causes students of behaviour modification more trouble than anything else. So let us start with a simple everyday example. As I write, my dog is pacing back and forth beside me, emitting panting and occasional coughing noises. He has been shaped into this strange pattern of behaviour by previous experience. Having tried all kinds of stimuli to get me to give him access to the great outdoors, he eventually hit upon coughing. Perhaps on some previous occasion of genuine throat-clearing, fearing for the state of my carpets, I jumped up and opened the door for him. But aetiology aside, the lesson has been well learned, and I think the deal is that he paces, pants, and coughs *until* I let him out for a sniff around the garden. In *his* case such behaviour has been *positively* reinforced by me. He gets his way a lot of the time and so the behaviour is well established in his repertoire. In my case, the behaviour of leaving my writing table (just in case he isn't fooling this time and to get rid of the distracting noise) is *negatively reinforced*. Contingent on certain behaviour from me, an unpleasant set of stimuli (noise and anxiety) are terminated. Dogs condition people too!

Here is another example of the negative reinforcement of behaviour. A man with a drinking problem wakes up feeling awful. He feels anxious, low, intensely miserable, and he has a craving for more alcohol. His family eye him suspiciously and engage in recrimination over the condition in which he came home the night before. He goes into the garage, pours himself a tumbler of whisky from his secret store, and soon after he feels better. The craving subsides, the world is a brighter place, and quickly takes on a pleasantly out-of-focus aspect, which distances him from his troubles and anaesthetizes him to the pain of everyday living. He takes another drink to intensify the effect. This man's initial drinking behaviour has been negatively reinforced. In the short term alcohol had the effect of reducing aversive stimulation, in the long term its effects on others will probably lead to its intensification, and so the vicious circle is continued. A useful way of clarifying the difference between positive and negative reinforcement is to imagine the usual Skinner box equipped with a loudspeaker or an electrified floor. To turn off an unpleasant level of sound or electric shock the animal operates a lever. On this occasion the behaviour is negatively reinforced since it *removes* a negative stimulus rather than providing a positive one. Any sequence of behaviour that reduces aversive stimuli will be readily repeated when the organism is faced with similar circumstances in future. So, analogously, we can think of the drinking response of the alcoholic as 'switching off' or at least 'turning down' the level of unpleasant physiological stimulation from within (anxiety, craving) and as distancing him from unpleasant social stimulation from without. Pain and anxiety are the most common forms of negative reinforcer. They encourage organisms to do something quickly to remove the causes of stimulation, or to escape from its effects: 'relief conditioning'.

To sum up:

> A negative reinforcer is a stimulus which, if *removed* contingent upon a certain response, results in an *increase* in the probability of that response.

Conditioned reinforcers

The *conditioned reinforcer* provides an important point of connection between the classical and operant models reviewed above. This term describes the process by which anything which is regularly associated with the reinforcement of an operant, eventually acquires an independent reinforcement value of its own. If then, we were to switch on a flashing blue light every time we reinforced the disc-pecking behaviour of a pigeon with food, we would expect, from our knowledge of classical conditioning, that the pigeon eventually would respond to the light alone. The light becomes a conditioned reinforcer, since it eventually reinforces the disc-pecking behaviour of the pigeon by itself. The extent to which the pigeon's behaviour can be maintained in this way depends upon a number of factors. The first is contiguity: the proximity of the light and the interval of time that elapses between delivery of the goods and the light. Another factor is the number of times the light and the food are paired; the more often this happens the more reinforcing the light becomes. However, this power of 'reinforcement by proxy' is lost relatively quickly when all food is withheld (extinction).

One further animal example to get this clear. Animal trainers have a problem in trying to reinforce items of behaviour at a distance. They cannot constantly be popping eatables into the mouth of their charges after every piece of clever behaviour, and there is a limit to the extent to which behaviours can be chained together so that reinforcement need only occur at the end of the sequence. This is where conditioned reinforcers come in. In the training of dolphins for public performance (the really interesting question here being why performing animals reinforce the attending behaviour of humans) the trainer needs something to stand 'in lieu' of fish when the dolphin is doing tricks in the middle of a large pool. He uses the sound of a whistle which has previously been paired with feeding. This sound eventually becomes a reinforcer in its own right. In turn, certain attending, emotional, and motor responses in the crowd are reinforced by the relative absence of controls. Skinner (1971) has proposed that the less conspicuous the controlling features of complex behaviour, the more interesting and credit-worthy it becomes; hence, the attraction of apparently non-directive dolphin training.

These examples give us a clue to the function of conditioned reinforcers in everyday life. Stimuli, in the form of attention, praise, or grades, maintain responding when larger-scale positive consequences are long-delayed, as when someone is studying for a diploma, or working with a difficult case, where any substantial outcome is likely to occur in years rather than months. These are secondary events associated through learning with a 'primary' pay off, such as greater prestige or more money. The reader might like to think about just how 'primary' these reinforcers are. There is nothing *intrinsically* satisfying about any of these examples. They are each a link in a chain leading back to genuinely primary, biologically based reinforcers: warmth, food, hunger, sex, and so on. But then men and women often forego or endure these things to obtain dignity, prestige, or even diplomas. Such motives become functionally autonomous; and so which reinforcers are really primary?

Generalized reinforcers

There is, however, another part to this process. A situation where particular conditioned reinforcers were linked only to particular primary deprivation states, or primary needs, would limit responsiveness drastically, and produce stereotyped and ultimately not very adaptive behaviour. Where this happens the result can appear bizarre, and not very creditworthy: 'Everything Bill Smith does is with an eye to the main chance'; 'Fred thinks of nothing but food'; and so on. But in the natural environment, in most cases, conditioned reinforcers *generalize*. This is to say that they become associated with more than one primary reinforcer. A wide range of responsiveness is maintained thereby, because of the increased likelihood that one or other of the primary deprivation states, or something very close to it, is likely to be present at any given time. Money provides a good example of a generalized reinforcer. We associate it with, and can procure with it, a wide range of goods, and therefore, whatever deprivation state we happen to be in, or whatever sources of stimulation happen to be near us at the time, there is a good chance that money will enhance the possibilities of satisfaction. For this reason tokens are used in certain behaviour modification programmes, for example those aimed at shaping the pro-social behaviour of chronic mental patients. These tokens can then be exchanged for a wide range of goods and services, and for access to special privileges (see page 155).

Skinner also cites sensory feedback, and the successful manipulation of the environment as examples of generalized reinforcers:

'A baby appears to be reinforced by stimulation from the environment which has not been followed by primary reinforcement. The baby's rattle is an example. The capacity to be reinforced in this way could have arisen in the evolutionary process, and it may have a parallel in the reinforcement we receive from simply "making the world behave". Any organism which is reinforced by its success in manipulating nature, *regardless of the momentary consequences*, will

be in a favoured position when important consequences follow.'
(Skinner 1953:78, my italics)

This example has obvious implications for the question of how artistic behaviour and creative endeavours are to be explained in behavioural terms (Skinner 1974). Further examples of generalized reinforcement are provided by approval, attention, affection, esteem, control, and so forth. In the case of a 'disruptive schoolboy', recently referred to me, attention undoubtedly provided a generalized reinforcement of bad behaviour. It was in short supply at home and in the school, *except* when he deliberately and noisily drew himself to the attention of school teachers normally reluctant to disturb what was called a 'good phase'. Attention had this effect because of its association with most things of value. Attention usually precedes, and is concurrent with, reinforcement in a social setting, and because of this it acquires its own behaviour-strengthening effects. It becomes worth having even when mixed in with irregular amounts of other stimuli intended to punish. Because these contingencies operate in a vaguely reliable way, the behavioural connection of attention with pleasure is eventually quite difficult to remove.

To sum up, a generalized reinforcer is a conditioned reinforcer that strengthens several types of behaviour in several situations.

Some further general points about reinforcement

(a) The reinforcement status of a stimulus is established by observing the *effect* that this has on behaviour by experiment: whether through the controlled experiments of researchers, or through the necessarily less well-controlled assessment procedures employed by therapists. The principles, at least, are the same.

(b) We are not surrounded by stimuli which it is possible to classify on an *a priori* basis as reinforcers. These properties are not of the stimuli, so much as of the organism on which they impinge and its previous learning experience. Such questions are decided by observation of effects.

(c) Behaviour is reinforced, not people. To say that Mr A is trying to reinforce Mary, is sloppy and misleading, except as a form of deliberate shorthand where all concerned know that it is Mary's assertive behaviour that is the target of positive reinforcement.

(d) Reinforced responses can be thought of as 'semi-automatic', in the sense that sometimes we behave in a very stereotyped way in response to contingencies, and think about it afterwards. Sometimes we think about the reasons for our behaviour *as* we behave. At other times stimuli give rise to memories, thoughts, and feelings about potential actions, which we perform later, and which are affected by these. In any case the consequences produced play an important role in determining how often, and in what circumstances these responses are used in future.

(e) 'Unconscious' learning can occur; that is, we may not always be able to specify the precise nature of the reinforcement contingencies that elicit certain responses from us.

(f) Patterns of positive and negative reinforcement are often inextricably intertwined. The taste of the whisky in the practical example on page 54 would be positively reinforcing and the (probable) build-up of 'frustration' (state of physiological arousal) in my dog (page 53), which my opening the door for him would put an end to, would ensure that his behaviour also receives negative reinforcement. Eating is both positively reinforced (food tastes nice) and negatively reinforced (it reduces hunger). The task in assessment is to identify such broad patterns as these.

THE SHAPING OF BEHAVIOUR

By selectively reinforcing features of a behavioural performance, or by reinforcing only those responses that occur at a certain level, we can gradually alter the nature of a response. Skinner worked with pigeons in this way to produce unusual neck-stretching movements and eventually a repertoire that included playing ping pong with their beaks! Using the same basic principles Isaacs, Thomas, and Goldiamond (1966) have shaped the behaviour of a chronically withdrawn schizophrenic patient whose typical behaviour consisted of sitting silently and staring into space. During a ward meeting the therapist pulled out a piece of gum and noticed that the patient's eyes moved in his direction slightly. The patient was given the gum and once the response was established, performance levels were gradually increased. The stages in this were: head turning; eye contact; holding out a hand; vocalizing, for example, saying, 'could I have some gum please?'; then more complex speech. At each stage only slightly exceptional behaviour was reinforced, and this is the key feature of operant shaping.

Referring to the shaping power of the natural environment, Skinner had this to say:

'Operant conditioning shapes behaviour as a sculptor shapes a lump of clay. Although at some point the sculptor seems to have produced an exclusively novel object, we can always follow the process back to the original undifferentiated lump, and we can make the successive stages by which we return to this condition as small as we wish. At no point does anything emerge which is very different from what preceded it. The final product seems to have a special unity and integrity of design but we cannot find the point at which this suddenly appears. In the same sense an operant is not something which appears full grown in the behaviour of the organism. It is the result of a continuous shaping process.'

(Skinner 1953:91)

Shaping, when systematically applied, is a therapeutic technique of considerable importance (see Chapter Six) as when the social worker selectively praises a parent for responding more matter-of-factly and calmly to an over-demanding child. Over time, reinforcement becomes conditional on longer and/or more complex sequences of behaviour.

Sometimes the shaping of *verbal behaviour* is important for therapeutic purposes (Skinner 1957). For example, in the case of an excessively shy and unassertive individual, speech containing self references, expressions of opinion, or statements of intention, can be selectively strengthened by increased attention and approval.

FADING

Fading is the process whereby control of a sequence of behaviour is gradually shifted from one set of reinforcers to another. This process is central to socialization, where, for example, parents gradually fade out the regular positive reinforcement of sitting at the table for meals until the behaviour is maintained by purely non-verbal approval and by conversation, plus the signalled threat of disapproval for breaking social rules. Similarly, a reinforcement programme that begins by encouraging adaptive behaviour in a child with the use of sweets or toys, can hardly continue in that vein forever. Apart from the possible side effects of obesity and dental caries, satiation effects will quickly reduce the effectiveness of such programmes! In any case, the aim of behavioural programmes is to bring adaptive behaviour under the control of naturally occurring variables. Fading in this type of programme can be accomplished by the use, alongside material reinforcers, of praise, affection, and so on, so that the former can be given less often or in smaller quantities as the behaviour comes to be maintained by the conditioned reinforcers.

Although fading is a common enough feature of daily life and of childhood experience, my impression is that far too little attention is given to it in therapeutic settings. Perhaps it is the fault of the still-dominant medical model which tempts us to think in terms of 'cure' rather than adaptation. Or perhaps it is the setting up of behaviour modification programmes that reinforces our own therapeutic behaviour because it is the most exciting part? The relatively mundane business of ensuring that any effects produced can be maintained in natural settings, smacks a bit of 'after care', and is (mistakenly) seen as a less important activity. However, research into the long-term effects of some quite impressively conceived behavioural schemes, shows just how dangerous it is to assume that behaviour changed in one setting will stay changed in another, when artificial reinforcers are no longer available. This point is particularly important in residential and hospital social work, where in the past, 'train and hope' programmes, as they are called in the business, have produced high levels of relapse.

DISCRIMINATIVE STIMULI

Discriminative stimuli (usually abbreviated to S^ds) are stimuli which (as a result of learning) signal to us that reinforcement may be available for particular forms of behaviour. They are especially important in complex social settings, and much of the process of human socialization is taken up with establishing finely tuned responses in relation to such cues. Where they have not yet been learned, behaviour can seem 'out of place' – as when children innocently repeat phrases such as: 'Why *are* you such a bore Uncle Fred?' Social gaffs of various kinds can often be put down to a failure to attend to available discriminative stimuli (see *Figure 3(2)*).

These stimuli are important in our work with clients, in that, if we learn what signals tend to precede particular behaviours, we may

Figure 3(2) A failure of discrimination?

Source: 'The man who asked for a double scotch in the Grand Pump Room at Bath.' In H. M. Bateman (1975) *The Man Who . . . and other stories* (edited by J. Jensen). Reproduced by permission of Eyre Methuen Ltd. and London Management Ltd. © H. M. Bateman 1975. The original of this cartoon is on display at the City Art Gallery.

be able to intervene at this early point in the sequence. In addition, clients can sometimes be taught to attend to these signals in a critical way, and to institute pre-rehearsed self-control procedures (see page 198). If feelings of boredom reliably trigger excessive eating, or a particular sort of conversation within a peer group reliably predicts aggression, then action can sometimes be taken to divert behaviour into another, more adaptive, channel. Also, attention to these antecedent factors can allow us to interrupt a sequence of problematic behaviour *before* it becomes fully developed. Thus, in the case of a child, withdrawal of attention, or a small sanction, might be used, whereas later, much stricter or elaborate measures would be necessary, bringing with them unwanted side effects.

Stimuli can also acquire a negative signalling value. These have the sub-title *delta stimuli* ($S^\Delta s$) and come to indicate, by regular association with a particular outcome, that no reinforcement is likely to be available for a given course of action.

In cases where a client's behaviour is 'overgeneralized', where, for example, he fails to discriminate between those people who are out to punish him for previous misdeeds, and those who wish to help him, an extra emphasis on identifying the differences in settings, behaviour, probable intentions, demeanour, function, and so on may aid future discrimination.

Let us now consider the effects that different patterns or schedules of reinforcement have on behaviour.

SCHEDULES OF REINFORCEMENT

So far we have been discussing the way in which different stimuli, and connections between stimuli, affect the elicitation and maintenance of behaviour. The next set of considerations stems from the fact that stimuli impinge, or can be artificially presented, in different *sequences*. This can have a marked effect: (i) on the rate and level of acquisition of responses; (ii) on the way responding is maintained; and (iii) on the resistance the behaviour shows to extinction. Therefore, such factors are of considerable clinical importance (Ferster and Skinner 1957).

The following factors are the most potent in their effects on behaviour.

(a) The number and ratio of responses receiving reinforcement in a sequence.

(b) Whether this pattern is regular or irregular.
(c) The interval between responses.
Each of these will now be discussed in turn.

Fixed ratio schedules

Descriptions of this type of schedule are usually abbreviated to FR, with an index number following, giving the number of responses which has to occur before reinforcement takes place. Thus FR6 equals six responses of a particular kind before reinforcement occurs. Natural environment contingencies rarely provide so regular a pattern. A piece worker, who receives payment according to the number of items of work produced, is on an FR schedule, as is the school child who gets a star for every three marks of B+ and above.

FR schedules have the effect of speeding up responses: the more items of appropriate behaviour performed, the greater the number of reinforcements supplied. Thus their chief characteristics are their high and stable levels of responding, and (as with continuous reinforcement schedules, see below) the fact that their effects are relatively easily extinguished. Secondary features are that the accuracy of the responses monitored on this schedule need be no more than adequate to obtain reinforcement; number of outputs, rather than quality of outputs is what is being reinforced. Indeed, if the ratio of response to reinforcement is high then a certain amount of 'trimming' occurs, that is, embellishments (which might provide opportunities for shaping) are dropped in the interests of speed, and, following reinforcement for a long sequence, the frequency of responding may well drop temporarily as another long series looms up. Obviously, if the ratio is too large the behaviour extinguishes altogether in the normal way.

Fixed ratio schedules are used in practice when a high, fast, and regular rate of discrete and easily definable responses is required. The rate can be varied so that it is favourable to start with and then increased later by gradual steps.

Continuous reinforcement

This is said to be occurring when every occurrence of a target behaviour is reinforced: this is the way in which many behavioural treatment programmes start off. The aim is to establish and strengthen a particular sequence as quickly and effectively as possible, and it is therefore worth knowing that experimental evidence shows clearly that reinforcement on a continuous schedule works fastest and best, in this regard. If a client only rarely engages in eye contact, then every single appearance of this behaviour should be positively reinforced with whatever works – perhaps increased attention, perhaps a smile, perhaps a favourable comment. Once the new behaviour is established, a different approach is required to maintain it.

Behaviour monitored on a continuous reinforcement (CR) schedule is easily extinguished. That is, if reinforcement stops, apart from a brief 'spurt', to test out the contingencies operating, the response rate drops like a stone. This fact has obvious implications for practice, and in particular the question of how to maintain desirable behaviours without artificial reinforcement after the social worker has disappeared from the scene. Most workers concerned with advising on behavioural programmes are familiar with this 'straight up and straight down' phenomenon present in the case data, where adequate behaviour is maintained on a continuous schedule until the client is 'better', then the case is closed. Three months later it is re-referred in virtually the same state, and behaviour modification is said 'not to have worked' or to have produced only short-term, 'symptomatic' benefits.

The real point is that no thought has been given to 'immunizing' the new behaviour against extinction by exposing it to little irregular periods of non-reinforcement. To resist the onslaught of natural environment contingencies behaviour is best *developed* on a continuous schedule and *maintained* on a variable schedule.

Differential reinforcement of other behaviour (DRO Schedules)

Another way to speed up acquisition is through providing a set of contingencies which 'contrast' one particular behaviour with others in the repertoire. To do this we continuously reinforce the desired sequence while placing nearby, competing, less desirable behaviours on extinction (as in the case discussed on page 153).

Intermittent schedules

There are two categories of intermittent schedules: (i) ratio schedules; and (ii) interval schedules. In the case of a ratio schedule, reinforcement occurs after a certain *number* of responses; that is, it might be given for every three conversations held with one particular nurse. In the case of an interval schedule, reinforcement occurs after a given amount of time has elapsed; that is, it might be given for every twenty minutes spent in the rehabilitation unit. The next important influence is whether the ratios and the elapsed intervals of time determining reinforcement in the two cases above are *fixed* or *variable*.

Variable ratio schedules

These schedules have very powerful behaviour-maintenance effects and provide built-in resistance to extinction (referred to above). With variable ratio (VR) schedules reinforcement occurs for an average number of responses. But the important thing is that the precise ratio of reinforcement to responses is variable over a given period. Thus, reinforcement may be experienced for every sixth, tenth, fourteenth, and tenth response – in sequence. This schedule would be called VR10 since the mean is ten. A good example of a VR schedule in everyday life is the 'fruit machine' where the excitement is derived from the unpredictability of reinforcement.

With this schedule the individual cannot easily predict when the next 'score' will occur, and so, not only is response maintained at a high and stable rate, but the quality of response is good since there is often experimentation to 'perfect' the response and so bring on the reward; the response can thus be shaped. Where reinforcement or punishment of a particular kind occur on a very variable schedule this can lead to what Skinner has termed 'superstitious behaviour' (Skinner 1953). The organism 'guesses' at the contingencies defining certain consequences, and tries out variations in behaviour to see whether this makes a difference or 'changes its luck'. Throwing salt over the left shoulder after a spillage, to avoid bad luck, is an everyday example of this.

If VR reinforcement is terminated completely the rate of responding tends to stay level for a considerable period (just in case the next sequence produces the long awaited pay-off) and drops only slowly.

While resistance to extinction is a considerable advantage when the issue is how to maintain new behaviours acquired in therapy it is an equally considerable disadvantage when trying to remove maladaptive behaviours from the client's repertoire. The reason is that most behaviours acquired through interaction with the natural environment are reinforced on variable interval schedules. Billy's mother does not respond with cuddles *every time* he has a tantrum; she did at first (continuous reinforcement), then she decided against this mollycoddling and ignored the next two tantrums. The third was a really bad one and Billy's mother found she couldn't ignore it and that there must be something the matter. The next tantrum was ignored completely, the one after that Billy was smacked, and the one after that Mrs B tried pleasant diversionary tactics. When the social worker called six months later she advised Billy's mother to completely ignore tantrums from now on 'so that they would extinguish'. Nineteen tantrums later mother gave up the scheme and told the social worker that behaviour modification sounded like a load of old nonsense; the social worker replied that it was 'certainly not a panacea' and wondered if she still had a copy of Melanie Klein at home. (See *Figure 3(3)*.)

In natural settings even more complex schedules operate, with the different types reviewed here combining and alternating to produce different effects on behaviour. Knowledge of these different patterns can help the social worker to identify them correctly during assessment and to develop combinations of techniques, either to counter them, or to exploit them for therapeutic purposes.

PUNISHMENT

The phenomenon of punishment requires discussion in some detail, not because it has a special place in the repertoire of behavioural techniques, but because of its controversial nature. First, it is important to distinguish punishment from negative reinforcement. It is commonly believed that negative reinforcement is just a fancy term for punishment, but this is not the case. Punishment is the effect of applying an aversive stimulus contingent upon a certain response thus decreasing the probability that the response will be emitted in similar circumstances in future. Imagine a Skinner box where the pressing of a lever always resulted in a shock or a loud noise. This punishment would result in a *reduction* in the performance of this response, or its complete suppression. Distinguish this contingency from one where the occupant of the box had to press the lever to *turn off* the unpleasant noise. This would negatively reinforce lever-pressing behaviour, and make the response more likely in similar circumstances in future.

Figure 3(3) Bitter sweets

Source: Posy Simmonds, *The Guardian*. Reprinted by permission of A. D. Peters and Co. Ltd.

The aversive stimulus referred to above may also take the form of a removal of positive reinforcement – as in the deprivation punishments of childhood. Two terms which the reader may encounter in the wider literature are: positive punishment, for the *presentation* of an aversive stimulus; and negative punishment for the *withdrawal* of a positive stimulus. The important points here are: (i) that in both cases the effect of the stimulus is to weaken the response that it follows; (ii) negative punishment (deprivation) is less likely to produce unwanted escape or strategic-avoidance behaviour.

The use of the word punishment in the behavioural psychology literature is somewhat different from our everyday understanding of the idea. It differs in two ways. First, it does not necessarily imply that anyone is deliberately setting out to inhibit certain behaviour. Second, there is no implication that the subject was necessarily doing anything 'wrong', or that the aversive event was retributive in character. (This closely parallels the position with positive and negative reinforcement, see page 00.) Through trial and error, or 'accident', certain environmental or internal physiological consequences occur that inhibit the behaviour with which they are associated. In other words, punishment is a naturally occurring phenomenon as well as something people do to each other deliberately.

Many of our clients live in extremely punishing environments, which is why so many of them withdraw from the constructive problem-solving attempts that look, to those not directly involved, like an obvious solution to their difficulties. An example of this kind of suppression of adaptive responses is the familiar situation of a multi-problem family, who, on balance, experience fewer aversive consequences by 'muddling through' at a very 'unsatisfactory' level, than through attempting to get to grips with their difficulties. When choice-making behaviour, or self assertion in any particular direction leads to punishment, then apathy results. Another familiar example of this phenomenon is that of the psychiatric patient whose attempts at communication with the outside world produce adverse reactions, resulting in the gradual closing off of this source of reinforcement, and the potentiation of alternative, day-dreaming and fantasy responses.

Social workers need therefore to know about the effects of punishment since unfortunately it is a particular feature of the environment of those with serious personal and social problems. Indeed it is the most common method used for the control of all kinds of social deviance. It is chosen for the following reasons.

(a) It is easy to formulate punishment contingencies – much easier than trying to discover precise deficits in social skills which result in inadequate performance, and easier still than trying to find reinforceable behaviour incompatible or competitive with maladaptive behaviour. Interestingly, and perhaps for this reason, when students in my own behaviour modification classes are presented with case material describing deviant behaviour they usually spring immediatedly into discussions about ways of suppressing such behaviour through punishment – though generally they would be against such things!
(b) Rewarding low-level adaptive behaviour, in the context of a serious maladaptive performance, calls for clear discriminations – not only on the client's part, but on the part of outside observers. Often the community and its representatives are unable, or unwilling, to make such fine distinctions; to do so would look too much like condoning the bad behaviour that happens to occur in the same context. It is safer and more comfortable to attribute behaviour entirely to durable, internal predispositions.
(c) Having decided to suppress behaviour (the effects of punishment, properly applied, are often quite dramatic) the short-term suppression of unwanted behaviour reinforces the punisher. Furthermore, he is seen to have done something definite and clear cut about the problem.
(d) Another reason for the popularity of punishment, is that it is believed to act as a source of vicarious suppression for similar behaviours in others, as in 'making an example' of offenders.

But there are many problems associated with the use of punishment.
(a) Naturally enough, it induces escape behaviours in those on whom it is used. These can be at least as maladaptive as the original problem-behaviour, and the negative reinforcement of successful responses in this class can give rise to a new generation of difficulties. For example, a child may learn that he can escape punishment by lying really dramatically and convincingly.
(b) Punishment gives rise to revenge motives. A good way of avoiding its unpleasant effects is to remove, or act against, the source of these. If this is the social worker, however benign his intentions, he may be left either with no-one to work with, or with a client who will regard his every suggestion as a signal to do the opposite.

(c) Punishment alone, whether arranged or accidental, gives no guidance as to what alternative behaviours might be more effective than the response that is being discouraged.
(d) Punishment acts as a *general* suppressant. It tends to have a 'blanket effect' removing wanted as well as unwanted responses from the repertoire, sometimes leaving nothing much for the therapist to work with.
(e) Unless profound, punishment has only short-term effects, and influence based on visible coercion is influence easily disregarded once the heat is off (Festinger 1957).
(f) Punishment can easily generalize to its users. Someone who makes regular use of it will find it hard to use positive reinforcement effectively with the same client in the future.

These problems need to be kept in view when the social worker is putting together programmes that have a necessary control element, particularly when they involve children. These points do not add up to a case for the complete abandonment of punishment as a technique, rather they are intended to serve as a reminder that most of our clients already inhabit environments rich in aversive stimuli, and only rarely will it help to add to these artificially.

There are occasions when punishment can be used to suppress quickly behaviours that interfere seriously with attempts to reinforce other performances positively. Lovaas (1967) used punishment (contingent electric shock) to suppress self-injurious behaviour in autistic children. Left to extinguish by itself this behaviour continued until thousands of self-administered blows were given. In one case, two shocks reduced this rate to zero – where it stayed for good, allowing physical restraints to be removed and a language teaching programme to begin.

The important point in this example, is that punishment was used briefly, and in the context of a wider programme reliant upon positive reinforcement principles. Analogously, the occasional slap in the context of a normally loving and affectionate family does no harm, and can sometimes help the child to discriminate between behaviours constituting mild naughtiness, and more seriously offensive behaviour. Social workers cannot have their heads in the clouds about punishment. It is not a very large feature of the repertoire of behavioural procedures appropriate to our field, but as an *effect* it is all around us. Some clients may even see the very presence of a social worker in their homes as a punishment, however benign and liberal our own interpretation of the purposes behind the visit.

Theories of learning 71

CASE ILLUSTRATION, SHOWING THE EFFECTS OF OPERANT CONSEQUENCES ON BEHAVIOUR

Background

Mark, aged ten, was referred to the Social Services Department via the Education Welfare Service (the department held a supervision order on an elder brother following two instances of minor theft). Junior school staff were greatly concerned about Mark's disruptive behaviour in class and were beginning to use psychiatric terminology to describe this. Expulsion was likely unless something could be done.

- In common with his brother, Mark's childhood had been somewhat troubled. A history of marital difficulties between parents, and two lengthy periods of separation from them while in the care of relatives, had been the most distinctive features.
- Family life seemed to have settled down of late and the social worker handling the case had filed increasingly optimistic reports about this. However, it was known that parents had often disagreed to the point of violence about disciplinary practices in the home – mother favouring the strict enforcement of rules, but father expressing a 'boys will be boys' philosophy – this, in the social worker's view, to excuse some of his own rather wayward behaviour.
- Mark was not a bright child and had reading difficulties requiring remedial teaching.
- With the somewhat hesitant cooperation of the school authorities an investigation of Mark's disruptive behaviour began in its natural setting. Four student social workers took it in turns to observe lessons. They were introduced just as 'students' and unobtrusively sat at the rear of the classroom.
- Data recorded by these observers revealed the following. (i) 'Disruptive behaviour' usually meant 'Mark leaving his desk', but after that he would occasionally make loud noises, slamming down objects, teasing, hitting, and pinching other pupils, and generally interfering with their work. (ii) Some teachers had more difficulty with Mark than others. (iii) The most common methods of dealing with Mark were: reasoning with him, or speaking sharply to him – both of which seemed to have only a marginal and temporary effect; trying to distract him, which only worked in the short term; placing him outside the door – which he did not seem to object to at

all and which again had no effect whatever on his subsequent behaviour; the occasional slap, which likewise had little discernible effect on him. By and large teachers tried to ignore him, most operating a 'sleeping dogs' policy where they could.

- The working hypothesis developed in this case was that Mark's classroom behaviour was largely a product of the following contingencies. (i) When Mark was at all well-behaved (which records showed was a fair proportion of the time) he was ignored. Most teachers were wary of him and left him alone if they could. (ii) Conversely, whenever Mark caused a disturbance he received immediate attention from his teacher on virtually every occasion. (iii) Attempts to punish Mark were ineffective, not only because they were half-hearted, but because of his exposure elsewhere to much more serious forms of it. (iv) Mark's reading difficulties made it hard for him to join in lessons – he was bored and a little embarrassed by this and escaped from these conditions by amusing himself with other more interesting, if dubious pursuits.

The reinforcement patterns operating here were thought to be as follows.

- Mark was *positively reinforced* with attention (a commodity in short supply at home, and particularly in his earlier life). A further contrast between consequences of good and bad behaviour was provided by the fact that teachers would stay away from him when he was not being difficult, and in any case saw all too little to reward in what they called 'his attitude to schoolwork in general'. Thus teachers were only persuaded to reward extended runs of good behaviour. These occurred very rarely.
- Mark's frequent tendency to get out of his seat, and his disruptive behaviour, were also *negatively reinforced*. The work was difficult for him to succeed at because he just did not possess the skills required, and so he became bored. If called upon to contribute to class work, he usually made a mess of things. Thus leaving his seat and disruptive behaviour had the effect of terminating, or reducing, boredom, embarrassment, and worries about failing. On one occasion, Mark automatically placed *himself* by the door after a confrontation with a teacher!

The attempt to reverse these reinforcement contingencies, to provide positive reinforcement for remaining seated and concentrating on school work, and none for disruptive behaviour, is described in Chapter Six. This approach is called *differential reinforcement* (see page 148) and its principles are central to the practice of behaviour modification.

Modelling and vicarious learning

So far, we have examined (i) the means by which new responses are generated through stimulus association, often in chain-like fashion (classical conditioning); (ii) the way responses are established in the repertoire or lost from it as a result of the consequences they produce (operant conditioning).

We can now turn to a third process, derived from the other two, called variously, *observational learning, vicarious learning, modelling, or imitation*. Different authors give somewhat different meanings to these terms, but since there is considerable overlap, and disagreement is rife, I suggest that for practical purposes they be treated as virtually synonymous. This works so long as we remember that 'modelling' generally implies *social* imitation. These processes are the means by which new responses are acquired, reinforced, or extinguished, *at a distance* (vicariously), through observation of the behaviour of others. A large proportion of the behavioural repertoire of each of us is developed in this way, not through direct personal experience in the first instance, but through watching what others do in particular circumstances and how they fare as a consequence.

Modelling is the process through which we learn the speech patterns of our parents; learn to walk like our favourite film star; pick up a new dance craze; learn how to behave in strange surroundings; how to approach members of the opposite sex; how to pick a fight; how to intimidate others; how to approach decision-making in as neurotic a way as our parents; how being aggressive gets people their own way, or not. Modelling is a powerful influence in human socialization, and its importance has been enhanced considerably by the arrival of the mass media. Through modelling we select, observe, and learn to imitate in approximate form elements of the behavioural performances of others every day of our lives. When we are in certain circumstances, under threat or in strange surroundings for example, we become avid modellers and search around for clues about how to behave. Similarly, at certain stages in socialization, during adolescence in particular, models are actively sought and copied as the young person experiments with different styles of behaviour. Paradoxically, this is done as a way of establishing a *distinct* identity.

As in the case of the other forms of learning reviewed above, we can acquire both useful or destructive, good or bad, self-enhancing or self-defeating responses through observational learning. The process is exactly the same. Albert Bandura (the foremost researcher in this field and a staunch advocate of modelling as a therapeutic device) makes the point that were operant conditioning the only means by which human beings could acquire a behavioural repertoire, then the planet would be littered with the mangled corpses of those whose responses had been ineffective in controlling their particular bit of the environment:

> 'In laboratory investigations of learning processes experimenters usually arrange comparatively benign environments in which errors will not produce fatal consequences for the organism. In contrast, natural settings are loaded with potentially lethal consequences that unmercifully befall anyone who makes hazardous errors. For this reason, it would be exceedingly injudicious to rely primarily upon trial and error learning and successive-approximation methods in teaching children to swim, adolescents to drive automobiles, or adults to master complex occupational and social tasks. If rodents, pigeons or primates toiling in contrived situations could likewise get electrocuted, dismembered, or bruised for errors that inevitably occur during early phases of learning, few of these venturesome subjects would ever survive the shaping process.'
>
> (Bandura 1969:143)

Skinner's analysis of what happens when we observe the behaviour of someone else and then perform it ourselves takes the standard operant view outlined in *Figure 3(4)*.

Figure 3(4) Observed behaviour: the operant view

S^d ——————————— R ——————————— S^r

In *Figure 3(4)* S^d represents the discriminative stimuli present in the modelled performance, R denotes an overt matching response, and S^r the reinforcing stimulus which follows this performance.

It will be immediately apparent that although this explanation may approach sufficiency in very controlled conditions of deliberate response-matching, where considerable prior learning has taken place (for example, a dancing class), for many everyday modelling situations it is inadequate. First there is the problem of acquisition, that is, how the observer comes to acquire the new set of responses in the first place. Second there is the problem of the retention of a modelled behaviour pattern for days and weeks before it is performed overtly. We may go to the cinema and observe a particularly cool, collected performance by an actor and not try to re-enact aspects of this until we are next confronted with the office panic-monger.

An experiment to demonstrate the role of reinforcement in modelling was performed by Bandura (1965). Children watched a film of an actor displaying aggression. The reinforcement conditions under which this behaviour was performed were systematically varied. In one variation the actor was punished; in another, rewarded with praise and sweets, and in another, no particular consequences were seen to result from his behaviour. Immediate post-exposure observations of children from the audience under controlled conditions showed noticeably different levels of aggression. The highest and most varied levels of aggressive behaviour came from the groups who had seen the model's aggression reinforced or attract no negative consequences. For them the violence was seen to pay off, so they imitated it at the next opportunity.

Post-performance reinforcement undoubtedly plays a part in the modelling process as this experiment demonstrates, but as a complete explanation it is somewhat inadequate. Paying attention to what other people do in interesting or stressful situations is likely to be reinforcing in itself. (Here too Bandura's argument that modelling *can* occur in the absence of reinforcement seems a bit thin.) He means, one supposes, deliberately presented reinforcement. But there is likely to be plenty of naturally-occurring generalized reinforcement for response-matching surrounding any behavioural performance which is sufficiently distinct to catch our attention. Also there is a key role here for the *anticipated* reinforcement (S^d) of any imitation which will add new response-options to the stock. The individual with a wide range of possible responses to whatever circumstances he happens to find himself in, is more likely to be able to obtain greater satisfaction, and more likely to be able to deal more effectively with aversive stimuli. In this sense, the knowledge that novel responses are being stored in memory as behavioural 'capital' for later use, might itself reinforce attentional and response-matching behaviour.

The rest of the modelling process occurs in symbolic form. That is, it is *cognitively mediated*. We think ourselves into the role of the performer, imagine and, to some extent, experience the emotional accompaniments that he might be experiencing (easy in the cinema and on television because of the cues provided by accompanying music). Next we anticipate how successful we would be in performing this behaviour and what the probable outcome would be for us in given circumstances. The member of a gang who watches others breaking down a fence with particular skill need not perform similar behaviour on the next fence he or she comes across. A variety of different conditions (S^ds), some of them social in origin, will determine when the behaviour 're-emerges'. In the meantime, aspects of the performance are represented in memory.

While there is no reason to suppose that cognitively mediated response-matching obeys different laws to those already outlined, this conclusion is somewhat uncomfortable for a discipline that dislikes straying far from the directly observable. Skinner's counter-argument is that so long as we can predict with reasonable accuracy that particular signals which enter the 'black box'[1] re-emerge in a particular form, then we need not concern ourselves too much about what goes on inside.

Another form of modelling where covert factors (feelings this time) play a large part in the acquisition process has been called *empathetic learning*. The fact that we tend to 'feel along' with the performances of a model (as a result of a lengthy process of classical conditioning) tends to make us want to re-perform the behaviour to obtain internal reinforcement from the various states of arousal that are known through vicarious experience to accompany it. In the example of the gang breaking down the fence, according to Bandura and Rosenthal (1966) the behaviour would be re-performed by an observer, with the aim of re-producing, perhaps in amplified form, the emotional 'kicks' that once accompanied watching someone else do it. The current status of this theory as an explanation of modelling is viewed by Bandura as similar to that of the operant conditioning model. Such factors may well be at work, and may play a relatively large part in modelling under certain conditions, but they are background rather than central features in most cases:

[1] The analogy is borrowed from physics, where the properties of particles are inferred from comparisons before and after being subjected to forces inside an apparatus (black box). The process inside is invisible.

'Sensory-feedback theories of imitation may therefore be primarily relevant to instances in which the modelled responses incur relatively potent reinforcement consequences capable of endowing response–correlated stimuli with motivational properties. Affective conditioning should therefore be regarded as *facilitative* rather than as a *necessary* condition for modelling.'

(Bandura 1969:132; my emphasis)

COGNITIVE-MEDIATIONAL THEORIES

Theories of observational learning which emphasize the importance of the mental representation of the sequence to be re-performed are called *cognitive-mediational theories* (Bandura 1969; 1977). They concentrate on the hidden stages that occur between observation and performance – the inside of the 'black box'. Two systems are said to be at work here to represent a performance in our heads for later retrieval: a process of imagination and a verbal process. Performances are encoded into particular image-sequences and word-symbols and stored in memory.

Let us look now at an experiment that demonstrates the role of such symbolic representation in modelling (Bandura 1965). In this study children were asked to pay attention to filmed sequences of quite complex behaviour. One group of children were just instructed to watch carefully; one group were asked, as well as paying attention, to speak along with the models on the screen and describe and label the models' behaviour out loud; another group were instructed to watch attentively, but to count rapidly at the same time (to prevent the encoding of information). When asked to re-create the sequences they had seen, the children in the 'verbal-labelling' group were much more effective at remembering than the next group (the watch-silently group) and produced yet more accurate responses than the group that had had to engage in a competing activity.

Most of us will have had the experience of talking ourselves through a difficult or unfamiliar task – either out loud, as in childhood, or subliminally ('under our breath'): 'Right now, that's the gasket back on, and now I put the large locating screws on the left so as not to confuse them with these smaller ones over here . . .'. The point here is that it is the encoding and organizing of complex modelling stimuli by the brain that ensures accurate reproduction. The more complex the information, the greater the degree of organization and splitting into sections required; or the greater will be the reliance on external cues to reproduction, as in those instances when we have to depend on the promptings of manuals and schedules of various kinds. By the same token, we can reinforce ourselves for both approximate performances, and during the mental rehearsal of a complex performance. This occurs through the tagging on of images of ourselves coping with, and mastering, the environment in which we plan to use the modelled performance − pictures of approving smiles from our peers as they see us deal with the boss politely, but *firmly* this time. Also, through self-talk: 'You're doing fine'; 'That went down very well'; and so on. The therapeutic derivatives of this phenomenon are discussed in Chapter Seven.

So far we have seen that offshoots of both classical and operant conditioning procedures play a part in getting us to attend to, and reproduce for ourselves, the behaviour of others. But neither of these processes fully account for this form of learning, which is made possible only through the process of cognition that allows us to re-enact, in symbolic form, the little dramatic performances we have selected from the behaviour of others and that we anticipate will be useful to us. The following diagram from Bandura (1977) *(Figure 3(5))* provides an economical summary of the various stages of the modelling process. The reader will see that the first list of factors is associated with the characteristics of the modelled stimulus, and what it is about it that we selectively perceive and attend to ('attentional process'). The second list relates to the coding, organization, and storage of a 'mental script' of the performance. The third set concerns the rehearsal of modelled performances, and the fourth the factors that decide the place of the performance in the repertoire − how often it is likely to be performed, whether it will be developed further, or lost, and so on.

THE USES OF MODELLING

Modelling procedures are useful in a wide range of circumstances, particularly the following.
(a) To remedy behavioural deficits. Clients often just *do not have* in their repertoire the behaviours necessary to solve their problems. They may simply never have learned them, or they may have lost them because of intervening experiences. In this case there may be little or nothing for the worker to shape − however ingenious his or her programme.

Figure 3(5) Component factors governing observational learning in the social learning process

MODELLED EVENTS →	ATTENTIONAL PROCESSES	RETENTION PROCESSES	MOTOR REPRODUCTION PROCESS	MOTIVATIONAL PROCESSES	→ MATCHING PERFORMANCES
	Modelling stimuli	Symbolic coding	Physical capabilities	External reinforcement	
	Distinctiveness	Cognitive organization	Availibility of component responses	Vicarious reinforcement	
	Affective valence	Symbolic rehearsal	Self observation of reproductions	Self-reinforcement	
	Prevalence		Accuracy feedback		
	Functional value				
	Observer characteristics				
	Sensory capacities				
	Arousal level				
	Perceptual set				
	Past reinforcement				

Source: Bandura (1977). Copyright Albert Bandura 1977. Reprinted by permission of Prentice-Hall, Inc., Englewood Cliffs, N.J.

(b) To reduce interfering anxiety. When individuals are forced to cope despite considerable social and behavioural deficits, their actions usually become stereotyped and awkward. They tend to avoid any circumstances where they know they will not perform well (S^Δ), or will be punished, and experience anxiety if they cannot manage to do this. Anxiety can enhance a performance up to a certain level, but beyond this optimum level interferes progressively with performance (Hebb 1972), resulting in increasingly inadequate and poorly discriminated behaviour. This, in turn, sets up a vicious circle leading to greater anxiety and more generalized avoidance. Modelling techniques can be used to demonstrate and teach better coping behaviours more likely to lead to reinforcement. Certainly the rehearsal of these new behaviours, to a point of reasonable competency, usually carries with it a 'desensitization effect' (see page 216). Fears are lessened therefore both by vicarious extinction (Bandura 1969) and by operant extinction – that is, by watching someone else perform the target behaviours without apparent anxiety, and then practising under relatively benign conditions (Rachman 1972).

(c) Modelling can also be used to re-establish behaviours which were in the repertoire of the individual but which have been lost or suppressed because of lack of available reinforcement or through punishment. If these are present at a very low level, then shaping is likely to be a lengthy and labour-intensive process. Sometimes short cuts can be attempted by modelling the required behaviour and showing it obtaining reinforcement.

In my view, we have now passed the point where exclusively behaviouristic conceptions of learning can account (without undue contortion) for the phenomena under review.

Cognitive learning

Several writers have argued that there is a type of learning – leading to the acquisition of new and visible responses – which is substantially independent of the associative mechanisms on which classical and operant conditioning depend, and on which modelling effects have been seen partly to depend (Michenbaum 1977; Lazarus 1971). There are various labels for this: *cognitive learning*, *insight learning*, *latent learning*, and so forth. Each of these terms refers to an overlapping set of concepts that lay stress on the importance (particularly in complex learning tasks) of understanding, imagination, prior knowledge, memory factors, and creative intelligence – the results of various forms of 'cognitive structures'.

Let us take the notion of 'cognitive structure' first. Skinner's view is simply that private events lie outside the boundaries of a true science, except to the extent that their influence can be reliably plotted by referring to overt behavioural correlates. However, to the extent that this can be done, he argues, we do not need to bother with hard-to-get-at internal processes of mediation, since we already have a more parsimonious and therefore superior theory (Skinner 1974). Skinner's analyses in this field, though economical and often persuasive, often leave one with the feeling that they are too 'pat'. The mental leap from the Skinner box to the roof of the Sistine chapel is hard to make in one go! Creative problem solving is surely something *entirely* different. Investigators of complex learning argue that crude and uncoordinated stimuli affecting an individual ought to result in crude and uncoordinated responses – unless, that is, something extra is added inside the 'black box'. The 'extra something' must be the effect of complex cognitive structures, that is, symbolic, mental 'maps' stored in memory, from which, and to which, items are added and subtracted, and between which interchanges can take place to create new orderings of information, and hence new response options. We are probably all intuitively aware of something like this going on when we come across a new idea that functions, at both a conceptual and an emotional level, as the final piece of an uncompleted jigsaw puzzle and enables us to see a new 'picture'. We have inside our heads the facilities to put items of information derived from incoming stimuli on 'hold'; dredge up information from memory of similar influences, run a series of simulations akin to computer models, select the best one (that is, the best matching and the one most likely to lead to reinforcement), and then behave according to this programme, changing course in the light of feedback on the environmental effects produced.

The main idea here is that of anticipated reinforcement, gauged through the setting up in systematic form of 'thought experiments': 'Now what would happen if I did x rather than y?' The answer is likely to be based on prior experience of similar situations. This sort of postulate has given rise to the notion of *coverant conditioning* (Homme 1965) where 'operant thoughts' are reinforced or extinguished according to whether they add constructively to a problem-solving formula likely to pay off for the individual when it is translated into behaviour, and to the extent that they give rise to pleasurable emotional responses. Thus, when we think of solving our financial problems by robbing a bank, the thoughts are usually extinguished quite quickly by other associations about the possible consequences, except where, 'just for the fun of it' (that is, for the emotional feedback), we deliberately control the mental drama to make sure we get away undetected.

Analyses of this type of problem-solving behaviour in traditional stimulus-response terms are also available (Skinner 1974), but they are exceedingly complex and cumbersome and quite often the game is just not worth the candle. The view that environmental influences do not simply enter the brain as stimuli and leave as responses, in 'ping-pong' fashion, is hard to resist. Just what kind of cognitive 'pinball machine' they do go through before they re-emerge as effects – often pretty divergent and unusual effects at that – is hard even to guess at, at present. For me the important question is, can we successfully intervene through the medium of language to alter cognitive patterns, mental maps, ways of seeing and so on, so that more adaptive *behaviours* are generated?

Let us try to develop the idea further through analogy. If we think of cognitive structures as forming a proposed plan for a building project (future behaviour), could we alter the shape of the eventual building by changing the plan – or does it all still depend largely on how the builder has done things in the past (learning history); whether he has the skill to do anything different (repertoire); whether he could be bothered to work on a building of a different shape (short-term reinforcement); whether such a building would 'work' or whether it would collapse in the face of environmental stresses (long-term reinforcement)? These questions need to be approached with caution. As we saw in Chapter One the automatic assumption that changing thinking changes behaviour has often led to ineffective methods being used in the past (Sheldon 1978b).

What then is the form of a 'cognitive structure' and what effects can these be seen to have on behaviour? It could be argued that once again we are in danger of reifying an activity and making it into a 'thing'. We infer that we have cognitive structures because the private processing of information about environmental contingencies tends to follow certain patterns. We quickly learn that stimuli are not

Theories of learning 83

always what they seem, that not all brightly coloured tablets are sweets and that not all 'sincere offers of help' are sincere offers of help. Therefore to respond to the surface features of stimuli could be dangerous. The behaviour of *interpreting*, then, readily attracts reinforcement. As an activity, it contains the following elements.

(a) An examination of sensory data in great detail.
(b) The action of looking at the *context* of stimuli (a pie cooling in the kitchen evokes quite a different set of responses to a pie cooling in a field).
(c) Responding to the images which stimuli evoke in our heads through classical conditioning. For example, if I write *red car* it is virtually impossible for you not to 'see' a red car. This image may be followed by an association with Redcar (the place), then with horse racing or any other number of items linked with the image through prior experience.
(d) The action of looking at relations between stimuli: two sets of stimuli are not just one set plus one set. Their conjunction can produce a quite different implication. The client who assures her social worker that things are getting better to the accompaniment of non-verbal signals of anxiety, might be said to be 'adopting a strategy' (for any one of several different purposes). Only further interpretation of these conjoined events, perhaps followed by some careful prompting or probing, will discover the true meaning or intent contained in the behaviour, that is, the effect it is designed to have, or the internal state it is designed to conceal.
(e) Stimuli produce a range of conditioned associations previously stored in memory. These are the raw material on which future computations about how best to behave are made. In addition they help to trigger and sustain emotional reactions which then enter the equation themselves as inhibitors or enhancers of particular behavioural options. Thus if we recall that last time we were in a particular kind of fix we 'brazened it out' and this image is accompanied by very pleasant feelings enhancing recalled actions, then unless there are powerful contra-indications present in the current environment, we are unlikely to hesitate for long before repeating this sequence.
(f) We use the facility of language (inner speech) to talk to ourselves about contingencies: 'Now wait a minute, someone may simply

have dropped this pie, there's bound to be a logical explanation, bit surreal though, shades of Magritte ... Wait 'til I tell the family'; (image of astonished and attentive family).

(g) The use of previously reinforced and shaped problem-solving strategies. We manipulate data in pre-set ways. There are many possible variables here. For example, we may have learned that *speed* in decision making is the crucial thing, and so select a course of action on the basis of little detailed evidence that this plan will 'pay off'. Or we may tend to 'weigh' such issues (scan and re-scan the data) because we have learned that precipitate action leads to regrets later. Similarly, we may approach a problem (a complex set of contingencies) on the assumption that it provides yet further evidence that others are out to get us. Or, in the absence of any well-practised methods of computing likely outcome, that it provides yet further evidence that we are 'getting past it' and can't cope any more. These *thinking styles* give rise to 'self-concepts', that is to views of our likely efficacy in influencing the environment, our abilities in discriminating among complex stimuli, and so on.

(h) 'Insight learning' may occur. The process here is one of scanning outer (environmental) stimuli, and inner (physical/emotional stimuli) and by manipulating, or even deliberately suspending, the rules by which such events are assessed, coming up with highly original responses. In man, these creative responses often attract generalized reinforcement (see page 56). They produce a feeling of mastery over the environment, cleverness, etc., and so are accompanied by pleasant feelings. Together these factors give the experience of 'insight', or creative problem solving, its unique 'Eureka!' feel. Additionally, most kinds of problem-solving, however refined, take place against a background of negative reinforcement. We often experience profound relief when we reach a tenable solution to a problem which has been baulking us, or use our 'wits' to escape a seemingly unavoidable obligation.

(i) The development of rules. Human beings can produce what seem like entirely novel and spontaneous responses because they learn the abstract rules that govern the relation and succession of stimuli, and the likely effects of particular actions. Rule-following behaviour is sparked off by hosts of discriminative stimuli present in the environment, and the application of existing rules to new combinations of stimuli can lead to new combinations of responses. This kind of computation gives to human behaviour its special 'knight's move' characteristics.

Now it could be objected that not all thought processes are so heavily strategic. For example, in the case of 'daydreaming' or contemplation, the thoughts we experience are not driven by an urgent need to come up with a quick behavioural policy. The philosopher Gilbert Ryle has this to say about thinking of this kind:

> 'Not all pondering or musing is problem tackling. While some walking is exploring and some walking is trying to get to a destination, still some walking is merely strolling around. Similarly while some meditating or ruminating is exploratory, and some, like multiplying, is travelling on business, still some is just re-visiting familiar country and some is just cogitative strolling for cogitative strolling's sake.' (Ryle 1979:28)

This is an important distinction, but not one which seriously threatens the analysis already developed. We know from studies in physiological psychology that the brain cannot easily do nothing, not even in sleep. It is just not 'wired up' that way (Blakemore 1977). The system is at an optimal level of arousal when it is working away. Much below this level, as in sensory deprivation experiments, strange things begin to happen. Perceptual distortions and even full-blown hallucinations can occur. These are symptoms of 'stimulus hunger' (see Heron 1957).

Ruminative thoughts, although not about urgent behavioural decisions, nevertheless are likely to be connected to more distant general contingencies. Thus, we ruminate about our long-term future without too much anxiety, and without feelings that a solution must necessarily be found quickly. External stimulation of even a slightly unusual kind disrupts this 'coasting along' and replaces it with thought patterns geared more directly to short-term problem solving. There is undoubtedly a role for reinforcement here too, and it is likely that relatively non-specific thinking would be maintained by conditioned reinforcers (see page 54).

If these assumptions are roughly correct, then there is no reason to view private, cognitive events as in some way disconnected, non-physical phenomena which have little to do with behaviour, nor to assume that they obey principles markedly different from those contained in the various theories of learning reviewed above.

If the phenomenon of interpreting and thinking about stimuli and their response connections complicates matters rather, then the fact that, in man, 'the environment' usually means 'the social environment' multiplies these complications many times over. A response to a response to a response, is a common-enough occurrence in everyday life. Sane people do not try to draw such complex interrelationships schematically, but this is not to say that they completely defeat a rigorous analysis.

The American psychologist Albert Bandura has developed such an analysis stage by stage over the last twenty years and it has come to be known as Social Learning Theory (Bandura 1977).

Social learning theory

This is a formulation that rests heavily on theories of vicarious learning (see page 73), especially modelling. The formulation shares many of the assumptions of the cognitive theorists, and yet in Bandura's view it is compatible with many of the basic tenets of traditional behaviourism. As a theory then, it is well placed to integrate a number of current trends in the discipline – although arguments still rage over its credentials as a *behavioural* theory.

Here are two quotations that should give you the flavour of social learning theory:

'Humans do not simply respond to stimuli; they interpret them. Stimuli influence the likelihood of particular behaviours through their predictive function, not because they are automatically linked to responses by occurring together. In the social learning view, contingent experiences create expectations rather than stimulus-response connections. Environmental events can predict either other environmental occurrences, or serve as predictors of the relation between actions and outcomes.' (Bandura 1977:59)

And on the question of determinism and whether behaviour and the learning function is powered from inside or outside the organism:

'Environments have causes, as do behaviours. It is true that behaviour is regulated by its contingencies but the contingencies are partly of a person's own making. By their actions, people play an active role in producing the reinforcing contingencies that impinge upon them. As was previously shown, behaviour partly creates the environment, and the environment influences the behaviour in a reciprocal fashion. To the oft repeated dictum, "change contingencies and you change behaviour", should be added the reciprocal side, "change behaviour and you change contingencies". In the regress of prior causes, for every chicken discovered by a unidirectional environmentalist, a social learning theorist can identify a prior egg.' (Bandura 1977:203)

Questions of ultimate causality do not worry Bandura much. The fact that man is above all things a social animal means that he both creates, and is created by, these special environments. It is Bandura's view that behaviour within this huge closed circuit is dominated by two sets of influences.
(a) *Outcome expectations:* the estimate of a person that given behaviour will lead to certain outcomes.
(b) *Efficacy expectations:* representing the conviction that one can successfully execute the behaviour required to produce a specific outcome.

These two influences are differentiated because a person can believe that a particular course of action will produce certain outcomes, but may have serious doubts as to whether they are capable of performing the necessary behaviour to bring these about.

These are the constituent parts of Bandura's concept of *perceived self-efficacy*. According to him *all* psychological change procedures, whatever their type, are mediated through this system of beliefs about the end result of an action and the level of skill required to perform it adequately (see *Figure 3(6)*).

Figure 3(6) Efficacy and outcome expectations

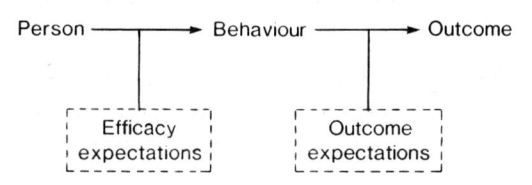

Person ———→ Behaviour ———→ Outcome

        Efficacy   Outcome
        expectations   expectations

Source: Adapted from Bandura (1977), by permission of Prentice-Hall, Inc., Englewood Cliffs, N.J.

Of these two elements, efficacy expectations are the most important. Attempts to modify outcome expectations by verbal persuasion alone have relatively weak and temporary effects, particularly in the face of contradictory experiences (Lick and Bootzin 1975). Similarly, so-called placebo effects, though they may have an enhancing effect on therapy, are unlikely to provide a sufficient basis for lasting change, and will rarely serve in place of a logically constructed programme of help (McGlynne and Mapp 1970; Sheldon 1978b). The main effect on outcome expectations is through the strengthening of efficacy expectations.

Bandura (1978) lists the following sources of efficacy expectations.
(a) Performance accomplishments: gained through participation, and desensitization to threats inhibiting an approach to the feared circumstances. (Bandura sees reinforcement simply as an *incentive giving* or *regulating* influence, cognitively mediated and reflected upon.)
(b) Vicarious experience: gained through watching others perform (modelling).
(c) Verbal persuasion: by suggestion, exhortation, guided self-instruction, interpretations, and so on.
(d) Reducing fears associated with particular performances by imagining oneself coping in a step-by-step manner. Other approaches include: relaxation techniques; biofeedback;[2] systematic desensitization; and symbolic exposure (imagining worst fears for lengthy periods as a way of extinguishing them (see page 216)).

Bandura suggests that the main effort of the would-be helper should go into directly modifying thoughts and feelings which affect perceived self-efficacy. This is in line with many of the treatment procedures and styles already made use of by social workers. But (referring to research into pathological fears), Bandura adds a word of caution and this is the point where his theory is connected to mainstream behavioural practice:

'Developments in the field of behavioural change reveal two major divergent trends. This difference is especially evident in the modification of dysfunctional inhibitions and defensive behaviour. On

[2] The use of amplifying instruments to provide a visible or audible measure of certain physical responses, for example, blood pressure, or 'anxiety level' as represented by the Galvanic skin response. 'Lie detectors' work on this principle.

the one hand, explanations of change processes are becoming more cognitive. On the other hand, it is performance based treatments that are proving most powerful in effecting psychological changes. Regardless of the method involved, treatments implemented through actual performance achieve results consistently superior to those in which fears are eliminated to cognitive representations of threats. Symbolic procedures have much to contribute as components of multiform performance-oriented approach, *but they are usually insufficient by themselves.*' (Bandura 1977 : 78, my italics)

Objections to Bandura's theory fall into three groups. First, those which object to it on the grounds that it is less *parsimonious* (economical) than existing formulations, and that the predictions made by the theory can be adequately explained by existing knowledge. (See, for example, Eysenck's cogent analysis: Eysenck 1978.) The argument here is that there is no need for Bandura's theory, since classical conditioning theory does the job of explaining in a more simple, and more easily verifiable way. Second, there are objections that Bandura's theory contains ambiguities (Teasdale 1978), particularly in the precise differences between outcome and efficacy expectations. Third, there is the view that there is as yet too little experimental evidence to support Bandura's contention that behavioural change only occurs through a strengthening of perceived self-efficacy.

At this stage then, cognitive-mediational theories of this type need to be approached with some caution. They offer the possibility of a meeting ground for therapists of different persuasions, and yet they retain intact certain important links with established behavioural practice.[3] Additionally, they are attractive in that they deal in an ungrudging fashion with the private 'world within the skin', and, despite the awesome difficulties, try to do this in a scientific way. Further, they are likely to be welcomed by those working outside controlled clinical settings, who have to rely to a considerable extent on programmes that aim to develop *self*-control (see page 198).

Against these attractive features must be weighed the fact that the classical and operant theories of behavioural change have served us very well and continue to do so. They are sophisticated theories, well grounded in scientific research, and they have given rise to exceptionally reliable and well-documented therapeutic approaches. I have

---

[3] At a theoretical level there are obvious links with Kelly's (1955) theory of personal constructs, and, at a clinical level, with 'Rational-Emotive' therapy. See Ellis (1979).

already given some indication of the places where existing foundations of behavioural change are relatively inadequate, and will not repeat these points here. The question of whether cognitive-mediational theories and their therapeutic offshoots can plug these gaps remains to be seen. My own position is that existing theories provide a barely adequate explanation of the various problems that fall within their scope. A strong skeleton structure, if you will. This provides a secure framework on which to base experiments in areas where the therapeutic implications of existing theories are difficult, or indeed impossible to implement. (For example, the hard-to-motivate families struggling with a range of problems at once, which make up a solid proportion of any social worker's caseload.) As long as the established standard of evidence, and the established ways of evaluating therapeutic outcome, are kept in sight, what is there to lose (except possibly some time spent in chasing red herrings)? Certainly there could be much to gain. I suggest that those concerned with the practical development of behavioural methods declare cognitive behavioural theory a 'free enterprise zone' for the next few years, and assess the profits and losses at the end of that time.

We have seen so far that the special nature of human behaviour is conferred on us through what Pavlov called 'the second signalling system' – language, and through it the facility for inner speech and complex imagery, which enables us to act upon the environment in an extraordinarily strategic way by conducting mental experiments to see what *might* happen if we did A or B, *before* we actually do it. On the face of it then, there is a prime facie case for supposing that in some cases we may be able to intervene effectively in the causal chain at *this* point: (i) by suggesting an alternative evaluation of the data on which the client is basing decisions; (ii) by challenging actions based on negative self-concepts which do not seem to us justified by the evidence or by any comprehensive view of the individual's future potential; (iii) by trying to substitute different imagery from that evoked by existing stimuli; (iv) by trying to get the individual to consider *new* evidence on their existing view of personal efficacy; (v) by presenting a different interpretation of the likelihood of certain positive or negative consequences occurring; (vi) by trying to reinforce a different pattern of self-commentary to run alongside particular actions.

To this list I would add the rider: that effectiveness is likely to be strongly influenced by the extent to which the therapist can ensure

Theories of learning 91

that the trial *behaviours* that occur as a result of such approaches are reinforced.

We have some evidence on the effectiveness of attempts to change behaviour by changing ways of thinking about it. So far studies report rather less attainment of goals in comparison with traditional behavioural methods (Marzillier 1980), but it must be stressed that as yet there is too little data to draw firm conclusions. However, the reason why cognitive and social learning formulations of behaviour deserve our special attention goes beyond the mildly encouraging research results referred to above. There are a number of important anomalies to explain in research into the effectiveness of existing behavioural methods (see Russell 1974). Studies into the effects of relaxation and progressive exposure to fear-provoking stimuli (desensitization)[4] have shown that in some cases useful effects can be obtained (at least until someone blows the gaff) through the use of 'placebo effects' of various kinds (McGlynne and Mapp 1970). This research can be countered with the view that placebo effects (pseudo treatments) are themselves susceptible to an analysis in learning theory terms. But the notion that clients could lose crippling fears just because they are induced to *believe* that they can, is somewhat outside the conceptual boundaries of established behavioural practice and this has to be admitted.

[4] The increasing use of rapid exposure techniques (see Chapter 7), in preference to slower desensitization approaches, enables us to side-step some by the implications of this research, but it is cautionary nonetheless.

4
Emotional reactions

Behavioural science is often accused of neglecting the emotional dimension of human existence. While this view continues to surprise some behaviourists familiar with the extensive literature on this topic within their discipline, it is perhaps an inevitable reaction. Any discipline that has, in the past, discouraged inference to internal goings on, and has ruled out introspection and subjective assessment as valid approaches to scientific or clinical phenomena, must tread this ground very warily. The argument that behavioural psychologists have probably done more than other schools to try to put the investigation of the nature and influence of emotion onto an objective footing, fails to convince. Partly this is a matter of stereotype, and partly it is a matter of disciplinary territory. Once the decision has been made to reject and therefore not to bother to read about behavioural topics, because they constitute a 'narrow, mechanistic, unfeeling doctrine', the view that this may not be the case, is unwelcome. But most of all, the general public and more than a few social workers too, baulk at the necessarily unemotional treatment of emotion when it becomes a subject of study. They prefer to hear more florid descriptions of its (admittedly) marvellous range and subtlety. This reflects a belief that it is better simply to experience emotion, rather than to analyse it. Anyone who has had to take *As You Like It* apart, syllable by syllable, or has dissected a Mozart piano concerto, note by note, will tell you there is something to be said for this point of view. But if we wish to understand something as completely as possible – even something beautiful and profound – then we have to analyse it thoroughly.

This means, certainly in this case, that if we wish to help someone with 'an emotional problem' – that undifferentiated catch-all of social work assessment – then we need to know what emotions are, what instigates them, whether they cause behaviour or are a concomitant of it, and whether, or how, they can be changed. Sometimes this can even leave us with a greater respect for that which has been analysed.

Certain basic forms of emotional responding are inborn, for example, fear, crying, smiling, and so on. This does not mean that they are unaffected by environment, which shapes these reactions from the moment of birth and teaches us how to cry so as to attract our parents' attention, and later when to suppress crying, and what to fear and what not to fear.

The experience of these basic emotions is closely allied to physiological changes that occur in the body predominantly as a result of external stimulation. The main systems of the body involved here are the sympathetic nervous system – mentioned already as giving rise to fight and flight reactions – and the parasympathetic nervous system which acts in juxtaposition to this. The relationship is analogous to the dual-control of limb movements by extensor and retractor muscles.

When some aspect of the environment acts upon us and triggers either a primary physiological reflex, or a powerful conditioned reflex of the 'Oh Lord, here comes the boss' kind, a number of biologically functional (but not necessarily socially functional) things occur rapidly inside our bodies.

(a) Heart rate increases, vasecontraction puts up the blood pressure, and hormonal release (adrenalin) maintains this.
(b) We start to breathe more rapidly.
(c) Skin pores dilate to aid cooling of the body.
(d) The blood sugar level rises to meet the potential increase in energy demands from the muscles.
(e) The pupils of the eyes dilate to let in all available light.
(f) The salivary flow dries up and keeps our throats clear for rapid mouth breathing.
(g) Blood flow is directed to the vital centres (that is, the brain and large muscles).
(h) Movements in the gastro-intestinal system are greatly reduced and in extreme cases the bladder and rectum contract.
(i) The capacity of the blood to clot is strengthened by chemical and enzymic action.

(j) Muscle tone increases as an aid to rapid movement.

As previously discussed, these mechanisms help to prepare the body for effective action in the face of danger. Other stimuli evoke different combinations of effects – as in the case of sexual arousal where some of the above mechanisms are involved, but are accompanied by powerful sensations of pleasure and the release of different hormones.

Neuro-physiologists have located specialized centres deep within the brains of animals which seem to be responsible for producing pleasure and pain. Olds (1956) inserted fine electrodes into the brains of laboratory rats, carefully placed in the region of the hypothalmus to stimulate such 'pleasure centres'. The rats in their experiments operated a lever controlling the mild electric current continuously, foregoing food, water, and the opportunity to mate to so stimulate themselves. They continued to do this to the point of exhaustion. It may be that similar centres in the brains of humans provide the physiological basis for reinforcement. A repositioning of the electrode produced equally strong pain and avoidance reactions.

There are several theories of emotion that build upon these basic physiological components. These are now discussed in turn.

According to the James-Lange theory of emotion (see James 1890) it is our perception of combinations of physiological changes of this type that we call 'emotion'. Hence James' famous dictum to the effect that 'we do not run away because we are afraid' – this is to misinterpret cause and effect according to this view: 'We feel fear *because* we run away'. The cause of our behaviour here is the escape-behaviour-provoking stimulus, whether genetically programmed or learned by association. The bodily changes experienced are, in the first place, concomitant not causal. (See *Figure 4(1)*.)

Figure 4(1) Emotional arousal (James-Lange theory)

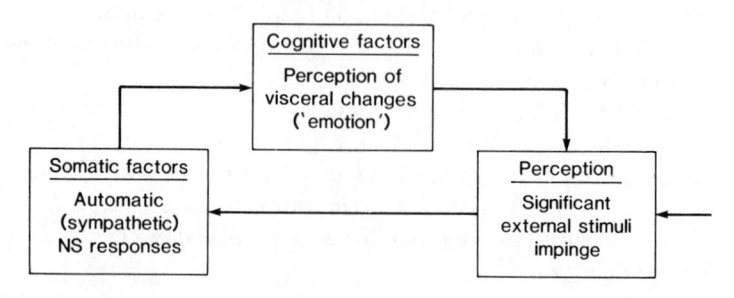

This is the dominant theory (in the sense of being best known) and is more or less accepted by the majority of behaviour therapists. However, it has long had its opponents, even within the scientific community. For example, in itself it fails to explain convincingly how we come to be able to appreciate the vast differences between varieties of emotional experience. The bodily changes described above, though they may occur in slightly different combinations or at different levels of intensity, are relatively crude. One critic (Cannon 1927) pointed out that the nerve supply to some of these relatively insensitive internal organs is insufficient to account for the tremendous speed and intensity of emotional reactions. Having tried (and failed) to induce replica emotions in individuals by chemical and other means (for example, the injection of adrenalin) he turned his attention to the role of the thalamus in the brain's central core. In association with the Danish physiologist, Bard, he developed the view that this centre acted as a kind of 'telephone exchange' for incoming stimuli, redirecting 'messages' to both the cerebral cortex and (via the sympathetic 'trunk lines') to the other organs of the body concerned with emergency action. The key difference here is that the brain is seen as the seat of emotion (see *Figure 4(2)*).

Figure 4(2) Emotional arousal (Cannon-Bard theory)

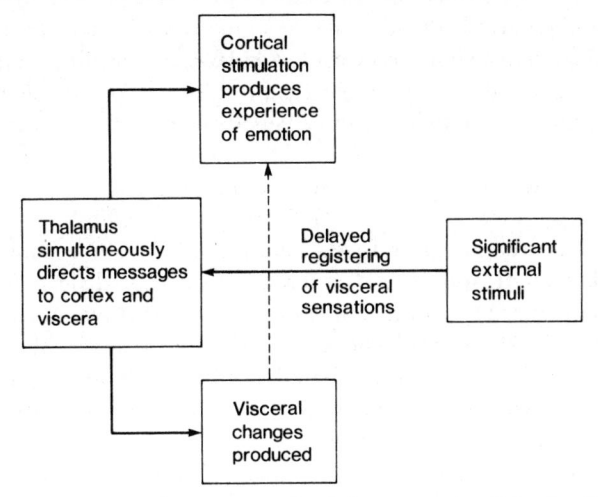

```
                    ┌─────────────┐
                    │ Cortical    │
                    │ stimulation │
            ┌──────▶│ produces    │
            │       │ experience  │
            │       │ of emotion  │
            │       └─────────────┘
            │              ▲
┌───────────────┐    Delayed      ┌────────────┐
│ Thalamus      │    registering  │ Significant│
│ simultaneously│◀── of visceral ─│ external   │
│ directs       │    sensations   │ stimuli    │
│ messages      │                 └────────────┘
│ to cortex and │
│ viscera       │
└───────────────┘
            │       ┌─────────────┐
            │       │ Visceral    │
            └──────▶│ changes     │
                    │ produced    │
                    └─────────────┘
```

Source: Adapted from *Introduction to Psychology*, seventh edition by Ernest R. Hilgard, Rita L. Atkinson, and Richard C. Atkinson, copyright © 1979 by Harcourt Brace Jovanovich, Inc. Reprinted by permision of the publisher.

More recent research has identified centres for the processing of emotion-arousing stimuli in the hypothalamus and the limbic system. One ingenious method of studying the relative parts played by concomitant visceral responses and by higher centres is to study people with spinal cord lesions placed in emotion-arousing circumstances. In this way the dimension of visceral feedback is controlled out. There is no doubt that people handicapped in this way experience something that they refer to as a kind of emotion and that they can act upon. But it seems that it is qualitatively different from what most of us feel. Here are some of the comments made by a subject in the study:

'It's a sort of cold anger. Sometimes I get angry when I see some injustice. I yell and cuss and raise hell . . . but it doesn't seem to have the heat. It's a mental kind of anger.'
(Hilgard, Atkinson, and Atkinson 1979:336)

The final theme of research into this question is that of the role of cognition, appraisal, and memory in emotion (see Schacter and Singer 1962). It may be (in line with the James-Lange theory) that the visceral changes we experience as emotion *are* relatively undifferentiated (in line also with the Cannon-Bard conclusion) but that an overlay of cognitive factors gives them their special and apparently discrete flavouring. Most of us are familiar with pictures in social psychology texts which show contorted faces or specific gestures and ask us to guess the emotion being expressed, without the help of the usual contextual factors. It can be very difficult to do so, particularly where facial expressions are involved. There is common sense in the view that waiting for an important exam to begin, and going out on a first date produce, objectively, rather similar sets of feelings – a tightening of the abdominal muscles, palpitations, blushing, an inability to think straight, and so on. An increasingly accepted view is that fine gradations of emotion are the result of the cognitive labelling and *attribution* of visceral experience according to the nature of the evoking stimulus and our memories of similar experiences in the past. This view opens the way to an amalgamation of the various themes discussed so far (see *Figure 4(3)*).

Thus in some cases of mild arousal, cognitive variables will be predominant: in other cases of strong arousal, physiological variables will largely control behaviour, and thinking will merely reflect upon this. Where clients have learned that a particular collection of stimuli

Figure 4(3) Theories of emotional arousal

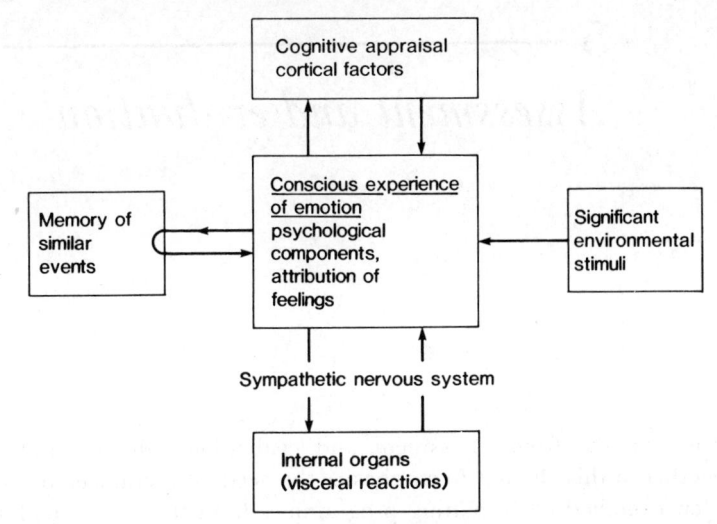

```
                    ┌──────────────────────┐
                    │ Cognitive appraisal  │
                    │ cortical factors     │
                    └──────────▲───────────┘
                               │
┌─────────────┐    ┌───────────┴──────────┐    ┌──────────────┐
│ Memory of   │    │ Conscious experience │    │ Significant  │
│ similar     │───▶│ of emotion           │◀───│ environmental│
│ events      │    │ psychological        │    │ stimuli      │
└─────────────┘    │ components,          │    └──────────────┘
                   │ attribution of       │
                   │ feelings             │
                   └──────────▲───────────┘
                              │
                  Sympathetic nervous system
                              │
                   ┌──────────▼───────────┐
                   │ Internal organs      │
                   │ (visceral reactions) │
                   └──────────────────────┘
```

are hazardous and respond with a high level of physiological involvement (experienced as 'anxiety'), this is certain to inhibit cognitive information-processing about how best to respond. Whether the threat, say of being in a group, has special properties in itself for the individual, based on myth, knowledge, or hearsay, or because of a prior learning experience, or because being in a group is associated with other feared happenings, makes little difference. The vicious circle of high emotional involvement, attempted escape behaviour, and/or faulty and inhibited adaptive performance, increases the likelihood of an adverse reaction. This further reinforces the perception of eliciting stimuli as constituting a threat. Behaviour modification techniques exist that are designed to extinguish, or control, the physiological component of conditioned anxiety by gradual or rapid exposure to the threat (see page 216). Recently, techniques have been developed that seek to change the cognitive basis of maladaptive responding: the unhelpful way in which the threat is perceived and evaluated (page 202). Both appear to be reasonably successful, which is fine from a clinical point of view, but not so fine from a theoretical standpoint since they start from different premises. However, the view of emotion as a process involving a range of different variables, as discussed in the preceding paragraphs, offers one explanation of how these different techniques can have similar effects.

5
Assessment and evaluation

Issues arising from assessment and evaluation will be handled together in this chapter to emphasize the need for therapists to consider a method of evaluating programmes from the outset. Unless data is gathered early on during assessment, to represent the *current* level of problems, then this begs the questions: evaluation in respect of what?; against what prior standard or level? Unless we have an accurate measure of the pre-intervention level and frequency of a problem, then, however rigorous the follow-up procedure, we can decide very little about our effect upon it.

In social work, our main experience is with qualitative evaluation procedures (attempts to assess what *kind* of change has occurred), rather than with quantitative methods (deciding how much change has occurred). Conversely, until quite recently, the behaviour modification field has been dominated by the latter consideration. However, outside very controlled conditions, evaluation exclusively in either form is a nonsense. There is little point in knowing whether Mary now spends more hours per week in conversation with other people than previously, unless we also have some idea of the difference this has made to her life and what she feels about her new activities. There is the argument that Mary would not persist in her new behaviour if she did not find it congenial, but this underestimates the demand effects present in therapeutic programmes, and it also assumes that everyone conducts long-term follow-up visits, which is naïve. There is no good reason why qualitative data about changed thoughts and feelings cannot be gathered in as rigorous a way as possible and used to supplement estimates of amounts of behavioural change, as the primary criterion of relative success and failure. This is certainly the approach adopted in this book.

Behavioural assessment is not just concerned with the problematic behaviour of individuals. Assessment procedures are also used to examine the links between behaviour and contingencies in the client's immediate environment. The apparently unreasonable or under-developed behaviour of the client may result from an unreasonable or a weak set of contingencies, as with the problem of institutionalization in hospital and residential care.

Distinguishing characteristics of behavioural assessment

The following discussion is intended to provide an outline of behavioural assessment and to distinguish it from other approaches with which the reader may be more familiar.

(a) Behavioural assessment is concerned with *who* does *what*, *where*, *when*, and with *whom*; it is also concerned to identify the 'withholding' of behaviours which it would normally be useful and reasonable to perform. It deals also with the consequences which actions have for all the parties involved in them – those who are said to *have* the problem and those for whom someone else's behaviour is said to *be* a problem. The emphasis here is on both *visible* problematic behaviour, and on the *absence* or the inadequacy of adaptive behaviour – where this could be used to reduce negative consequences for the client. Thus, early on in assessment, decisions need to be taken about (i) what behaviours are in *excess*: that is, what do the client and the person influencing him do *too much of*? An example would be aggressive behaviour well above what could be regarded as an unguarded response to everyday frustrations. (ii) What behaviours are in *deficit*: what does the client do too little of? For example: 'Mary has not spoken to any other resident at the hostel since she came here four weeks ago.' (iii) What behaviours occur in the wrong place or at the wrong time? For example: 'Fred approaches people in the street and tells them all about his personal problems, which reinforces their idea that he is an odd person. To some extent, this is an artificial distinction, since in the first example it could be said that the client *lacked* self-control or adequate coping behaviours for dealing with frustration. However it is useful in practice, and serves to remind the assessor to look out for what behaviour *is* and is *not* there.

(b) Behavioural assessment is concerned also with private sensations, such as doubts, worries, fears, and depression. Methods of assessing these predominantly internal behaviours will be discussed later. For now it should be noted that each of the internal conditions monitored gives rise to behavioural excesses or deficits: self-preoccupation, ineffective or ritual activity, in the case of worrying; motionlessness, a fixed expression, lack of attention to dress and hygiene, in the case of depression. People either *do* or *do not do* things as a result of emotional states, and before-and-after comparisons of these things can provide useful supporting data to how people *say* they feel. Having both kinds of information helps to reduce the influence of the demand effects mentioned above – clients trying to please by giving a false impression of improvement, or just living up to expectations in what they say.

(c) Considerable emphasis is placed on contemporary behaviour. The search for the long-lost causes of problems is regarded with suspicion for the following reasons: (i) there is no guarantee that they will ever be found and the exercise is costly in time and resources; (ii) when views as to the original causes of problems *can* be elicited they are not always agreed upon by the various participants, nor are they necessarily valid; (iii) going back into history can often serve to intensify bad feeling and can distract from the necessity of doing something positive in the here and now. However, the social worker must balance against this the need for clients to understand the nature of their problems and the ways in which various parties view its development. One solution is to limit history-taking to brief accounts of the *aetiology* of the problem (the pattern of its development) and to emphasize to clients that often problems are re-activated every day by what people do or fail to do, and by negative expectations which become self fulfilling. The more interesting question is: what maintains problematic behaviour in force, long after the original factors eliciting it have passed into history? More often than not Mr Smith scowls at Mrs Smith because of what happened yesterday and what he expects to happen today, not because of what happened on Jubilee Day 1977. However, if problems seem to be tied up closely with 'personality factors', that is, with typical and well-established ways of responding which vary little across settings, then it may be useful to take a *learning history*. This includes identifying behavioural excesses, deficits, and failures of discrimination as in (a) above; trying to find out how a particular pattern came about; how it has been reinforced; and, concomitantly, why it has proved resistant to change or extinction. This can help the social worker to formulate a more accurate treatment plan, but it still leaves him in the position of having to work with the contemporary manifestations of the problem.

(d) At some stage clear decisions have to be made with the clients about what sequences of behaviour need to be increased in frequency and/or strength and direction, and what sequences decreased in these ways. (The terms accelerated and decelerated are useful ones here.) Further questions include: what new skills would be required in order for the client to perform other more adaptive sequences?

(e) The concern for contemporary events in behavioural assessment is part of the wider attempt to establish the controlling conditions that surround a given problem. This analysis can be thought of as 'topographical' in that it is concerned with the 'surface layout' of the problem, and the aim is, metaphorically, to produce a 'map' of specified daily activities. Thus, in behavioural assessment we are concerned with such things as *where* things tend to happen and not to happen; what happens around the client or to him just *before* a sequence of the unwanted behaviour occurs; what happens around the client or to him *during* the performance of the behaviour; and what happens *after* the performance of the behaviour. This emphasis reflects our knowledge of the way the opportunity for certain sequences of behaviour is 'signalled' by prior events (S^ds) and how it is maintained by prior knowledge of reinforcing consequences. Any natural correlation or variance in these factors provides useful extra information, for example when Johnny wets the bed every night *except* when he sleeps with his brother or *except* when he stays at his grandmother's. Or when Mr Turner's bouts of drinking and exhibitionism always result in his daughter coming to stay with him until he feels better.

(f) Behavioural assessment takes place independently of the definitions and labels that others place on problems. We are concerned to find out what people who are said to have 'inadequate personalities' do; what 'schizophrenics' do and don't do; what it is that Joan says to make her parents describe her as 'insolent'; how someone with 'anti-social tendencies' actually behaves, and so on. There are good ethical reasons for building such a 'label' examining stage into our assessments, but it is also necessary if we are to reduce the element of subjective judgement present in most conceptualizations of problematic behaviour.

(g) The need for flexibility of approach is always stressed in social work texts on assessment. While it is a matter of common sense that assessment procedures that are rigid and forced will probably be self-defeating, there is at least an equal need to make assessments of problems as clear and specific as possible. Our main concerns here should be as follows. (i) To produce clear *formulations* of problems. That is, to put together a concise account of how the problem has developed and what maintains it. This does not have to be established truth – just a coherent view that is testable in practice. A good formulation leads to (ii), clear *hypotheses* about what might affect the problems under review. The chief characteristic of the good hypothesis is that it should be as 'risky' as possible (Popper 1963), that is it should be the sort of statement that can be easily checked up on. The statement: 'Mr Brown's low level of self-esteem is due to poor ego-development' is a poor hypothesis since there is little or nothing that could ever happen to disprove it. 'Mary's shyness with strangers is likely to reduce if she learns how to start conversations' is better. If Mary receives instruction on how to start conversations, begins to mix with strangers, and yet does *not* talk to them and does not stay long in their company, then the hypothesis, as it stands, is *wrong* and the social worker knows something more about the client and the problem confronting her. (iii) Hypotheses lead to both long-term and short-term goals. These too have ideal characteristics and they are similar to those just listed. The clear goal is one which provides definite feedback on progress towards some specific, and at least partially defined, end-state. Thus we need to tell from the goals we set with our clients whether our assessment policy is on the right track or not. The goal: 'to improve communication in the family' has little real meaning of its own. What will family members do more of, less of, do differently, do in different combinations, or in different places, as a result of family communication being improved? Will they have more rows? ('Tensions are less bottled up

Assessment and evaluation 103

these days in the Williams family – which is healthy') or fewer rows ('Mr and Mrs Williams have far fewer arguments than they did – which is healthy'). Alternatively it could be said that: 'John and Katy Williams spend less time in the house these days' (which is healthy?); or that Mrs Williams now devotes much more time to her husband (what do John and Katy think?). Obviously, 'circumstances alter cases'; the point is that some pre-described state – represented by actual behaviour – should be the target of intervention. The question of which particular future actions are desirable, acceptable, fair, feasible, and so on is a matter for consultation and negotiation with clients, and of conscience. If it turns out, as work progresses, that what is being aimed at is unlikely to represent any of these things, then the policy can always be re-assessed. Better a series of relatively short-term unequivocal, specific, and monitorable goals which can be replaced as necessity demands, rather than one, all-purpose, impossible-to-refute objective which allows almost any eventuality to be claimed as a success: 'Mr and Mrs Williams now argue constantly and the children are very worried about their parents' behaviour – but at least these hostilities are now out in the open.' I once saw something very similar to this written on an agency case record. The husband went to prison eventually for repeated assault – perhaps he 'came to terms with the latent aggression in his personality' there. I don't know.

Goals are points to steer by and the last thing anyone (or his passengers) needs, when trying to steer by a point, is a 'flexible' point. A flexible policy made up of a series of very definite points is a different matter. Francis Bacon put his finger on this problem some time ago: 'Truth arises more readily from error than confusion.' We can learn from our mistakes only so long as they are clearly identifiable as such, and cannot be massaged into the shape of half-successes.

Now that we have gained an overview of behavioural assessment we can start to examine the process stage by stage and in rather more detail (see *Figure 5(1)*).

Obtaining a general description of the problem

The ideal shape for any assessment procedure is, metaphorically, that of the tun-dish: wide-open to start with and convergent there-

Figure 5(1) Stages in the assessment of behavioural problems

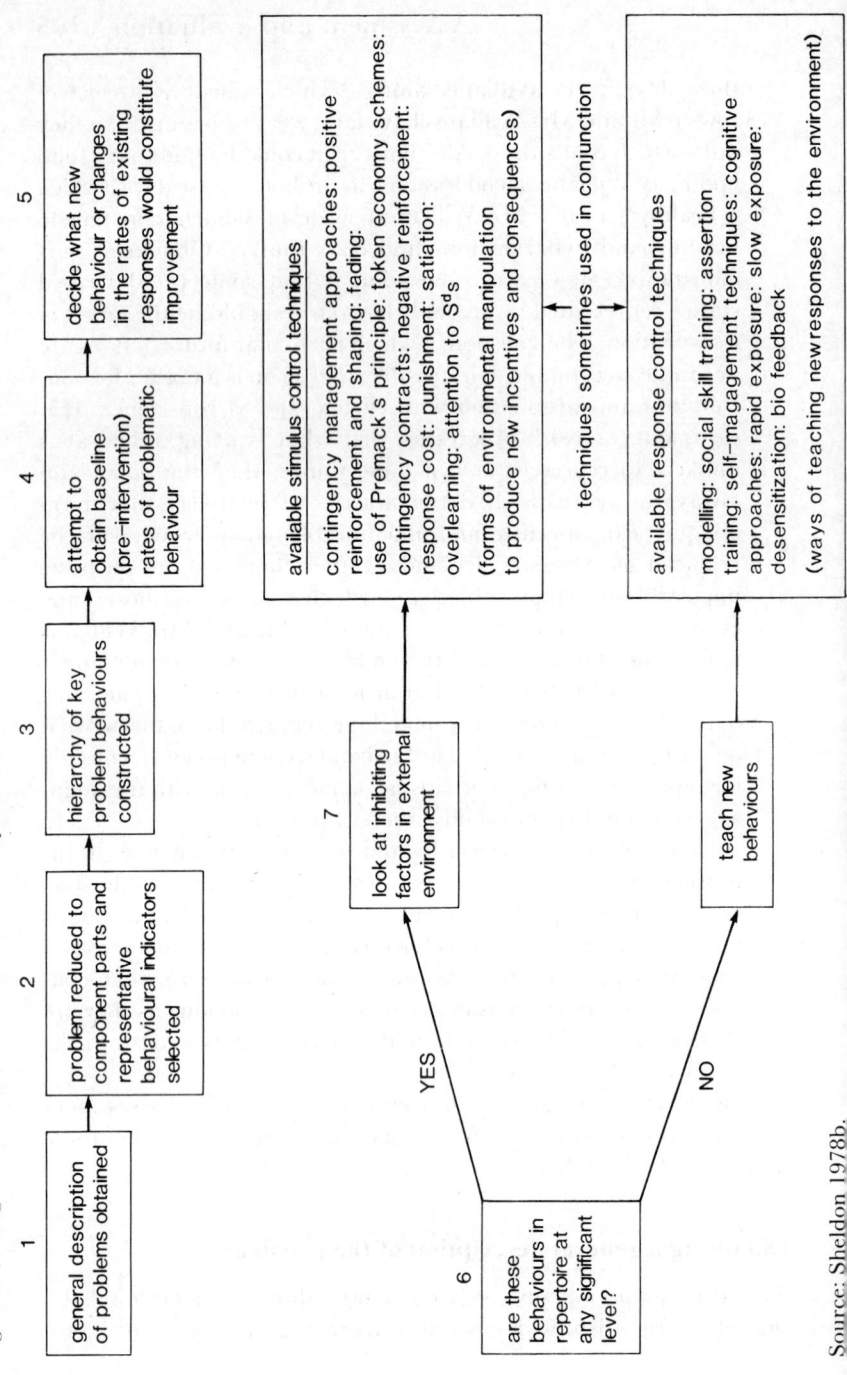

1. general description of problems obtained
2. problem reduced to component parts and representative behavioural indicators selected
3. hierarchy of key problem behaviours constructed
4. attempt to obtain baseline (pre-intervention) rates of problematic behaviour
5. decide what new behaviour or changes in the rates of existing responses would constitute improvement

6. are these behaviours in repertoire at any significant level?

YES → 7. look at inhibiting factors in external environment

available stimulus control techniques
contingency management approaches: positive reinforcement and shaping: fading: use of Premack's principle: token economy schemes: contingency contracts: negative reinforcement: response cost: punishment: satiation: overlearning: attention to S^ds
(forms of environmental manipulation to produce new incentives and consequences)

↔ techniques sometimes used in conjunction ↔

NO → teach new behaviours

available response control techniques
modelling: social skill training: assertion training: self-management techniques: cognitive approaches: rapid exposure: slow exposure: desensitization: bio feedback
(ways of teaching new responses to the environment)

Source: Sheldon 1978b.

Assessment and evaluation 105

after. The first stages of a behavioural assessment are little different from those recognizable to most social workers already and the sequence runs as follows.

(a) Obtain a general description of the problem from as many different points of view as time permits.
(b) Find out whom the problem affects and in what ways.
(c) Trace its course and development.
(d) Get some idea of the different parts of the problem and how separate or interactive they are.
(e) Assess *existing* motivation for change (for example, had the client and/or his family gone to any trouble to overcome these difficulties before and if not, why not?). The question of how motivated and motivatable the client or his family are, is answered further by experience of them and how they respond.
(f) Obtain an impression of the assets available in the client and other interested parties. The assessment of what is right with people often gets overlooked in social work.

There are two opposing categories of mistake that can be made at this stage. The first is that in the attempt to be task-centred and behaviourally virtuous, the worker can prematurely 'squeeze' out of the client's story all those things likely to complicate the business of reaching a clear policy decision in the case. These effects are well known in both clinical and research work, as is the tendency for interviewers to shape assessment data until it fits a favourite theoretical mould (Heine 1953; Sheldon and Baird 1978). The danger at the other polarity is that, unless prompted, clients fail to give an adequate account of the whole of their problems because they have forgotten things, because they make narrowly based decisions about what is relevant, or because they are responding to the theoretical preferences of other professionals with whom they have been in contact.

The point about shaping by other helpers is particularly important in social work because we are often left to deal with the casualties and cast-offs of other professions. For example, in the case of the agoraphobic client referred to in Chapter Three (page 46), the information about her fainting episode came out only in the later stages of the first interview. She had been taught by previous 'helpers' to respond to her problem as a manageable psychiatric illness and so viewed this episode as just another manifestation of whatever was wrong inside her head.

All preliminary conclusions about the range, scope, and development of the problem at which the social worker arrives ought to be shared with the client. No more than a brief summary of impressions is required, but this 'reading back' helps to cut down the risks of misunderstanding which are quite considerable in our field, as Mayer and Timms noted in their consumer research:

> 'There is almost a Kafkaesque quality about these worker-client interactions. To exaggerate only slightly, each of the parties assumed that the other shared certain of his underlying conceptions about behaviour and the ways in which it might be altered. Then, unaware of the inappropriateness of his extrapolations, each found special reasons to account for the other's conduct.'
>
> (Mayer and Timms 1970:77)

An outsider sitting in on the first stage of a behavioural assessment interview might be struck only by the number of times the client was asked to give examples; by the concern of the interviewer to know what was *done* as well as what was thought and felt; and by the emphasis on what sort of events tend to precede, follow, and accompany problematic behaviour.

Reducing the problem to its component parts

There are various suggestions about how best to start this process. I advocate the 'man from Mars' technique or some variant of it. This involves asking the client to say what an outside observer who knew nothing of the problem would see were he in a position to observe everything that went on. Clients often describe events in terms of their own part in them or according to the effect that other people's behaviour has on *them* – leaving out important information about what other people do on the periphery. A second tendency is for clients to diagnose 'intentions'. Remember that the statement: 'He snubs me every evening, just to put me down,' can be read from the husband's point of view as: 'She's waiting for me every evening as soon as I come home from work, just looking for trouble and finding fault; I ignore her, because I've found that's the best policy.'

Concentrating on who does what, where, and when, reveals that Mrs X hovers near the door when her husband returns from work and says things in an attempt to continue earlier arguments. Mr X tries to avoid this and comes home late, does not speak, and picks up his newspaper. We are not setting aside the client's interpretations here – neither the view that Mrs X is a 'nervous wreck and is always looking for a fight', nor the view that Mr X 'thinks he is better than everyone else and behaves as if I don't exist just to get the better of me and make me feel small'. We are simply trying to isolate the behaviour that leads to such views.

There is a third category of behaviour apart from deficits and excesses such as these; namely, 'failures of discrimination'. You will remember from Chapter Three that behavioural sequences are often 'cued' by stimuli that signal either the likelihood of reinforcement (S^d) or its probable absence (S^Δ). Failures of discrimination are an important consideration in behavioural work and the social worker should be on the look-out for these. The person who consistently fails to match his behaviour to that prevailing in the group as a whole, or the person who is assertive to all and sundry regardless of whether anyone is set to deprive him of his rights or not, both fall into this category. They fail to identify, or at least do not consider it worthwhile to respond to, orientational signals from their social surroundings. A useful device for gaining some preliminary ideas about what might be sparking off, and then maintaining behaviour in this way, is the 'A.B.C. Chart'. A. stands for Antecedents, B. for Behaviour (the performance), and C. for Consequences. It is an easy matter to instruct clients in the use of these simple charts and they often give valuable information (see *Figure 5(2)*).

Figure 5(2) An example of an A.B.C. Chart

Time	A What happened just before?	B What happened?	C What happened just after that?
12.30 p.m.	I sat at the table and asked Billy to come for his dinner	Billy threw a tantrum for ten minutes and went upstairs	I took his meal upstairs. Billy ate it and gave me a cuddle
2.00 p.m.	I was in the kitchen washing up.	Billy cried for 20 minutes.	I coaxed Billy out of his mood and played with him for half an hour
3.30 p.m.	I started to get Wendy's tea	Billy threw his toys all over the floor and tugged at the electric plugs	I smacked him.
4.30 p.m.	I was in the kitchen washing up.	Billy had another tantrum for 15 minutes this time	Told Billy to stop or I would put him to bed. Gave him a cuddle and got Wendy to play with him.
5.20 p.m.	We were watching T.V.	Billy took his clothes off and went outside	Hurried him back in and sat him on my lap. We all watched T.V. together
7.10 p.m.	I told Billy it was time for bed.	Billy started to wail and wouldn't stay upstairs	Brought him downstairs for ten minutes.

108 Behaviour Modification

Most of the problems dealt with by social workers are compendium problems; they have lots of different parts to them and the parts tend to interact with each other. The best way to begin the process of specification is to find out from clients what things go together and what things operate as separate entities. We begin then by pencilling in connections between events and bracketing other events off until we get *some* idea of how the whole system works. The next stage in the process of specification is to reduce each point of the total problem to discrete behaviours (see *Figure 5(3)*).

Figure 5(3a) Case record – the Thomas family

Client: Mary Thomas (26)
General problem: 'Lack of social confidence'; 'withdrawn'; 'excessively shy'.
  History of psychiatric care.

Problematic behaviours (information source = family)

Deficit	Excess
Leaves the house very rarely	Talks aloud to herself
Will not talk to anyone outside the family (except, very rarely, social worker)	Occasional bursts of over-activity (circles room rapidly for ten minutes)
Has to be bullied into a daily wash by relatives	Gives voice to unreasonable beliefs, for example, TV surveillance
Virtually no eye contact with social worker	Spends long periods staring through window
Shuffling gait	Stares fixedly at mother for periods of up to half an hour

---

Client: Mr Thomas (Father)
General problem: Will not stand up for himself at work and outside the house. Takes his worries and frustrations out on family members.

Problematic behaviours (information source = wife and son)

Deficit	Excess
When asked to work overtime at work will not refuse even though he feels very frustrated that he cannot refuse	Shouts at family. Presses Mary to discuss and defend her delusional experiences and then tells her she is mad

Deficit	*Excess*
Will not ask for overtime when he needs the money and waits to be asked	Drinks too much – at the pub for five evenings per week
Remains silent when juniors make fun of him; will not initiate conversation with colleagues	Fusses endlessly over his clothes
Is embarrassed to say pleasant things to his wife; 'feels a cissy'. Low level of sexual activity	

Client: John Thomas (Brother)
General problem: Rows with father followed by long periods of absence from home and long silences on his return.

Problematic behaviours (information source = mother and son)

Deficit	*Excess*
Ordinary, everyday conversations with father	Shouting at father
Does not talk to Mary and his mother in father's presence but will as soon as he goes out of the room	Long periods away from home without explanation

It is possible to further reduce items in these check lists and this may be necessary when it has been decided to concentrate work on one part of the problem. For example, for Mary, one can look in more detail at 'lack of social confidence'.

Figure 5(3b) Lack of social confidence (Mary)

Eye contact level is about a second every three to four minutes.
Sentences are faltering and often left incomplete.
Voice level is low with only occasional variations in pitch. There are sharp intakes of breath at unexpected moments in the middle of conversations.
Replies to direct questions are always brief – sometimes merely labels.
When door bell rings Mary walks immediately to her bedroom.
When Mary stares out of the window her lips are moving most of the time.
Mary spends only a few minutes per week out of doors.
Mary rejects all opportunities to meet other people unless forced to by relatives.

Some problems are easier to reduce to behavioural components than others. Generally speaking, the more interconnected and the wider the scope of a problem, the more difficult it is to decide where one piece of behaviour ends and another begins. In other cases problems may be mainly emotional in character and not reliably connected to a particular behavioural sequence of anyone else. When people are severely or clinically depressed, then it is very likely that this will show up in what they do *not* do. Self-care behaviours will be severely reduced and the client may spend long periods, head in hands, sitting in a corner. He may also express feelings of unworthiness to anyone who gets into conversation with him. In less severe cases, emotions and behaviour are not so clearly connected. For example, the client who feels a failure and whose marriage is going through a shaky patch may behave in an exaggeratedly cheerful and solicitous manner, thereby often making things worse. Social strategies and over-compensations are unlikely to escape detection completely, but they can cloud the picture initially.

In addition, there is the consideration that the person in a family exhibiting the most disturbed behaviour may not be the person who 'has' the problem. Children often react violently to family and marital difficulties either as a strategy for preoccupying or uniting parents, or to punish them, or to guarantee attention that would not otherwise be forthcoming. However, it makes little sense to proceed automatically to this conclusion, and to see all problems of childhood as 'symptoms' of a breakdown in the 'family system', and less still to assume that changing problematic aspects of family functioning will automatically result in a disappearance of the child's behaviour – which may be maintained by all sorts of other factors in the environment.

Behavioural indicators

A useful notion in complex cases such as the above is that of the *behavioural indicator*. An indicator is something that reliably detects the presence of something else, just as blue litmus paper turning red reliably denotes the presence of an acid. If, for instance, there is evidence to suggest that the disturbed behaviour of a child is caused by, or at least fluctuates in sympathy with, certain problematic behaviours performed by other members of his family, and if these behaviours are : (i) complex, interrelated, or hard to monitor on an

Assessment and evaluation   111

individual basis; (ii) are the antecedents of the child's behaviour; (iii) are the logical point of intervention; or (iv) cluster around factors not easily observed, such as the clients' feelings for one another, then the frequency of the child's problematic behaviour can be used as the barometer of success with the primary family problem. Monitoring in this type of case can be made more useful still, if qualitative data – for example, detailed self-reports about changed feelings – are combined with matching data from the first quantitative source.

CASE ILLUSTRATION

In a recent case referred to me, a twelve-year-old boy, John Pearson, was said to be 'obsessed with fire'. The problem seemed to be linked to the fact that his father, a previously active and affectionate man, had recently suffered an industrial accident and was now confined to a wheelchair. The father's reaction to this was one of (understandable) self-pity and complete self-preoccupation. The reaction of his wife was a mixture of doting and mild depression. The main hypothesis here was this: a not – in itself – very serious incident of arson involving an old allotment shed (committed with a gang of other boys) for once produced attentive responses from the family. Married brother and sister visited the house to talk over the problem, and the father was sufficiently aroused by this to express that he would discuss 'whatever was worrying his son' at any time: 'you have only to ask, son'. In this way, an otherwise random act of vandalism was powerfully reinforced. Another more serious fire followed, this time started by the boy alone. He was identified and a supervision order was made; another minor fire occurred and the police made it clear to the child and family in no uncertain terms that he was heading for secure accommodation. Actual fire-lighting ceased, but *talking* about fire, *fire*works, *fire* accidents, *fire* engines, and the leaving of matches around in odd places, became an ever-present feature of family life, and was cited by them as the most important (removeable) cause of unhappiness.

This boy's obsession with fire gained him the family's attention, jerked his mother out of a minor depressive episode, and produced some fatherly behaviour from dad. It also helped make the boy a reputation at school as a dangerous character, where previously he had been rather low in the pecking order. Moreover, he achieved all this without actually having to light another fire and risk incarceration.

During treatment, the behaviour in parents that instigated the problem was monitored only with some difficulty. Parameters included periods of conversation between Mr and Mrs Pearson; periods of conversation not related to fire-raising topics between father and son; attempts by Mr Pearson to wash and dress himself with reducing amounts of help, and so on. This side of the analysis left out important but subtle variables; Mrs Pearson's feelings of pessimism about the future; Mr Pearson's ruminations about money and the inadequacy of his compensation payment; the tension in the family when their son seemed to be deliberately but pointedly withholding 'fire-talk' – 'the calm before the storm', as it was known.

It *is* possible to construct behavioural definitions and measures for all the subtle behaviours just mentioned, but it would probably involve the social worker in a mass of detail and would require highly cooperative recorders. But when levels of fire-talk and long periods of silence were used as indicators of the complex variables that we might call 'the atmosphere in the family', it was found that the two matched quite closely. Subjective estimates of how the week had gone, other qualitative measures, and numerical data available on other behaviours, showed that whenever the father's self-preoccupation was particularly evident, so was talk about possible incidents involving fire. It made sense here to attack both sets of problems, but to give priority to John's, the danger being that his behaviour would obtain extraneous reinforcement from outside the family. (There is a description of the methods used on page 153.)

Throughout, the behaviour for which this child was referred remained the most reliable indicator of progress; it 'stood for' a range of other complex variables. Indicators are not 'the problem' just as failing to dress, wash, and smile are not depression, but a reflection of depression. The question that has to be decided is whether they are a reliable reflection or not. Mr Pearson could conceivably sob into his washbasin and sit ruminating in his best suit. To rule out such effects requires a little imagination, and as wide a range of different indicators as is feasible.

Problem hierarchies – deciding where to start

Once the problem has been reduced to descriptions of behaviour, behavioural deficits, and the contexts in which particular behaviours do and do not occur, the next stage is to establish the priorities of intervention. Two general features of the behavioural approach in this respect, are: (i) the importance of providing clients with an early experience of success in the field of problem-solving; (ii) accordingly, the policy of starting off modestly and increasing the scope of the programme later on, as positive results acrue.

Establishing priorities in a case can also depend on a number of other parameters. Here are some likely considerations.

URGENCY

Is anyone at serious risk because of the problem(s) under review? Questions of safety and the basic rights of individuals have obvious priority over future therapeutic possibilities. Below this level, is part of the problem likely to produce seriously adverse consequences in the near future, for example a further prosecution, expulsion from school, loss of job, and so forth?

CLIENT'S VIEW

It is a good general rule that 'the customer knows best'. Clients usually have an intimate knowledge of their problems and are quite often in the best position to define what the priorities should be. This is not, of course, an absolute principle, and the key notion here is that of open negotiation about what needs to be done. The social worker has all the benefits and drawbacks of a more distant perspective. The two views put together are unbeatable if the compromise can be effected.

MOTIVATIONAL FACTORS

Clients tend only to come (or be referred) for help when their own unaided efforts have failed. Most social workers have experience of trying to persuade families who have 'tried everything' to 'try it again . . . but systematically this time'. The point is that constructive problem-solving efforts may never have been reinforced and correcting this is an important priority.

FEASIBILITY

Programmes requiring intensive visiting, or, in residential settings, the concentration of staff on one small group, may be beyond the scope of available resources. However, if some small-scale positive changes can be brought about, then it is possible that the clients themselves will play a larger part in the programme later, so lessening the load.

MEDIATORS

Most behavioural programmes are highly dependent on the use of *mediators*: people in the client's surroundings who can record, prompt, and reinforce appropriate behaviour. The availability or otherwise of such people, their willingness to cooperate in the programme, and their likely teaching skills, are major factors in determining what the initial starting point should be.

INTER-RELATEDNESS OF PROBLEMS

Where problems are rooted in complex patterns of behaviour, the social worker must decide on the *centrality* of particular features. If teaching interview skills to an eldest son might help him to get a job, so enabling him to contribute to the hard-pressed family budget, reducing his level of frustration *and* the level of arguments in the family at the same time, and if this in turn would give Mr and Mrs X a breathing space to get to grips with some of their own problems, then this is the obvious point to start. For a small investment of effort the potential payoff is large.

CLIENT CAPACITIES AND INTERESTS

Sometimes the nature and scope of a programme is dictated by the intellectual and other personal capacities of the clients and/or mediators. Conversely, where clients have personal resources or enthusiasms which could be built upon, these too must be taken into account.

Dissipation of the energies of both social workers and clients is a considerable danger when complex problems are attacked on all fronts at once. The existence of a carefully planned hierarchy of problems – or problem elements – reminds everyone of this and is an aid to the strategic deployment of whatever resources are available.

Evaluation: the use of single case experimental designs (S.C.E.D.s)

We need now to consider how some idea of the *extent* of the problem chosen as a starting point can be gained. This is the point at which the assessment joins evaluation, and the first task is to decide how often behaviours or indicators relevant to the problem occur prior to active intervention by the social worker. This is called the *baseline stage*. It is not a measure of the problem before *any* help has been given. Sometimes just talking problems over, getting things clear during assessment, or feeling that there is someone on hand if problems get worse, will have a very beneficial effect. In such cases baselines record the *pre-specific* or *pre-active* intervention level of a problem. They provide a standard against which the specific problem-countering policy worked out by the therapist can be assessed. They do not alone provide a control for various background therapeutic effects.

BASELINE EFFECTS

Sometimes when clients set about measuring the extent of their current problems the situation improves. This so-called *baseline effect* is probably the result of focusing attention on specifics rather than generalities, and of the improvement in morale that a businesslike approach to problem-solving can bring.

RECORDS AND RECORDING

There are a variety of ways in which records can be kept. The graph is probably the best method since it provides information at a glance, and patterns and trends show up quite readily. However, graphs frighten some clients and the social worker needs to adapt the presentation of data to suit both the clients' expectations and their intellectual capacities. This said, graphs do provide powerful visual feedback on progress; if they are introduced in a matter-of-fact way and explained in simple terms, they pose few insurmountable problems in the majority of cases. But if graphs are rejected by the client, the social worker needs to use his ingenuity. Students of mine, working with mentally handicapped youngsters, have used recording devices such as the 'posting' of tiddleywink counters into a moneybox and the pasting of cut-out cartoon characters onto a board as recording methods. Only a few clients refuse to keep records if the scheme is carefully explained and adapted to their needs. A larger problem is the aversion to graphs and counting felt by social work refugees from the Maths curriculum.

On this issue of recording, it is my experience that clients respond favourably to the following: (i) the clearly demonstrated assumption on the social worker's part that effective helping requires careful assessment; (ii) a sympathetic but matter-of-fact approach and time spent explaining how best to keep records and what problems might arise; (iii) reinforcement for record-keeping; (iv) simple, well-produced proformas with clear instructions written on them; (v) the social worker actually using the records in front of clients and going over the data with them.

Record entries need to be made as soon as possible after the target behaviour has occurred. Clients often try to remember numbers until a single 'totting up' session at the end of the day, but this is full of pitfalls and should be discouraged. Sometimes a recording device needs to be portable. No-one is going to carry a chart around all day, and no parent is going to run downstairs at 3 a.m. to record on a wall that his son is out of bed for the fourth time. A variety of methods can be used, including postcards, golf-counters, marks on sticky tape around the wrist, and so on.

METHODS OF GATHERING DATA

Direct observation

This method is applicable where the problem behaviours occur at a high frequency and so a relatively short period of observation gives a good idea of current rates. It can be used only where the presence of a non-participatory observer is not likely to be a distracting influence.

Time sampling

Time sampling is used where it is impractical or undesirable for an observer to spend long periods of time with the client. Instead, ten

Assessment and evaluation 117

five-minute observations – for instance – can be made at intervals throughout the day, perhaps by a mediator. This method is particularly useful in residential and hospital settings, but it can deal only with behaviours of relatively high frequency.

Participant observation

Essentially the same as direct observation, this method can be used where the presence of an outsider is less intrusive if he joins in whatever is going on. The behaviour under review needs to be somewhat independent of observer-effects, or a few dummy-runs need to be made so that the observer 'merges' into the background.

Mechanical, electrical, and other aids to observation

Tape recorders, video sets, one-way screens, and other such aids are increasingly available in child guidance clinics and other specialist centres. Once clients become familiar with such devices they tend to overlook their presence.

Observation by mediators

This method is very common in behavioural work. Parents, teachers, spouses, relatives, and peers can all be enlisted to record the incidence of target behaviours. The method is particularly applicable to field settings.

Self-observation

Again, this method is very useful in field settings. The success of self-recording depends on: (i) a well-organized scheme; (ii) a very clear definition of what is to be counted so that the client is in no doubt; (iii) whether the behaviours under review are of a character to make deliberate distortion likely. It is a brave client who will report clearly on his own anti-social activities, and a brave social worker who will offer an amnesty on such behaviour for recording purposes and so run the risk of appearing to condone it. One alternative is to monitor the occurrence of positive (generally acceptable) behaviours which are incompatible with the problem behaviours under review. Decisions of this kind, and decisions about whether to use mediators instead,

118 Behaviour Modification

depend largely on the amount of cooperation the social worker can get from his client. Self-observation is used to assess behaviours that occur in private, at low frequency and/or beyond the range of mediators. On the whole it works well, and a client who will not cooperate with it is unlikely to cooperate with the therapeutic scheme that follows.

Reliability checks

It is possible to use these different methods in combination, thus adding greatly to their validity and reliability. Where self reports and reports of mediators agree substantially with each other, or with a period of direct observation, then greater confidence can be placed on findings.

INTERPRETATION OF BASELINE DATA

All scientific data require interpretation; only rarely will a self-evident conclusion jump off the page. This is especially true of the kind of data gathered in natural settings, which are at best a compromise between rigour and relevance.

   The first point of consideration is the length and stability of the baseline measure. The aim in baseline recording is to obtain a typical sample of behaviour and so recording must continue long enough for odd fluctuations and recurring patterns to be seen in context. It may be that a pattern of aggressive behaviour on Mondays, or in the presence of another particular group of people, will emerge. It may be that the last two days just happen to have been particularly difficult or particularly good, giving an artificial impression. Over a longer period such effects will show up and can give much valuable information. (Examples of S.C.E.D.s with both stable and unstable baselines can be found in *Figures 5(4)* and *5(5)* on pages 119 and 120.) But the ideal length for a baseline depends on several different factors.

(a) Some behaviours, for instance eye-contact patterns, obsessional behaviours, or periods of rumination in depression, are likely to occur at a high rate, and so observation over a period of two or three days will give some idea of the stable frequency. The social worker must use his judgement here. If different things happen on different days then it may be useful to see how this affects the data. A daily time-sampling approach may be the answer (see page 116).

Assessment and evaluation 119

(b) Where behaviours occur at low frequency, for example conversation in a withdrawn schizophrenic patient, enuresis, or stealing, baseline data need to be collected over a longer period.

(c) In all cases the ideal to aim for is a *stable* measure where there are no great or untypical swings in the rate of performance. This is not to say that there must be *no* fluctuations, just that these must roughly cancel each other out (as in *Figure 5(4)*), or cluster around the median, with only one or two exceptions outside the range. In cases where data are very difficult to interpret, simple statistical techniques are available (see page 246).

(d) Ideally, the more recorded observations of the behaviours being monitored the better. In practice this usually means the longer the baseline period the better. However, a balance has to be struck here between therapeutic considerations and the need for careful assessment. Although clients will sometimes suffer problems stoically for months or years, the arrival of professional help can make further delay difficult to bear.

Below is an example of the simplest kind of S.C.E.D., the A.B. design, which makes a straightforward 'before and after' comparison. A comparison between this example and *Figure 5(5)* on page 120 should illustrate the difference between stability and instability at the baseline stage.

Figure 5(4) Example of an A.B. design with an unstable baseline

Uncontrollable temper tantrums[1] in a five-year-old child

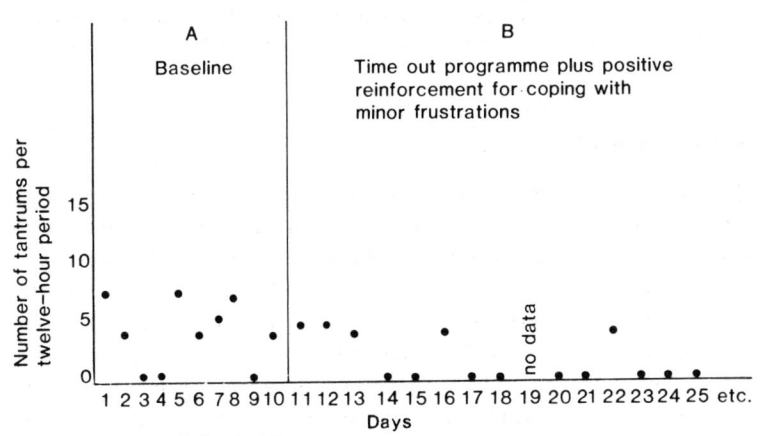

[1] Operationally defined with parents.

120   Behaviour Modification

Figure 5(5)   Example of an A.B. design with a stable baseline

Baseline data from classroom management scheme for a 'disturbed' nine-year-old boy

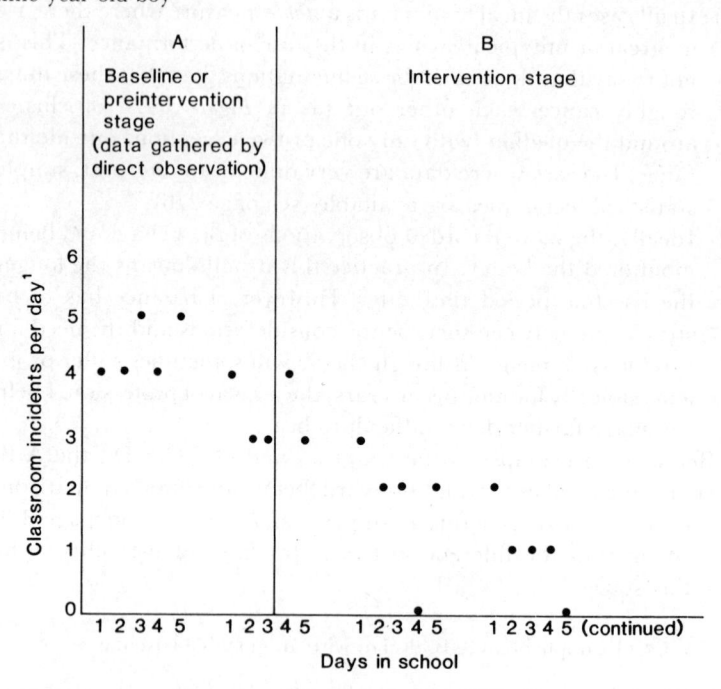

```
                A                              B
        Baseline or                    Intervention stage
        preintervention
        stage
        (data gathered by
        direct observation)
```

[Scatter plot: Classroom incidents per day¹ (0–6) vs Days in school, showing baseline points around 3–5 incidents and intervention points declining to 0–2 incidents across four 5-day blocks, with "(continued)" after the final block]

¹ Predefined with teachers as any combination of: Interfering with the work of others; causing physical pain to others; leaving his seat and failing to return within one minute of first being asked; making loud noises, or noises continuing long enough to distract other pupils.

Setting target levels

The next stage in the assessment sequence is that of setting target levels. The client and the social worker have to decide what would constitute a significant improvement in the case, remembering that in some cases it is not the behaviour *per se* that is the problem, but the rate at which it is performed, or the setting in which it occurs. We all lose our temper occasionally, but some people lose it every day and do not feel that they should try to keep it just because they are out with friends. It is a useful check on the usefulness of a programme, and often a spur to everyone concerned with it, if target *levels* are written

Assessment and evaluation 121

in next to goals as soon as these have been formulated. A simple statement such as: 'Mrs A. will consider that her son's behaviour has substantially improved if he returns home within fifteen minutes of the agreed time'; or 'Billy will have achieved his target when he can dress himself unaided', will usually suffice.

The next decision to take is whether the behaviours which will constitute an improvement are already in repertoire at any significant level. (See *Figure 5(1)*.) The decision as to which group of behavioural approaches we are likely to select treatment from depends on the answer to this question. We need to know whether the person whose behaviour we would like to change *ever* engages in behaviours or levels of behaviours *anything like* the target behaviours. If so, then these operants might be reinforceable. If not, or if the behaviours are at a *very* low level, it makes more sense to concentrate on teaching and developing new behaviours. From this distinction is drawn the twofold classification of behavioural approaches used in this book: *Stimulus Control* techniques (designed to change the behaviour through changing the environment and the consequences it produces for different behaviours) and *Response Control* techniques (designed to alter the range, type, or level of responses that the client has in repertoire, or to equip him with completely new ones (Bandura 1969). Obviously, there are close connections between these two groupings, and many programmes will include elements from both – as when a new sequence of behaviour is first modelled and then approximate performances are positively reinforced during rehearsals with the client.

The rest of this chapter is concerned with the various methods by which behavioural programmes can be evaluated and in particular with further examples of single case experimental designs. This approach to evaluation is not dependent upon the use of formal behavioural techniques. So long as the user is willing to link expected outcome to behaviour in some form, any method can be used. Whether the use of other methods is advisable in a particular case is a separate question.

A.B. designs

The reader will see from *Figures 5(4)* and *5(5)* that the recording of the target behaviour (or some reliable indicator of it) is continued after the start of the programme designed to alter it. A.B. designs are a considerable advance on impressionistic case studies, but they are still *quasi-experimental* rather than fully experimental. They offer good correlational evidence of outcome; but we cannot be sure from them which of the many variables introduced into a case is the really potent one. It could be the social worker's own behaviour; 'placebo effects' of various kinds; or particular elements in the programme. Any or all of these could be producing the effect. In the short term, this may not appear to matter much, because the social worker's main job is helping people with problems, not researching psychological techniques. But in the long term, we need to think about sifting and refining our different approaches to different types of problem (Sheldon 1978). Patterns do emerge between workers and between problem and client groups in a series of A.B. designs, but there is need for caution in interpreting data gathered in this way, as the following hypothetical example *(Figure 5(6))* will demonstrate.

Figure 5(6) Diagram showing misleading interpretation of an A.B. design

Hypothetical natural course of problems encountered on discharge from psychiatric hospital

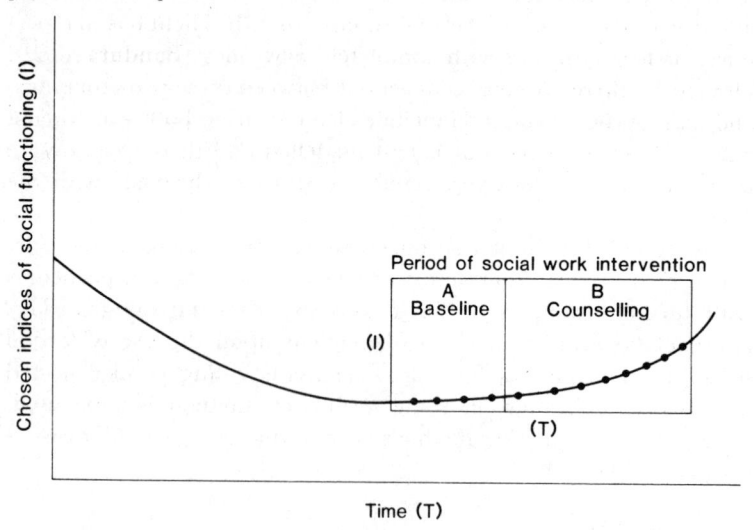

The centre graph gives all the appearance of a successful therapeutic encounter, but the larger graph reveals a 'natural' pattern in the course of the problem, under the control of other variables.

If the social worker samples behaviour at a particularly fortuitous point in the 'natural' development of a problem, he can easily be misled. Although this is a hypothetical illustration, it is not a hypothetical problem. Patterns of this kind do occur. Manic depressive behaviours follow a cyclical pattern, and a wide range of other problems are known to remit spontaneously. There are several things we can do to guard against such distortions in our data.

(a) We can get to know something about the research in the area of the problem we are trying to deal with. If the research literature suggests that a particular problem is resistant to treatment, yet we are managing quite respectable gains, then we are justified in concluding that this is probably not a quirk in the development of the problem.
(b) We can monitor over a longer period, that is, extend the baseline period, and watch for trends of this kind, which are seemingly independent of the things the social worker is doing.
(c) We can arrange follow-up visits. This procedure is relatively inexpensive, can be greatly reassuring to clients, and need not be carried out by the worker who handled the case originally.
(d) We can employ a more sophisticated design (see below).
(e) We can look very carefully at the differences between baseline-phase and intervention-phase rates. The ideal outcome in this respect is for a clear and fairly rapid distinction to emerge between the two phases. *Figure 5(7)* proves little about effectiveness, whereas *Figure 5(8)* is rather more suggestive of it. In *Figure 5(7)* the 'trajectory' of the behaviours under review is already well established, and the probability is that such a well-established upward trend would continue. In *Figure 5(8)* the difference between the two stages is well marked.

FOLLOW-UP DATA

A follow-up visit can solve many of the problems associated with simple A.B. designs. The fact that there is no tradition of this – even in clinical social work settings – is something of a scandal. Follow-up assessment is straightforward when a particular group of problematic behaviours has been reduced to nil (or virtually nil) prior to closure, since it requires only a visit, a telephone call, or a pre-paid letter, to establish whether or not the position is still the same three months later. Similarly, when the client has not experienced any great difficulty in recording items of behaviour he can be advised to continue to do this until the follow-up contact. But not all cases fall into these categories and so another strategy is required if we are to

Figure 5(7) Social confidence problem in an ex-psychiatric patient

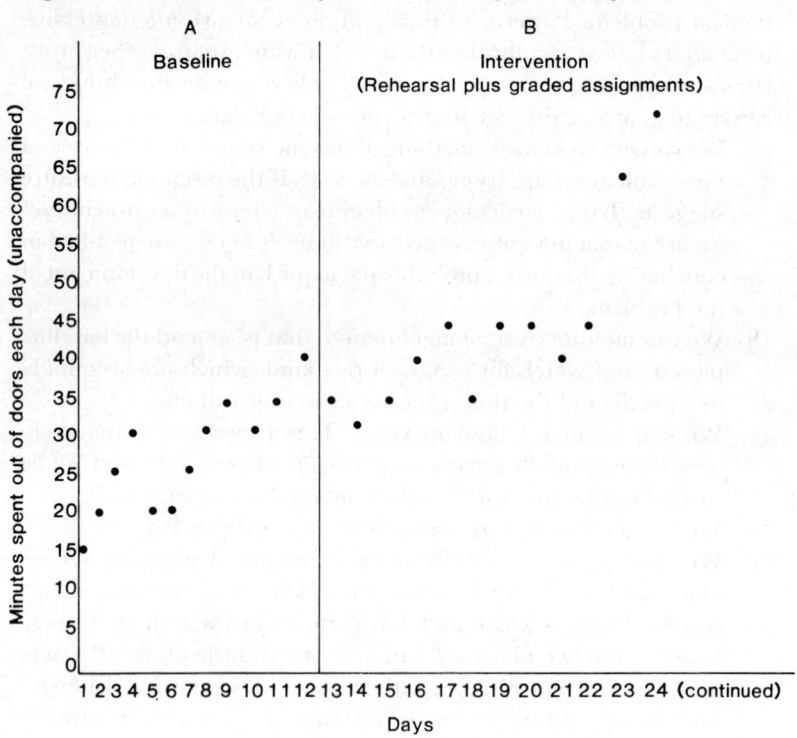

Figure 5(8) A school attendance problem

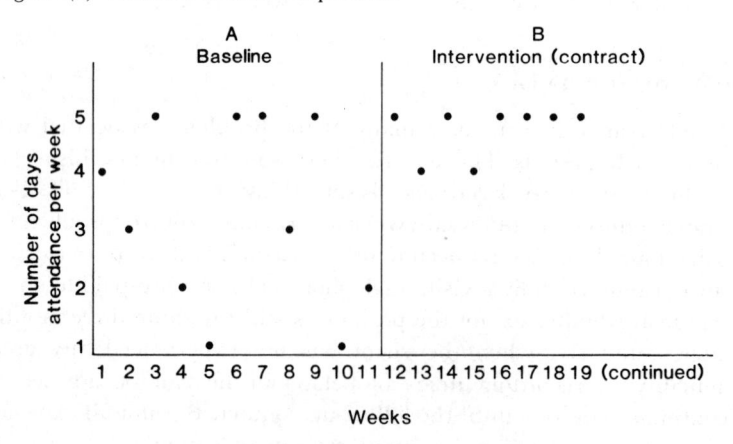

improve upon the client's subjective impressions of change. I have found the following approach useful.
(a) The follow-up visit is fixed in advance at the time of closure.
(b) The client is instructed to repeat the original measurements (or to try and have some other person do it) for a suitable period before the visit is to occur.
(c) Rates at closure are compared with the average rate recorded just prior to follow-up. This is not foolproof; clients occasionally report that things have been untypically better during the pre-follow-up recording phase – perhaps because of the impending visit. This is particularly true of cases involving children. But then this in itself tells us something about what is effective in controlling the behaviour in question: brief, intermittent, maintenance visits might be indicated.

Figure 5(9) is an example of an A.B. design with a follow-up period built into it.

Figure 5(9) Assertion training[1] with a withdrawn psychiatric client

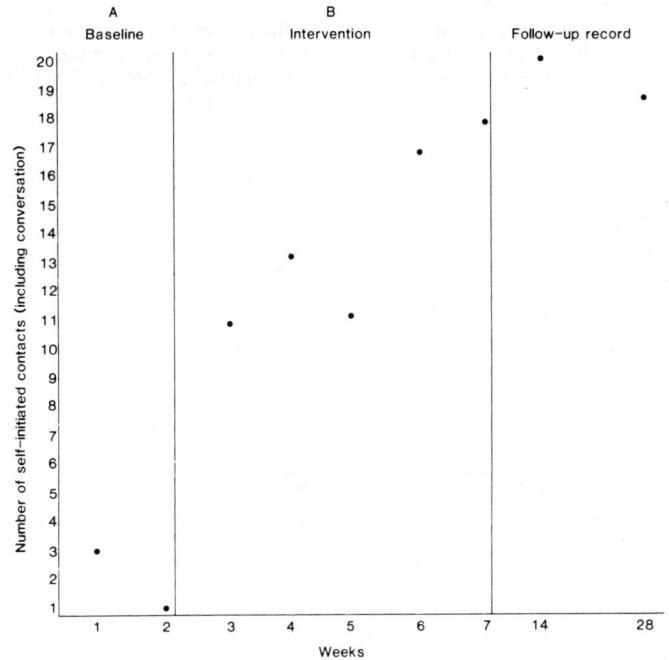

[1] The programme included modelling and rehearsal, graded assignments, plus a back-up reinforcement scheme.

B.A. designs

B.A. designs offer a limited but useful way of monitoring how much learning has taken place as a result of behavioural programmes. They may also be used where a case is too urgent to allow the normal period of baseline recording. But once again, clear gains in the B. phase, plus a later follow-up period, are necessary if interpretation is to rise above an educated guess as to whether outcome is due to social work intervention or other factors.

Figure 5(10) provides an example of a B.A. scheme designed to produce clear feedback on expenditure for a family with chronic financial problems. In this family, budgeting and rudimentary financial record-keeping were known to be virtually non-existent. Therefore there was no point in a detailed baseline phase. In this example we see that although the behaviours established by the budgeting

Figure 5(10) Budgetary control in a family in chronic financial difficulty

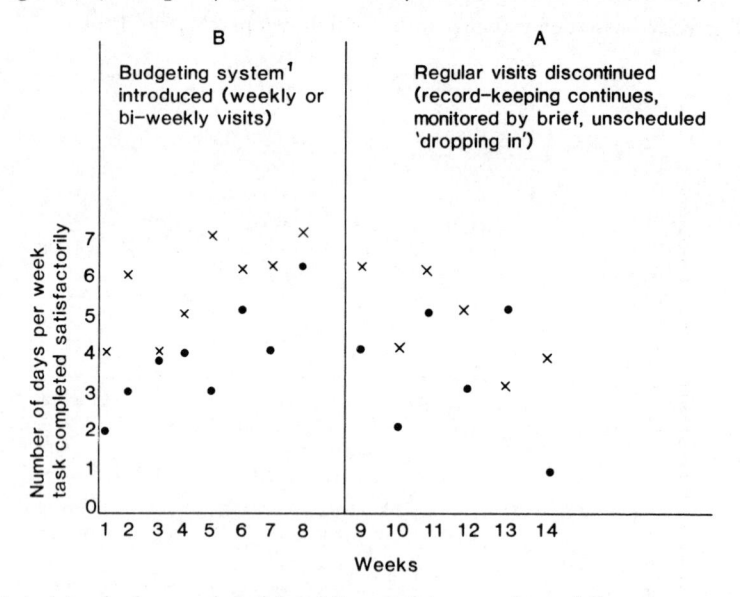

× task involved conversion of electricity units into approximate daily costs.
● task involved keeping daily spending within budget, including payment against arrears (separately monitored).

[1] Programme consisted of simple financial record-keeping, training in electricity meter reading, plus reinforcement for accurate records. The ultimate success of the scheme was judged by the family's financial state (bills paid, payment books kept up-to-date, and so on).

programme were still in existence following the main effort to establish them, they were in gradual decline thereafter, and so some sort of 'topping-up' attention was required.

A.B.A. designs

The A.B.A. design is an advance on the simple A.B. approach, since it includes a return-to-baseline phase at the end. Like the B.A. design above, it offers a useful means of checking whether learning has taken place as a result of a programme. *Figure 5(11)* is an example from a child guidance setting. In this case the item of behaviour being measured (night-time interruptions) is an *indicator*, since the social worker thought that the problem might really be a sexual and a marital one. Her hypothesis was that mother and child were in unwitting collusion and that mother was quite pleased to have her son in the marital bed, since it removed the threat of unwelcome sexual advances from her husband. The couple were eventually referred for sexual counselling, but, though this was remarkably successful, the problem of the child remained. It started as an indicator of another related problem but became a problem in its own right, requiring direct attention. The design is further complicated by

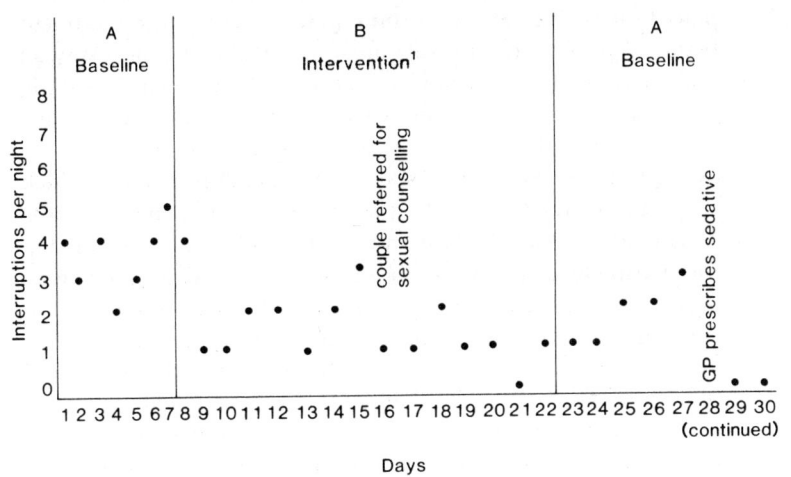

Figure 5(11) Sleep problems in a four-year-old child

[1] Reinforcement programme used model farm animals, stories, sweets, and a star chart.

128   Behaviour Modification

the prescription of a hypnotic by the family doctor. Whatever happens after this medical intervention (which was effective, but could not be said to have solved the problem in the longer term) should not be used as evidence in the evaluation of the social work programme *per se*: this is messy, but typical.

The A.B.A. design has the following problems associated with it.

(a) If the B. phase is exceptionally long, then some of the criticisms of the A.B. approach apply; that is, the social worker can be less confident about whether it is the therapeutic input that is responsible for the changes recorded, or something else.

(b) Similarly, where a lengthy intervention phase is used, one would expect, even hope (as can be seen from *Figure 5(11)*), that learning would occur. In operant programmes where the worker has tried to change the contingencies in the client's environment, confusion can arise as a result of learning effects. Let us suppose that relatives of a psychiatric patient firstly respond to, and enquire into, the content of delusional talk as usual, just recording its occurrence (A. phase); then, on advice, they withhold attention from delusional talk (B. phase); then they stop the monitored programme and do what they always used to do; how are we to interpret the result from a case-research point of view if the delusional talk remains at low level in the second A. phase? Has some learning (in this case, operant conditioning) taken place? Or is this behaviour quite independent of the treatment being applied to it? The only answer to this question is to wait and see whether the behaviour returns. If not, then something new has been learned. In such cases a return to baseline amounts to a reversal rather than a suspension of the programme. In this example relatives have to start doing something again which they have learned not to do, that is, respond to delusional talk. This kind of reversal procedure can be useful to check whether the treatment policy is the correct one, and whether the behaviour varies regularly under its influence. But then it needs to be succeeded by a further treatment phase (A.B.A.B., see below).

(c) Where two different treatment methods are introduced sequentially, perhaps because of changes in the assessment, or lack of success, then specific results are easily confounded. The correct name for this type of approach is A.B.C.A. – in other words, baseline – intervention strategy One – intervention strategy Two – return to baseline. If a new treatment approach is introduced at the *end* of the first treatment phase, perhaps to supplement it, then this is called an A.B.BC.A. design. The sequence is: baseline – treatment One – treatments One and Two combined – baseline. The example shown in *Figure 5(11)* is technically an A.B.BC.A. design since, although sexual counselling had only just begun by the end of the first treatment phase, it might have had a rapid effect, which could have combined with the long-term effects of the initial B phase and resulted in the modest gains of the second baseline phase. The point is that in these more complicated variations of A.B.A. the *relative* potency of the different treatment approaches is very difficult to establish. Each new phase which is added *could* be helped along by what has gone before, and two methods in combination, superseding one or both of these methods applied separately, can have very different effects (Hersen and Barlow 1976). This is not a serious problem from the therapeutic point of view since it is the treatment 'package' that we want to evaluate. However, if the social worker is trying to find out which type of approach is likely to be more effective with a family – perhaps with an eye to future work – then a separate return to baseline must follow each separate treatment phase.

A.B.A.B. designs

This is undoubtedly the most satisfactory procedure from an experimental point of view, although we shall see that application may be hindered by practical and ethical considerations. A.B.A.B. designs can be used in those cases where (i) it is possible clearly to define and separate out the target behaviour; (ii) the behaviour is likely to respond markedly to pre-planned environmental changes (contingency management). Therefore the widest application of this evaluation method has been in operant work with children.

In this sequence the problematic behaviour (or its chosen indicators) is recorded prior to intervention in the usual way (A.). The main treatment programme is started (B.). When this shows a positive effect it is halted for a period (A.). A comparison between the two phases is made, then the treatment programme is restarted (B.) and further comparisons are made at the end of this phase (see *Figure 5(12)*). Results obtained by this method are extremely reliable, since there are two points at which the behavioural effects of treatment and no treatment can be compared. This fact does away with the criticisms which, strictly speaking, can be made of A.B., B.A., and (to a lesser extent) A.B.A. designs from the case-research point of view. However (the point is worth reiterating), even those comparatively simple designs represent a *considerable* advance on what has passed for evaluation hitherto, and A.B.A.B. approaches cannot be universally applied.

The idea of halting a successful programme just as it is getting into gear is often viewed with misgivings by social workers and obviously there are cases where it would be dangerous and unethical to suspend treatment to make an independent check on the efficacy of treatment procedures. But safety considerations aside, if a particular pattern of behaviour can be seen to vary with the contingencies applied to it, then this is very well worth knowing and treatment procedures can always be re-established – presumably to the same effect. Another consideration here is the very positive 'demonstration' effect that this type of design can have. Where parents see that the problem goes away if they stop attending to particular anti-social behaviours in their children and concentrate on others, only to reappear when they reverse these conditions, then a powerful lesson has been learned.

Two examples of A.B.A.B. designs are given below (see *Figures 5(12)* and *5(13)*). The first shows a clearly successful programme; the second is broadly successful, but the results are difficult to interpret. (Some of the details of these cases will be familiar to readers from earlier discussions.)

To prevent learning factors interfering too much, suspension or reversal needs to follow quickly on the establishment of a stable trend towards improvement.

Let us concentrate for a moment on *Figure 5(13)* since it demonstrates many of the problems of trying to evaluate rigorously in a field setting. The reader may be able to see several compromising features. The scheme starts off well: the first baseline period is of reasonable duration considering the state of tension in the family (more details on page 133), and is just about stable, with the rate hovering between four and eight items per day in a range from two to ten with a clustering around four and five items per day. But the baseline shows a downward trend (regarded as untypical by the parents and probably a demand characteristic of 'baseline effect', as discussed on page 115). In addition, the treatment phase begins with a worsening of the problem, which continues for a while until the programme of ignoring

Figure 5(12) Evaluation data for contingency management scheme for coping with aggressive talk about fire by a twelve-year-old-boy

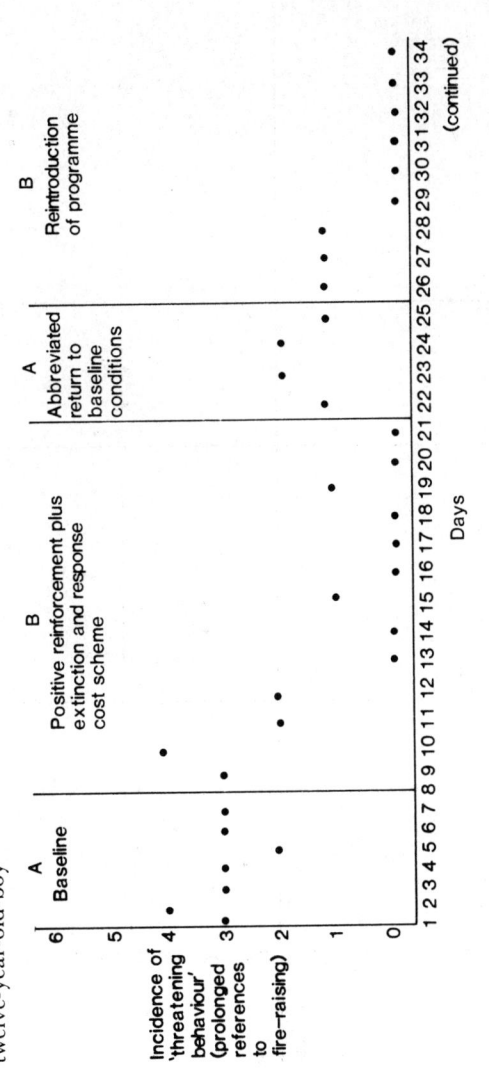

Source: Sheldon and Baird (1978).

Figure 5(13) Contingency management scheme for reducing delusional talk in a twenty-four-year-old psychiatric out-patient

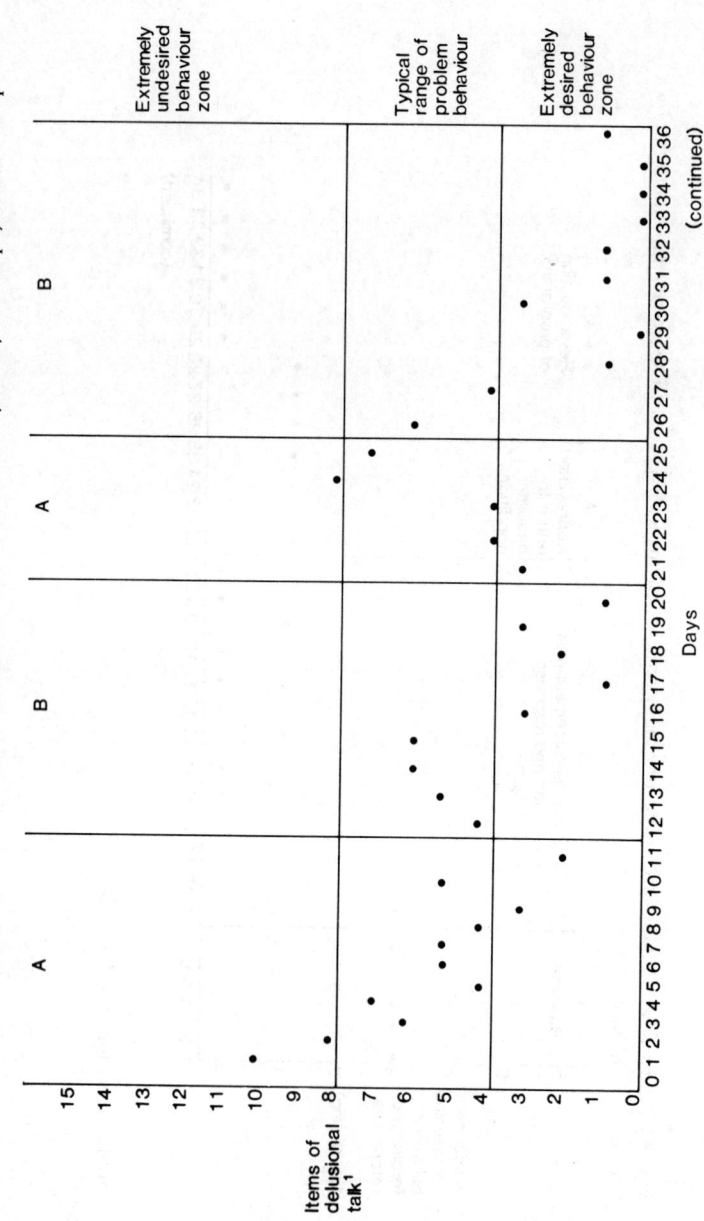

(continued)

[1] Operationally defined with relatives.

Assessment and evaluation 133

delusional talk begins to take effect. In the second return to baseline (a reversal in this case, because parents were instructed to resume their old practice of asking for clarification of delusional references and trying to reason their daughter out of them), there is an upward trend which continued until near the end of the second A. phase. Then the rate begins to fall again and so confounds somewhat the effect of restarting the programme – which produces a relatively stable and confidence-boosting downward trend.

This scheme, using parents and a younger relative as mediators, continued for another forty-six days, during which time the incidence of delusional talk (mainly the reporting of feelings of surveillance) never rose again above two incidents per day. For twenty-two of these days it stood at nought. A brief follow-up at six months revealed a maintained level of improvement of roughly this order, punctuated here and there by the odd sharp increase, which the mother was able to relate convincingly to various family episodes.

Figure 5(12) represents a more complicated case (described in detail on page 153) but produces less complicated results. Here the return to baseline phase was abbreviated because of the tensions within the family and the not inconsiderable fire risks involved in this case. Despite the misgivings of the client's father, the 'demonstration effect' of suspending treatment was very powerful indeed. It produced a real 'shot in the arm' when the family saw that the behaviour was partly under their control and not caused by some sinister mental illness. However, the requirement that a promising treatment phase should be temporarily suspended and reversed raises ethical problems, and this design needs to be used with caution and common sense. But blanket objections to the use of such methods need to be seen in the context of the equally pressing ethical consideration of whether the service being provided is effective.

B.A.B. designs

B.A.B. designs are ideal for operant work where for various reasons it would be unwise to delay treatment until a baseline can be established. This design can be used where target behaviours are clearly dependent on identifiable contingencies and these are subject to manipulation.

Figure 5(14) is an example of a B.A.B. design. In this case the 'urgency' which precluded baseline recording stemmed largely from the fact that the little West Indian boy was the only black child in the nursery school, and the impression that he 'did not fit in' was growing among certain staff members. He spent most of the day sitting alone and rocking gently, having little or nothing to do with the other children. Descriptions of him as 'solitary' and 'withdrawn' began to circulate.

Figure 5(14) Withdrawn behaviour in a four-year-old nursery school child

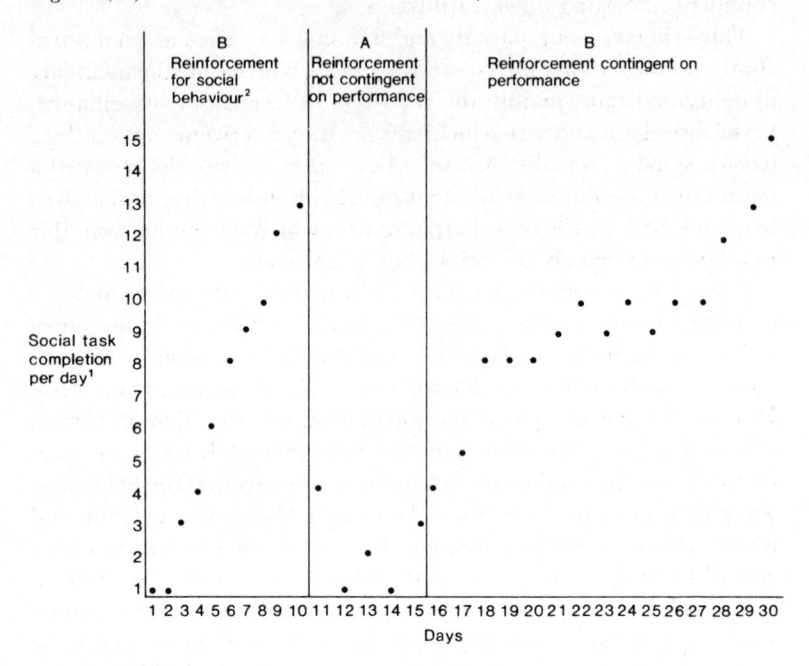

[1] Predefined tasks (behaviour shaping, ranging from showing interest in play of others, to solitary play nearby, to participatory play).
[2] Approval plus sweets (given by nursery staff).

Multiple baseline designs

The multiple baseline design uses each defined element of a problem as a control for the others. There are two distinct advantages with this approach: (i) it does away with the need for a suspension or reversal phase; (ii) the worker can try out one method at a time in a complex case. The approach is really just a series of A.B. designs run in a particular sequence. The procedure is as follows.

First, the pre-intervention rate of each different target behaviour is recorded. When a stable rate appears in one behaviour, the treatment programme is applied first to that behaviour. During the next stage two things need to be noted: (i) the difference that intervention is making (if any) to the first target behaviour; (ii) whether the base rates of the other behaviours to which the treatment variable has *not* yet been applied are changing substantially (co-varying) with the target behaviour. If *not* then the programme is applied to the next behaviour and after a suitable interval the procedures outlined above are applied again. This process continues until the scheme is in operation for all the target behaviours. *Figure 5(15)* gives an example of a multiple baseline design applied to a range of disciplinary problems experienced by a single mother and her children.

Multiple baseline designs have a wide range of uses with social work clients who have a number of different problems. However, the approach has the following drawbacks. The behaviours under investigation have to be fairly discrete; in other words, the occurrence of each must be assessed as substantially independent of the others. To the extent that the start of the first B. phase produces a marked co-variance in the other base rates, the experimental principle of using the other behaviours as a control is confounded. It may be that the procedure being used is particularly potent, or – later on – that generalization is occurring. But this cannot just be assumed (however beneficial the result) and the sequence collapses into a concurrent series of A.B. designs.

MULTIPLE BASELINES ACROSS SETTINGS

Another multiple measurement approach is the 'baselines across settings' design. With this, problems in different settings are baselined and the treatment variable is applied to each in sequence according to the principles outlined above. For further details of the different types of design available, consult Hersen and Barlow's comprehensive handbook (1976).

Other factors in the use of S.C.E.D.s

A wider range of single case evaluation procedures is available than there is space to discuss in the present volume. The main approaches likely to be applicable to social work have now been outlined, but there are one or two other issues remaining.

Figure 5(15) Multiple baseline design[1]

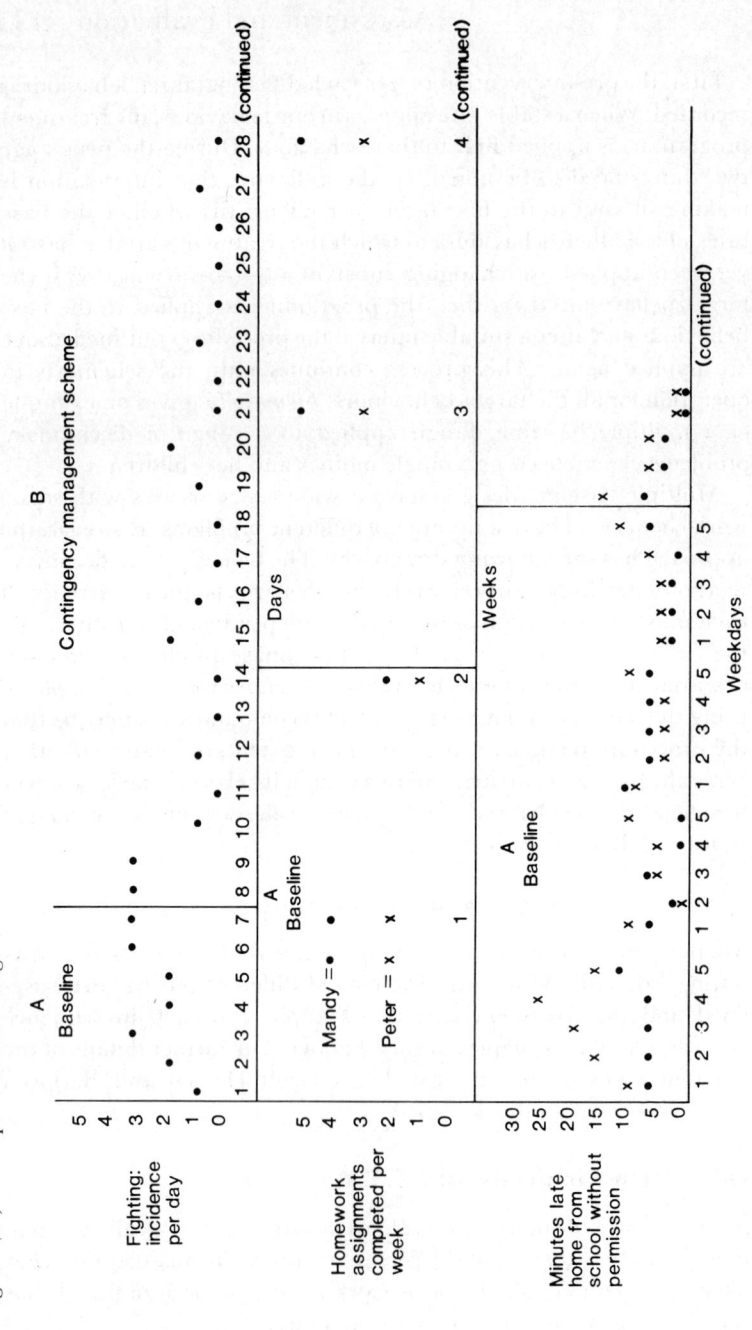

[1] Programme equals: reinforcement of cooperative behaviour with star chart, sweets, models, comics, plus extra TV time and bonus outings with social worker, determined on a sliding scale. Also agreed rates for deprivation of privileges.

Assessment and evaluation

First, assessment and evaluation procedures of this type do not have to be used in a 'mechanical' way. The question of balance between rigour and the intrusiveness of a particular approach must always be given careful consideration. This is not to say that at the first sign of difficulty the principle of rigorous case evaluation should be abandoned in favour of some vague notion of the need for general flexibility. But, where necessary, these procedures can be changed and reconstructed, as long as due care is given to their subsequent interpretation.

Second, these designs hold out the possibility that in certain areas of social work we could see the emergence of the practitioner-researcher, someone who contributes to the literature specific information and potentially replicable results drawn from his own caseload; someone who is more than a passive consumer of other people's theories.

Qualitative assessment and evaluation

At various points in this chapter I have argued for a combination of quantitative *and* qualitative information as the sensible basis of both assessment and evaluation. When considering qualitative change, we are interested in the character and in the general social effects of a new behaviour, rather than in precise changes in the rate of its occurrence. However, we must avoid the trap of seeing these different types of assessment variables as completely different things. An increase in the level of self-assertion, though recorded as a quantitative change, can produce notable qualitative changes; perhaps in the way that the client sees himself, or in the enjoyment he now gets out of life.

Sometimes the changes produced by behaviour modification seem (at a qualitative level) artificial or stilted, because, initially, new behaviours are being grudgingly or mechanically performed. It should be remembered here that the availability of new sources of reinforcement produced by the behaviour can often change the way these things look and feel, given time.

THE ASSESSMENT OF COGNITIVE AND EMOTIONAL FACTORS

People respond to their circumstances according to the way they 'see' them, and so the first priority of this dimension in assessment is to get the client to discuss his interpretation of the contingencies that surround his behaviour. Here we are investigating *beliefs* about future events and behaviour. If a client believes that the powerful fear reaction she typically experiences on going out of doors alone will cause a heart attack, then this can only increase her apprehension and the level of her avoidance behaviour. Similarly, if a group member believes that the leader is out to show him up, then even the politest enquiry will bring forth a defensive reaction.

A useful concept here is that of the *personal construct* (Kelly 1955). The psychologist George Kelly has developed an elaborate theory of cognition and behaviour change which has always had strong advocates, but which has been somewhat neglected in social work. At a very basic level, Kelly's view is that we are constantly experimenting with our environment; erecting hypotheses, observing results, and developing our own individual 'theories' about how the world works. But sometimes our theories are based on flimsy evidence, sometimes the experiments we conduct are biased or inadequate, and sometimes we draw erroneous conclusions from the data available to us. Notwithstanding this, not only are we likely to act upon our constructs, but existing constructs will also have an effect on our future experimentation with the environment.

However, constructs can also be functional, in that looking at a problem in a particular way makes life easier for us. They are also subject to the rules of reinforcement. If we have developed a view that X is, administratively speaking, a bit sloppy, then X's future behaviour is always viewed through this 'filter'. Behaviour which tends to contradict this construct is seen as a 'fluke'; the fact that X has more to do than many others with whom his performance is compared is either not perceived, or is attributed to past administrative bottlenecks, which should have been avoided. Similarly, once the construct 'Y is a schizophrenic' is developed, his daily behaviour is likely to be screened for instances of bizarre behaviour, and the many occasions in the day when this does not occur are seen as periods in which bizarreness is 'latent', or even deliberately disguised.

As assessors we are concerned to know about the thinking styles, beliefs, and constructs clients have developed in the area of their problems. In other words, we need to know what their model of this bit of their reality looks like. We have to hypothesize about their hypotheses. Here is a list of mental events on which we might concentrate our investigations.

(a) Perception: what kind of events does the client usually attend to and what does he ignore?
(b) Images: what mental-picture associations does the client report when experiencing problems, or when he is in the vicinity where they occur? Watch out for exaggerated imagery, for instance being held up to ridicule, dying of fright, or bursting into tears after a reproof.
(c) Inner speech: what does the client typically say to himself about his performance? He may say: 'This is hopeless, I'll never be able to do it. I'll make a fool of myself for certain [image]; better to get it over with quickly.'
(d) Constructs: what theories does the client have about his problem, and about his own role and the role of others in it? He may apply the principle 'others will always get you if they can', and this will colour all his actions.
(e) Emotional accompaniments of cognitive events: what kinds of emotional events accompany cognitions? For example in (c) above, anxiety about a particular social performance may be replaced by relief when the client issues his declaration of surrender to himself (negative reinforcement).
(f) Thinking styles: how does the client typically respond to problems? For example, he may jump to unfounded conclusions on little evidence; he may think fatalistic thoughts; he may see unjustified connections between events, or he may not connect present events and past behaviour at all. His thinking may be imaginative or concrete, divergent or convergent. He may be capable of constructive speculation, or not.
(g) Information and beliefs: what does the client believe will happen if he attempts to solve his problems? What information are these beliefs based upon? Is this adequate or inadequate knowledge? For example: 'There's no possibility of someone from my background getting that job – it never happens.' The client may feel that he has evidence for his view (and of course he may be right), but it may be incomplete evidence.

Many of the existing assessment aids employed in behaviour modification can be adapted for the assessment of the cognitive accompaniments of behaviour. The client can be asked to keep records of his thoughts in particular circumstances, in diary form, for example. Or in the initial stages of assessment he can be asked to tick various prepared statements about thinking patterns and how often they

occur. A number of different scales are available (see Thomas 1974).
As to the rating of various levels of emotion or fear known to accompany certain problems, in my experience it is more useful to construct a simple scale with the client, and to train him to discriminate between various points on it. There is good evidence that given practice, clients can report accurately on levels of arousal, when compared to various physiological measures. *Figure 5(16)* gives an example of a simple fear scale.

Figure 5(16) Fear scale

Terrified, felt I was going to pass out or die. Would do anything to get away. Panic-stricken.	Sweating profusely, very tense, wanted to run away.	Heart beating fast, some sweating, tight muscles.	Attention fixed on object or thought. Feeling tense. Conscious of heart rate.	Only mildly anxious or a little uneasy.	Calm
5	4	3	2	1	0

Such scales can be used as a device to control subjective reporting of arousal since – among other things – they focus the client's attention on the different physiological components of the arousal he tends to experience in given circumstances. With practice they can be used as a partial basis for assessment (to establish in what circumstances high and low value responses occur), and as a partial basis for evaluation (rates may be compared before and after therapy).

The single case design format can also be applied to thought patterns given a reasonable level of client cooperation, as demonstrated in *Figure 5(17)*.

Behaviour therapists are interested in cognitive events for two reasons only: (i) to test the hypothesis that if patterns of thinking (self-statements, and so on) can be altered by training and therapy, then the problematic behaviour which they accompany will also change (this is to assign to thoughts the role of mediating variables and discriminative stimuli); (ii) to give us clues as to the type of consequences that maintain unwanted behaviour and prevent the emergence of more adaptive approaches. As with all types of assessment 'the proof of the pudding is in the eating', and we are most interested in how the client subsequently *behaves*, as a result of our intervention.

Figure 5(17) Example of the assessment of an internal behaviour (fantasies about sexual exhibitionism involving children)

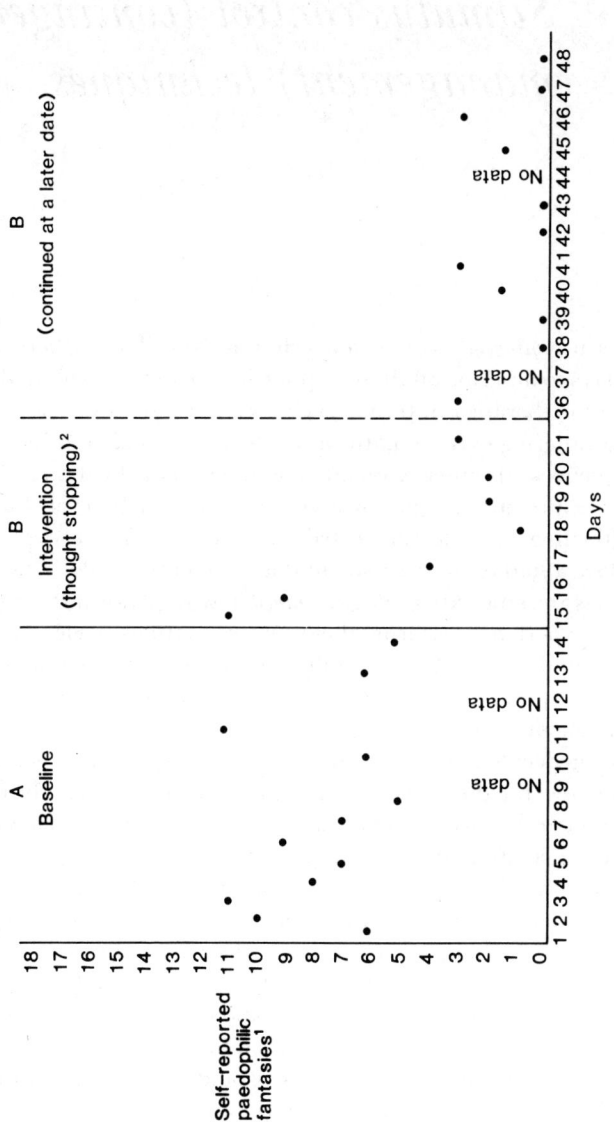

[1] Prolonged over approximately five seconds (estimate).
[2] Client is instructed in ways of terminating these images by forcing himself to imagine a contradictory scene (see page 211).

6
Stimulus control (contingency management) techniques

The term *contingency management* (Homme and Tosti 1965) is used nowadays to describe all those applications of the operant model that involve the therapist in trying to change, control, or develop behaviours by altering existing patterns of eliciting stimuli and reinforcing consequences. In other words it is assumed that the desired behaviours are already in repertoire at some significant level, but need strengthening, as demonstrated in the *stimulus control* section (Bandura 1969) of the assessment diagram on page 104. That is, the client has to some extent *already learned* how to perform these behaviours, but perhaps performs them only in settings irrelevant to the problem under review, or very infrequently, or at only a weak level. It is on these questions that the decision whether or not to use operant reinforcement techniques rests.

Having decided that the target behaviours are in repertoire to some degree, the therapist must look next to the factors in the client's environment that are failing to elicit and maintain these behaviours – or that are eliciting and maintaining undesirable responses in competition with them. This may be just a question of coming up with a rearrangement of existing contingencies – as in a case known to me, of a mentally handicapped young man who was a chronic absconder from hospital. It was suggested that the staff should occasionally supply the interesting car rides he was known to enjoy, but which currently he had only when being returned to hospital under escort, (so reinforcing his running away). These would now be given for behaving well around the hospital and *not* running away.

Stimulus control techniques

Alternatively, it may be necessary to produce an entirely new set of contingencies, for instance: 'If there are three clear days without a single incident of fighting, John and Marion will be taken to the sports centre for one hour by mother.'

Set out below is a summary of the range of possibilities for changing behaviour by manipulation of the contingencies that surround it.

(a) Where the problem results mainly from an insufficiency of certain behaviour, it may be possible simply to identify and *positively reinforce* a low-level adaptive response so that it is 'amplified', performed more frequently, and its place in the individual's repertoire is strengthened. In other words, we can work to improve the 'pay-off' for desirable behaviour.

(b) A performance may be *shaped* by the selective reinforcement of approximately similar behaviours, until they become progressively more like the desired behaviour.

(c) Where the problem results mainly from an excess of unwanted behaviour, it may be possible to identify and positively reinforce a response which is *incompatible* with the existing (unwanted) response. That is, we may be able to encourage an alternative activity, which could eventually replace the existing behaviour, or which prevents the individual from gaining reinforcement for the unwanted behaviour.

(d) Again, in respect of an excess of unwanted behaviour, it may be possible to apply *negative reinforcement*, so that whenever the individual *stops* this behaviour and performs some desirable alternative, an aversive stimulus is terminated. Here the *removal* of the aversive stimulus is made contingent upon the client refraining from undesirable behaviour and engaging in some more appropriate activity, and this serves to strengthen the alternative response.

(e) It may be possible to reduce the frequency of undesirable behaviour by extinction; in other words, just by removing the reinforcement currently available for it. In this way, unwanted behaviour is not encouraged by the positive consequences it brings.

(f) In certain cases, unwanted behaviour can be eliminated by *punishing* it whenever it occurs; that is, by ensuring that an aversive consequence results from its performance. More sophisticated adaptations of this principle are available, which attach different levels of punishment to different activities. These are called *response cost* schemes and involve the assignment of an agreed 'price' to each different pattern of unwanted behaviour, according to its seriousness. Such programmes may be useful where there is a range of different responses which the therapist is anxious to discourage in different degrees – a sort of inverted shaping approach.

(g) Behaviour may be either encouraged or discouraged by manipulating the stimuli which *elicit* it. Thus, it may be possible to do one or more of the following: remove or reduce the effect of the environmental cues (S^ds) which signal that reinforcement is available for a particular unwanted sequence; intensify the S^ds which trigger competing, desirable behaviours; intensify the cues which signal that no reinforcement will be forthcoming for unwanted behaviour (S^Δs); or remove the S^Δs which signal that no reinforcement will be available for desirable behaviour, so that it is more likely to occur.

Combinations of techniques

Items in the range of possible influences on behaviour given above are presented separately, so that each can be clearly identified. In a therapeutic programme it is very likely that a combination of such approaches will be used. For example, a scheme designed to extinguish unacceptable behaviour, by withdrawing attention from it, is likely to be augmented by a programme of positive reinforcement for acceptable behaviours, the aim being to shape the individual concerned towards a more acceptable pattern of attention-getting.

Selection of reinforcers

The popular image of reinforcement is that it involves someone in authority dispensing artificial rewards for good behaviour – such as sweets, money, or tokens. While each of these examples could serve as positive reinforcers in some circumstances, it can be misleading to think of reinforcement in terms of someone giving some *thing* to someone else. Tharp and Wetzel (1969) have suggested the term 'reinforcing event' as more appropriate to field-settings, since it is often impossible to specify exactly which part of the sequence is the potent element. Even where something tangible is being handed over in exchange for certain behaviour, it might well be the pleasant demeanour of the therapist that is effective, or the client's own sense of achievement (of which the tangible reward is merely a symbol, as when we earn stars or grades at school), or the fact that other people see him receiving preferential treatment. It is technically possible to conduct experiments to isolate the key factor, but this is rarely worth the effort involved, and so reinforcement often remains a 'package' of different influences presented contingently. The therapist must use his common sense here and not respond mechanically to his clients in the interests of accuracy. Words of praise for appropriate behaviour, which never vary in content or emphasis, quickly lose their reinforcing power.

Skinner has written interestingly on this point in his philosophical text *Beyond Freedom and Dignity* (1971). He suggests that in cases of admirable behaviour the prestige accorded to an action is inversely proportional to the visibility of the forces which control it. In other words, dignity, prestige, and honour are accorded to approved behaviour in direct proportion to the difficulty of identifying the reinforcement which maintains it: for instance, where it appears to arise spontaneously; where the individual has nothing very *obvious* to gain by performing a difficult task; and where the easiest explanation is that the behaviour is 'self-motivated' and completely altruistic.

The practical point here is that outside the animal laboratory reinforcement is a *process* – a series of events with special meanings. What is given cannot be separated off from the manner or context of its giving. There is a tension here between technical specificity (making sure that reinforcers are given contingently and are having their intended behaviour-strengthening effects) and naturalness (taking care not to make the subject feel that he is being artificially handled and manipulated, because most of us experience this as the opposite of reinforcement). The following general points about reinforcement practices arise from this discussion.

(a) Wherever possible, reinforcement for appropriate behaviour should arise out of the setting where it is performed and should be a natural concomitant of the performance. A set of contingencies expressed like this: 'If John helps staff and refrains from aggressive outbursts, which are distracting and time-consuming to them, *then* they will have time to spare to help him learn to ride his bicycle', is usually less resented than this: 'John can have twenty minutes supervised bike-riding if he refrains from aggressive behaviour and helps staff for three hours.' In the first example a causal link is made between John's uncooperative and time-consuming behaviour and what happens next. Staff have time to spare given a little help, but this is not the case if they have to spend the morning coping with John's bad behaviour. The consequence is a fact of life; it occurs fairly naturally, and is not just a therapeutic device.

(b) Where it is not possible to link naturalistic consequences to behaviour, and some more artificial scheme is introduced (as in the case of token economies in mental hospitals, or star charts displaying a record of good behaviour for children), then it is important that clients appreciate both the reasoning behind the scheme and that it is a temporary arrangement, designed to help the client gain control of his behaviour. For example: 'As soon as Robert has achieved the specified level of school attendance, and has broken the habit of avoiding lessons he doesn't like, the daily report cards will be discontinued.' This point is particularly pertinent to the design of contracts (see page 161), but it applies to all work with adults.

(c) Artificiality and feelings of manipulation are likely to be lessened where non-material reinforcers – such as praise, approval, affection, attention, and joint activities – are a main part of the programme. Where these are unlikely to be effective, material reinforcers should still always be accompanied by them. In this way acceptable, everyday rewards acquire a reinforcement value of their own, and represent a basis for the subsequent fading of the artificial (that is, socially untypical) features of the scheme.

At this point it may be worth re-emphasizing that reinforcers are not special in themselves. Events or objects become reinforcers because of the particular behaviour-strengthening effects they happen to have on the performance of a particular individual, in a particular circumstance. The only sure way to find out what reinforces a piece of behaviour is to make an educated guess: try it, and observe the effects. However, there are some general guidelines.

(a) We should try and observe the client in natural settings so that the consequences that normally follow behaviour can be determined. It may be possible then to reorganize these consequences (for example, by providing more attention for approved behaviour, and removing it from unacceptable behaviour).

(b) We should make use of Premack's principle (Premack 1959). This states that a high-probability behaviour can be used to reinforce a low-probability behaviour when the performance of the former can be made contingent upon the performance of the latter. The assumption behind this approach is that if patient A spends 60 per cent of his day looking out of the window, then this must be a powerful source of reinforcement for him. If the same patient can be induced initially to exchange one hour's access to the dayroom couch near the window for a few minutes of rehabilitation therapy, or conversation with ward staff, then a basis for shaping has been established. Premack's principle has had wide application in mental handicap settings and in work with chronically institutionalized psychotic patients, where it is difficult to discover interests by interviewing alone. Nevertheless, it also has a wide application outside these settings – whenever it is difficult to find a specific influence to which the individual might respond (see page 159).

(c) Probably the commonest – and most sensible – approach to deciding what reinforcers to employ is to ask the people concerned (the client, family, friends, staff, and so on) what is likely to be effective. In their work with problem children Tharp and Wetzel (1969) advocate the use of simple sentence-completion exercises such as: 'The person I most like to spend time with is . . .'; 'The best reward costing about 50p that I can think of is . . .'; or, 'The thing I enjoy doing most is. . . .'

(d) Reinforcement checklists are another method of giving an idea of what reinforcers to build into a programme. These cover a range of possible influences, from material rewards and objects to activities and the names of significant people. An example of a reinforcement checklist is to be found in Thomas (1974).

(e) Programmes can be based on generalized reinforcers (see page 56) if nothing more specific seems likely to be effective. Attention, approval, free time, money, exchangeable tokens, and so on, are usually quite potent since they are a prerequisite for other kinds of reinforcement. Money or tokens have the advantage that they can be readily exchanged for other sources of reinforcement, as well as taking into account the fact that appetites and interests change from day to day and setting to setting.

(f) Existing reinforcers can be *potentiated* if access to them is limited prior to the start of a programme.

The next set of factors concerns the feasibility of using particular types of reinforcement.

(a) Reinforcement needs to be powerful enough to compete with the already-present attractions of performing unwanted behaviours. It also needs to be durable over time. In addition, some thought should be given to the question of whether one type of reinforcement will affect behaviour in different settings (for example, both inside the home and outside, where there is competiton with the peer group). There is also the problem of satiation: if the programme is based on material reinforcers, or on one type of activity, it may be that after a certain number of sweets, coloured pencils, and trips to the sports centre, junior will have had enough of them! Often it is better to try to elicit *types* of activity and then to vary these systematically throughout the programme, or to offer a choice from a particular category or value grouping.

(b) There is little point in selecting reinforcers which will be technically difficult to present as a consequence of certain behaviour. Sometimes a token or signal of having earned a particular reward will act as a conditioned reinforcer (see page 54) and bridge the gap between performance and ultimate reinforcement; but, generally speaking, the shorter the interval the better.

(c) Another consideration is whether there will be someone around to act as the therapist's agent or mediator, to supervise and apply the new contingencies. Levels of cooperation, skill, and understanding of the programme are important considerations here (see page 19).

(d) The old social work maxim 'start where the client is' applies particularly to behaviour therapy. Clients will not respond to reinforcers if these are contingent upon performances (i) that are beyond their present capacities, or (ii) where the reinforcer on offer is simply inadequate to elicit and maintain large-scale changes of behaviour – in other words, is 'not worth it'. (See *Figure 6(1)*.)

Differential reinforcement programmes

These are probably the most widely used form of contingency management and involve the setting up of a contrast between the consequences of desirable and undesirable behaviour. Behaviours that we want to strengthen are positively reinforced, and behaviours that we would like to weaken are placed on what is called an *operant*

Stimulus control techniques

Figure 6(1) Level at which to begin a reinforcement scheme

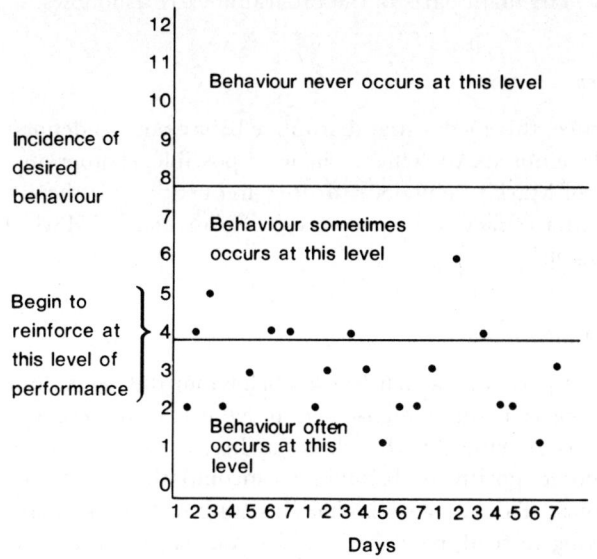

```
                    12
                    11
                    10   Behaviour never occurs at this level
Incidence of         9
desired              8
behaviour           ────────────────────────────────────────
                     7   Behaviour sometimes
                     6   occurs at this level       •
Begin to             5   •
reinforce at   ⎫     4   •      • •        •              •
this level of  ⎬     3        •     •   •  •              •
performance    ⎭     2  • •              •    • •       • •
                     1   Behaviour often
                         occurs at this •                •
                         level
                     0
                        1 2 3 4 5 6 7 1 2 3 4 5 6 7 1 2 3 4 5 6 7
                                          Days
```

This diagram shows the daily occurrence of a behaviour which is to be reinforced. The scatter may be divided into zones labelled as above, or alternatively, 'extremely desirable range', 'desirable range', and 'extremely undesirable range'. Reinforcement should first be applied at the top end of the 'frequently occurring' range, that is, should be given for daily rates of 4 and above.

extinction schedule (we arrange that no reinforcement should accompany such behaviours). To those factors can be added a third: the likelihood that in future, as a result of this clear demarcation, the client will be better able to *discriminate* between the two kinds of behaviour. That is, he will be more likely to know where, and when, each behaviour is, and is not, to be performed, as well as the likely consequences which attach to these different performances and settings.

CASE ILLUSTRATION SHOWING THE DIFFERENT ELEMENTS
OF A CONTINGENCY MANAGEMENT PROGRAMME

Here are some details from the case of the boy exhibiting 'disturbed behaviour' in school (hitting other children, running around the classroom, making disruptive noises), which readers will recall from page 71. The main parts of the programme are as follows.

Extinction

In practice, this meant that disruptive behaviour (as defined above) was to be ignored by teachers whenever possible. If other pupils complained of Mark's behaviour (as they frequently did) they were told in a matter-of-fact way to ignore it if possible, as Mark was just 'showing off'.

Positive reinforcement

Any short period in which Mark's behaviour did *not* contain any of the disruptive features mentioned above was to be responded to as quickly as possible by the class teacher, as a useful opportunity to reinforce positively behaviours incompatible with the target behaviours. This category included: sitting still, working at an exercise, trying to read, neat work, and so on. Where Mark joined in a group task – such as answering questions put to the whole group, or reciting an exercise – first the group would get the teacher's praise, and then Mark (and anyone else who came into this category) would receive a special mention for trying harder and for showing good progress.

The following reinforcers were used: physical proximity of the teacher and individual attention; praise and little displays of affection, such as a pat on the back (Mark would sometimes go through the motions of shrugging these off but undoubtedly looked for them next time); compliments on any work showing an improvement, whatever its absolute standard; ticks and initials on a card (see *Figure 6(2)*) which was taken home to show parents and could be redeemed for small monetary rewards, or bonus trips to the swimming baths, cinema, or whatever, with father. Limited financial aid was given to parents to establish this part of the scheme, and faded out later.

This classroom programme was complementary to a scheme already running at home. The daily progress card was used to link the two so that three initialled entries per day earned Mark a coloured star on his home progress chart, praise from parents, ten minutes extra TV time per entry, plus 10p for every three entries. A bonus

Figure 6(2) A typical progress record card

PROGRESS CARD		TO BE TAKEN HOME EVERY AFTERNOON		
MON	TUE	WED	THURS	FRI
Morning	Morning ✓R.T.A. ✓R.T.A.	Morning	Morning	Morning
Afternoon ✓R.T.A. ✓R.T.A.	Afternoon ✓R.T.A ✓R.T.A. ✓R.T.A.	Afternoon	Afternoon	Afternoon
Mark can earn ticks for 15 minutes good behaviour in class				

scheme was introduced to reinforce good weekly averages, so that initially, four stars a week resulted in an outing with father. All the rates in these various parts of the programme were gradually increased (with Mark's foreknowledge) as behaviour improved.

Other procedures

An important part of the programme was an augmented remedial reading scheme implemented by teaching staff. This was carried out by a favourite second-year teacher of Mark's who did not normally have this function. In the long term, this regular contact undoubtedly reduced his feelings of inadequacy and frustration in certain lessons.

Problems

The programme's weakest point was the extinction contingency for disruptive behaviour. Some behaviour was just impossible for teachers to ignore, either because of the risk of injury to other pupils, or because of the bad example set for the rest of the class. Existing approaches, such as standing outside doors, smacks, or taking notes home, had proved ineffective. Mark did not mind being put outside classroom doors as there was always plenty going on in the corridors; indeed this may have had a minor negative reinforcement effect since it put an end to classwork. Similarly, if sent home Mark would probably get a smacking from his mother, but then would be free to play on his own for the rest of the day.

Time out

A time-out from reinforcement scheme was therefore tried, and proved to be reasonably successful by at least bridging the gap until the positive reinforcement scheme took control of Mark's behaviour. A half-empty storeroom was used opposite the school secretary's office. A desk was placed there together with reading and writing materials. Extremely disruptive behaviour was first responded to by a special form of words, which gave Mark a clear option to sit quietly and get on with his work. If this failed he was unceremoniously removed by his teacher, without comment. This occurred on eight occasions throughout the course of the programme and the periods of absence varied from five to fifteen minutes.

Changes were necessary at various stages of the programme. The extra TV time contingency, for example, did not work when there was nothing of interest being shown, and so playing out of doors for an extra fifteen minutes was substituted as a reinforcer on these occasions.

Another problem was reported by the class teacher who, in the early stages of the case, found herself having to explain to other pupils why Mark was apparently receiving preferential treatment. She took advantage of time-out intervals to discuss with the class the idea that Mark needed special help. In this context the implication was that this help could not always be pleasant. An alternative approach might have been to involve other interested children in similar schemes, but geared to academic attainment or other individual considerations.

Cooperation from teaching staff increased steadily as the scheme began to pay off, and the social worker was increasingly free to concentrate on the home-based scheme, leaving the school programme to the teachers. However, there were some early problems over defining professional 'territory' and the readily available option of 'special facilities' for this child.

Follow-up of the home and school programmes at six months revealed substantial and well-maintained gains in the school setting and less dramatic, but still very useful gains maintained at home.

Stimulus control techniques 153

However, the main achievement in this case was that Mark continued to be taught at his ordinary school and at the time of closure was seen, in the words of the staff, as 'a bit of a challenge to disciplinary skills', rather than as a 'seriously disturbed boy' in need of 'psychiatric investigation' and 'special care'.

CASE ILLUSTRATION SHOWING USE OF A WIDER RANGE OF TECHNIQUES

In the case of the boy arsonist (assessment and evaluation data on pages 111 and 131), a wider combination of techniques was used, including the following.

(a) There was positive reinforcement of activities unconnected with periods of talk about fire and fire-related 'accidents'; self-selected activities included gardening projects supervised by his father. (This new behaviour of father's required considerable reinforcement from mother at first.)

(b) If fire talk occurred, father had instructions to come indoors at once (negative punishment: see page 68).

(c) A diary scheme: one-hour intervals without pointed fire references earned (i) pamphlets and information about agricultural and horticultural courses from the social worker; (ii) visits to a local nursery and farm; (iii) money to take to school. This diary was pointedly inspected by elder brother on his visits, and outings with him were made conditional on a rising standard of behaviour.

(d) Extinction scheme: all talk of fire was ignored or, if it could not be ignored, it was responded to with a graded series of deprivations (see *response cost* section below for further details).

(e) John was instructed that if he felt himself wanting to talk about fire he was to try to think about other things instead – outings, models, youth clubs – and if this proved unsuccessful he was to leave the room.

(f) Targets in all schemes were gradually increased. John knew the point of this and understood that the purpose of the scheme was to build a happier family life and to keep him out of trouble.

Response cost (negative punishment) schemes

The 'time out' procedure described on page 152 is one form of response cost. This technique involves the assignment of specific deprivations to different gradations of unwanted behaviour. Jehu (1972) quotes an interesting case entitled 'Time out from Reinforcement, or Techniques for Dethroning the Duke of an Institutionalized Delinquent Group':

> 'The subject was a sixteen-year-old boy named John, who severely bullied smaller boys and directed his followers to do likewise. The intimidating-aggressive behaviour paid off in that it was followed by compliance and submission from his peers. The staff found it difficult to detect and interrupt the process because the threats were often quite subtle. For instance, John had only to walk towards the television for the occupant of a choice seat to vacate it in his favour. The essence of the time out programme was that "when there is any reason to *suspect* that any child is being threatened, bullied or subtly intimidated, either directly or indirectly, by John *or his clique*, John is to be taken immediately to isolation", and this was expounded to the staff in some detail. After the regime had been in effect for six weeks they reported an appreciable decrease in John's aggressive behaviour.'

(Brown and Tyler 1968)

CASE ILLUSTRATION

A different form of response cost was used in the boy arsonist case (outlined on page 111). Talk about fire, fire accidents, playing with matches, and so on, were at first ignored whenever possible (operant extinction) but beyond a certain level of persistence they had to be responded to in some form. A graded series of possible responses was drawn up and given to the family. The instructions given may be paraphrased as follows.

> Whenever possible parents were to ignore the bad behaviour, but not to *studiously* ignore it. When the point has been reached beyond which it could not be convincingly ignored, they were to issue the first warning (an agreed formula designed to give John the option of abandoning the behaviour and doing something else). If the behaviour continued, mother was instructed to take her son by the hand and lead him from the room. He was told he could return in five minutes but that if behaviour was continued he would lose TV privileges, and an agreed sum of money allocated for him to take to

school. If the behaviour persisted he would be sent to his room for one hour. If he refused to go or re-offended at the end of this period, his brother, who was married and lived nearby (rather than the father who was physically handicapped), would be telephoned, and if necessary would come over and ensure that the scheme was complied with (this was rarely necessary). Specific instructions had to be given as to how the brother should behave – in general, neutrally – since contact with him was otherwise rewarding to John. A positive reinforcement scheme was also used in this case (see below), but it is doubtful whether it would have had a chance to work without the security afforded by this approach. Parents also felt more confident at being provided with an agreed and written-out formula to apply.

An important point raised by Jehu (1972), and also within the present author's experience, is the problem of deciding when an agreed rule has been broken. In the early stages of the case outlined above John adapted his behaviour to the new contingencies by becoming extremely subtle in his transgressions. A single match would be left in a conspicuous place, or he would hover dramatically at the window for a few seconds, and if questioned about this would reply that he thought he had heard a *police* siren 'or something'. Parents were bewildered by this and had to be persuaded by the social worker to trust their own judgement (as with the residential care staff in the case described by Jehu above). They were helped by another agreed formula: whenever they *suspected* John of leaving 'fire symbols' around or talking obliquely about fire, they were instructed to issue the warning described above, and to add to it in the face of John's protestations, phrases such as these: (Stage One) 'In my opinion you are trying to irritate us with silly talk about fires – you have no need to do this.' Stage Two: 'If we are wrong we are sorry but then since you do this kind of thing a lot we can't be blamed for any mistakes.' The response cost scheme was then applied on the basis of parents' considered *judgement* as to what was occurring.

Token economy schemes

In the past few years various forms of token reinforcement systems have been applied to behavioural problems found in psychiatric, residential social work, and special education settings. The results of these attempts can best be summed up as generally encouraging, but mixed (Krasner 1968; Ayllon and Azrin 1964; Montgomery and McBurney 1970). Before discussing these problems an introduction to the principles of token reinforcement is called for.

In essence, token reinforcement schemes are a group-level application of operant conditioning techniques. Schemes have the following general characteristics.

(a) An agreed list of behaviours which the staff implementing the programme would like to see strengthened – such as self-care skills, delusion-free conversation, negotiation without threat, participation in rehabilitation schemes, and so on.

(b) Tokens of pre-determined value are used to reinforce these behaviours, and these are exchangeable for a range of commodities (such as coffee, cigarettes, and toys) and privileges (such as access to TV, free time, and special sports equipment).

Programmes of this kind have two main effects. First, they develop and increase the frequency of behaviours likely to be useful to the client both inside, and, more importantly, outside the institution. Second, they provide opportunities for *discrimination learning* in that they encourage clients to distinguish which occasions and settings are appropriate for certain types of behaviour to be performed.

The tokens themselves derive their reinforcing power from two sets of influences. First, they act as *generalized reinforcers* in that, though worthless in themselves, they are symbols of access to a wide range of already well established reinforcers. In other words, even if one source of reinforcement is temporarily satiated (the client has enough chocolate and there is nothing on TV worth watching), then there are still likely to be other forms of reinforcement available. Second, to a much lesser extent, they can serve as conditioned reinforcers (see page 54). That is, their regular association with attention, praise, and tangible rewards gives them in some circumstances an intrinsic reinforcement value.

The advantage of using tokens in place of the actual reinforcers is that they only marginally interrupt the sequences of behaviour they are designed to influence. Handing an extra cup of coffee each to two chronically withdrawn patients in the middle of a rare period of conversation would probably see the end of it!

Points have been used as an alternative to tokens and these have the advantage that they cannot be misappropriated by other residents (see *Table 6(1)*).

Table 6(1) *A typical points system for use with children*

weekly privileges	price (in points)
allowance (pocket money)	1 000
access to bicycle	1 000
access to TV	1 000
games	500
snacks	1 000
permission to go into town	1 000
permission to stay up after usual bedtime	1 000
permission to come home late from school	1 000

Source: Phillips (1968).

The power of token schemes is well demonstrated by the following data (see *Figure 6(3)*) from the psychiatric field. Note how a range of pro-social behaviours are regularly performed by this group of chronic, institutionalized patients when contingent reinforcement is available, then drop to near zero when the same amount of reinforcement is available – but non-contingently – and then return to the previous level when the token scheme is reinstated (B.A.B. design).

PROBLEMS ASSOCIATED WITH TOKEN ECONOMY SYSTEMS

In an extensive review of token economy schemes, Hall and Baker (1973) take issue with Krasner's view (1968) that such programmes represent 'the most advanced type of social engineering currently in use' (leaving aside the wages system presumably):

> 'It is an unfortunate fact that these forms of engineering seem especially prone to breakdown – in the engineering sense, of course. Tinkerings by psychologists, psychiatrists, and others have not prevented several of these advanced social engineering projects from grinding to a halt.' (Hall and Baker 1973)

Remarking on the 'unique sabotage potential' (Miron 1966) of these programmes, Hall and Baker identify five crucial components of token economies in hospitals which can lead to failure. Four of these headings can be adapted to our purposes here:
(a) The first concerns client characteristics, with selection as the key

158 Behaviour Modification

Figure 6(3) Results from a token economy scheme

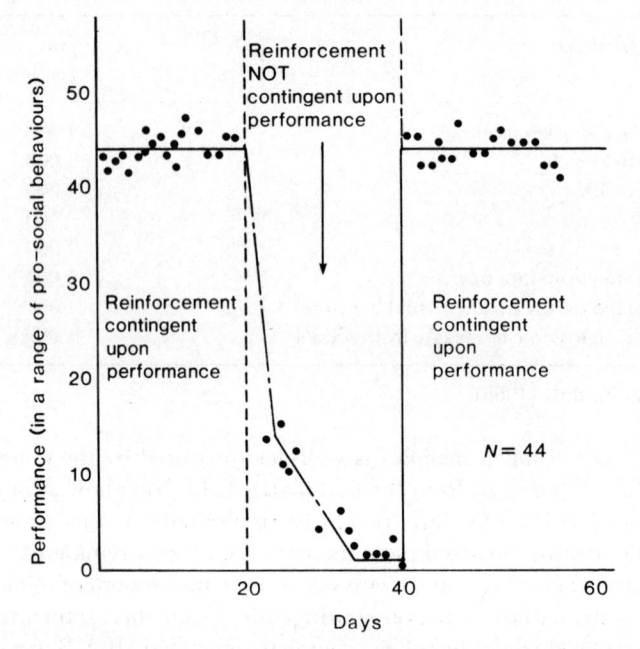

Source: Ayllon, T. and Azrin, N. H. (1965). The measurement and reinforcement of behaviour of psychotics. *Journal of the Experimental Analysis of Behaviour* **8**: 357–83. Copyright 1965 by the Society for the Experimental Analysis of Behaviour, Inc.

difficulty here. Where mediators have to cope with widely different types of target behaviours interfering with the emergence of these widely different problems, and markedly different intellectual capacities, then the demands on them are sometimes too great. Where initial selection poses problems then sub-grouping may be the answer.

(b) The mediators actually applying the reinforcement contingencies are essential to any operant reinforcement programme and may require special training.

(c) In addition, there is the need for support for staff, and a relevant question is: 'Who will reinforce the reinforcers?' It is often the case that after the initial interest of setting up the programme, the staff of volunteers in face-to-face contact with residents are treated as functionaries and just left to get on with it. Where this

occurs, and where doubts and problems arising from the programme are not discussed, the token system becomes 'token' in another sense. This point applies equally well to fieldwork programmes using mediators.
(d) Before setting up a programme it is necessary to ensure that everyone the client is likely to come into contact with understands its principles and will agree to abide by them. There is little point in encouraging non-acrimonious discussion within the house-system of a community school, if the Metalwork and Physical Education teachers insist on silent obedience. Discrimination between such settings will not always look after itself and neither will the generalization of programme effects to the outside world.

Use of Premack's principle

Readers will recall that the definition of this approach to selective reinforcement was that a high-probability behaviour could be used to reinforce a low-probability behaviour, provided that opportunities to perform the first could be made conditional upon the performance of the second. This principal is especially useful in cases where it proves difficult to find effective sources of extrinsic reinforcement – for instance, where there is nothing the subject values more than the reinforcement obtained from performing a certain (high-probability) behaviour.

CASE ILLUSTRATION

The following case of a four-year-old child brought up in a residential nursery, with one failed foster placement behind him, illustrates the principle. It was hypothesized that Ian had learned three things from his first years of life: (i) adult attention is a scarce commodity; (ii) if you want it you have to make a fuss and put up with the 'impurities' when you get it; (iii) when you get it, hang on to it.

Ian was placed with carefully selected foster parents, but after a short while and despite active social work support, the placement began to break down. Foster parents complained of the following behavioural problems.
– Uncontrollable temper tantrums, with Ian resisting comforting or diversion.

- At other times, excessive clinging to foster mother (this was seen initially as a transitory phase in the placement, but it did not go away as expected). Ian would hold on to foster mother for half the day, trying whenever possible to get on to her lap. Attempts to remove him resulted in tantrums.
- Entering foster parents' room at night. Occasional breath-holding when frustrated.

Procedure

This is a complex case and lack of space dictates that I concentrate here on the procedures used to modify Ian's clinging behaviour, using a scheme based on Premack's principles.
- Foster mother was instructed to pay special attention to Ian's occasional periods of solitary playing and whenever he seemed to be coming to the end of such a period (*before* he began to 'grizzle' or seek attention) she would invite him to come and sit on her lap and hear part of a story. It was made clear to Ian that this was a *reward* for playing quietly. Foster mother was understandably resistant to this idea at first but agreed to give it a try.
- At the end of five minutes of story-telling a 'natural break' was initiated. Ian was taken back to the scene of his earlier play activities and encouraged to resume, foster mother reassuring him that in ten minutes or so he could come back for part two of the story. If Ian attempted to clamber back before the time assigned, he was taken firmly back to the play area. If he persisted, foster mother would leave the room, leaving the book behind. If Ian followed and refused to be taken back, a 'time out' scheme came into operation.
- A darkroom timer with buzzer was used in the early stages of this case, and waiting for the signal for an interlude on foster mum's lap became a game in itself.
- Time on foster mother's lap (high-probability behaviour) was made conditional on increasingly long periods of play, or non-attention-seeking activities (low-probability behaviour).
- Other useful behaviours, not associated with tantrums or attention-seeking, were differentially reinforced with praise, sweets, and so on, as part of an overall scheme.

Ian eventually went to his local school – not without difficulty, but with considerably less than anticipated. His clinging behaviour reduced to easily manageable levels in thirteen weeks of therapy (due mainly to foster mother's grasp of the scheme and her ability to adapt it to new circumstances). Most importantly the therapy gave foster parents a 'second wind', enabling them to continue the fostering arrangement.

Contingency contracts[1]

This is a very promising procedure indeed, and particularly applicable to interpersonal problems. Contingency contracts are documents that specify behaviour which the parties to a problem would like to see performed. They rest on a particular interpretation of operant theory and this needs to be taken note of before describing their applications.

In many cases that get referred to social workers, it cannot be said that one person *has* the problem, or even that one person *is* the problem. The problem lies in the conduct of relations *between* people. This is particularly true of family and marital difficulties. Much of our behaviour in such settings is maintained on the basis of reciprocal reinforcement, and this process can best be thought of as an *exchange*, in which behaviour from person A is elicited and reinforced on the implicit understanding that behaviour from person B will be similarly treated. Within this process will be found different 'exchange rates' for certain behaviours which are differentially valued by the parties. Above all, in most relationships there is a tendency towards a relatively enduring balance or homeostasis maintained and controlled largely at an implicit level. Where this balance and the reciprocity which maintains it break down, as in the case of family problems or estrangement in marriage, then four kinds of things tend to happen.

(a) Helpful behaviours, which would normally be elicited by the everyday actions of the other party, have to be specially prompted and specifically controlled. Arguments occur about relative contributions – who has done what, what the real value of such behaviour is when weighed against the behaviours performed by others, and so on. Generally speaking, people are uncomfortable in the face of breakdowns of this kind, especially

---

[1] Parts of this discussion are drawn from my paper: (Sheldon 1980) *The Use of Contracts in Social Work*, BASW Publications.

since explicit prompting and aversive control rob behaviour of much of its dignity and spontaneity (Skinner 1971).
(b) The balance of mutual control shifts from positive reinforcement and positive shaping towards punishment, negative reinforcement, and negative shaping. Respectively: 'If you do X I shall retaliate with Y' and 'until you do A I shall keep doing B'.

In other words, control of really important behaviour is maintained by punishing transgressions, and by keeping 'the heat' on the other person until he performs actions close to those desired. This gives rise to the usual escape responses, which become increasingly sophisticated, so requiring more powerful aversive controls, and a negative spiral develops.

Figure 6(4) A useful hint

From time to time, I reward my husband by not pouring hot, scalding tea, over his bald head, first thing in the morning.

Must try it

Source: 'Private Eye', October 1980. Reproduced by permission of John Glashan.

(c) In such a context a relaxation of control tends to be taken advantage of by the other party, and an attempt to use positive reinforcement again is often seen as a *strategy* to be resisted.
(d) When reconciliation *is* attempted, either internally or with the

help of an outside agency, parties often start negotiations with an insistence that others must change their behaviour first. However, on the occasions when this happens the behaviour tends to receive little or no positive reinforcement for quite a time. Indeed, it is more often used to contrast previous behaviours (the 'about bloody time too' syndrome, known to most family social workers).

These few points all add up to a view of close personal relations as a system of reciprocal reinforcement that has its own mechanisms for maintaining balance. In the same way, a gyroscope will resist small buffetings and remain stable, but a stronger force will seriously disrupt the mechanism and then equilibrium is hard to regain. This model draws on both operant and classical learning theories. When potentially useful, conflict-reducing actions are not reinforced (either positively or negatively), they are likely to recur less often. Also, when the behaviour of another person is regularly associated with punishment, eventually this person's presence alone can trigger bad feelings – irrespective of what they happen to be doing at the time. This experience is well known to us all, and is what we mean when we say 'we can't stand the sight of' someone.

There is good empirical evidence that relationship problems and marital problems can be overcome by direct measures to re-institute reciprocal reinforcement. A comprehensive review of recent research in this field is to be found in Linehan and Rosenthal (1979).

The logical corollary of the views presented above is that the social worker seeking to improve interpersonal relations is unlikely to be successful if he works with just one part of this system – an estranged partner or an adolescent seriously at odds with his family. The reinforcement potential lies in the hands of people least likely to use it, and some sort of staged reduction of hostilities, based on the exchange model outlined above, is usually the best, if not the *only* workable policy. It is in this field of family and marital problems that contingency contracts have had their widest application (Stuart 1975). They arrange for the guaranteed reinforcement of adaptive behaviours, on the basis of an agreed exchange of actions which would not otherwise be performed – as when Mr Smith agrees not to quiz his son about who he has been out with, so long as he returns home by eleven.

THE DESIGN OF CONTINGENCY CONTRACTS

Contingency contracts are specific written agreements about future behaviour and they are based upon two major premises.

(a) That a definite, unequivocal, and publicly made commitment to a future course of action is more likely to be complied with than more implicit agreements reached about future behaviour in more casual and reflective forms of discussion – providing that the client does not feel that he has been unduly coerced into these decisions (Festinger 1957).

(b) That with many interpersonal problems, the most powerful reinforcers available for adaptive behaviours lie with the person experiencing the other half of the problem. Therefore a prearranged and simultaneous alteration in the pattern of consequences produced by key problem-related behaviours is the best way to proceed.

There is considerable empirical support for these two propositions and, in the field of interpersonal problems, contingency contracts are one of behaviour modification's success stories (Gambrill 1977). The aims of these contracts are similar to those of most types of operant scheme. The behaviours under review must be accurately defined, and the future contingencies which are to apply must not be capable of misinterpretation. Specificity is all. Where definitions of problems cannot easily be reduced to items of behaviour, then a good second best is to have an agreed list of examples to refer to, so that John's 'showing off', or father's 'unhelpful reminiscing', can still be accurately identified when they occur. In contract work there is an additional emphasis on negotiation *between* parties, and on identifying behaviours of equal 'value' to the participants so that in the presence of one, the other is much more likely to occur. In other words, considerable effort goes into striking an equal bargain, using sequences of behaviour as the medium of exchange.

Here is an example of a contingency contract *(Figure 6(5))* worked out between a fourteen-year-old 'skinhead' boy who was referred to social services by the police and his parents. The three main problems were: (i) a risk of him committing further offences (property theft, damage to public property, and so on); (ii) his increasing estrangement from his family, father having threatened to evict him several times; (iii) a real risk of violence between father and son (mother described their behaviour as a 'love-hate relationship').

Figure 6(5) Contract (Skinner family)

This is a contract between Mr and Mrs Skinner and John Skinner (aged fourteen). It aims to increase the level of happiness enjoyed by this family by making it clear to each member what the others expect, and what consequences follow both meeting and not meeting these expectations.

Mr and Mrs Skinner	*John*
Agree that if John returns home by 10 p.m. on weekdays and 10.45 p.m. on Saturdays, nothing will be said to him about where he has been or what he has been doing. If John is late they will ensure he forfeits time the next night.	Agrees that in exchange for the privilege of being allowed out late he will: (a) try hard to keep on time; (b) forfeit double time for each five-minute period he is late without an acceptable excuse and twenty minutes for each five-minute period after half an hour has elapsed past the deadline – regardless of excuses. The time will be forfeit on the following night.
Agree that if John will stay home every Sunday evening and one weekday, John will be allowed to attend two discos a month until 12 p.m., at which time he will be collected by father.	Agrees that in exchange for the privilege of being allowed to attend discos he will spend a specified time at home and will spend at least two hours of these days helping with household tasks, for instance, cleaning his bedroom, washing up, and/or gardening; and that he will telephone home before 11 p.m. to reassure his parents.
Agree that they will give £2 pocket money per week, 25p of which will be unconditional. Sister's pocket money will be similarly worked out and no extras given.	Agrees to forfeit money in up to 25p units if he fails to: (a) help around the house as defined; (b) telephone to reassure parents or is spiteful to his sister by social worker's definition.

continued

Mr and Mrs Skinner	John
Agree to accept John's comments on their behaviour as it affects him, and to involve him more in day-to-day decisions – such as where to go out together, or what TV programmes to watch.	Agrees that in exchange for the privilege of being consulted, and having his views listened to, he will try hard to keep his temper and limit direct criticism of parents. Failure to cooperate as defined by social worker means loss of one evening out.
Every Saturday father will spend at least three hours with John engaged in an activity acceptable to John if John meets the terms of this contract for one week. No mention will be made of past problems during these activities.	In exchange for going out alone with father, John agrees to: (a) stop provoking his sister into rows; (b) to listen more attentively to the points father makes, providing they are within the terms of this document.
Parents agree to address any worries about what company John is keeping to the social worker, and will not talk to John about them for the moment.	In exchange for the privilege of being allowed to choose his own friends, John agrees to call to see social worker briefly once a week after school and by appointment, and will be prepared to discuss his activities and their possible consequences.

There will be a fortnightly family meeting with social worker to discuss disputes and any problems arising from the use of this contract.

Signed .... Signed ....

Date ....

Source: Sheldon 1977.

This contract was abandoned after eight weeks of operation. It did not solve every aspect of the family's problems; father continued to idealize his own childhood and draw unfair comparisons between the somewhat anti-social views of John and his gang and his own golden youth. It was not possible either to influence John's behaviour outside the home directly. However, no further offences were committed, and parents thought that this was at least partly because John spent more time at home and had less interest in 'shocking' his family in retaliation for what he saw as their unreasonable treatment of him. This is speculative; what the contract achieved without question was an effective truce between the warring factions, the rules of which, as the contract was faded out, became part of their normal day-to-day behaviour.

Two general things can be said about contracts such as this:
(a) They work best when potential solutions to problems lie substantially within the gift of the parties directly involved. That is, where each of the protagonists genuinely possesses the power to alter things for the other(s) and satisfy them to some degree. There is little point in trying to produce an internal settlement in a dispute maintained largely by outside pressures.
(b) It is far better to agree relatively easily and substantially on something small, than partially and with difficulty on something grand. A Kissinger-type approach may look good on paper and produce lots of handshakes and *bonhomie*, but often the shooting starts again before the presidential jet (or, in this case, the departmental Mini) has landed back at base. As with other types of behaviour modification scheme, the all-important task of the early stages of contact with the clients is to provide a positive experience of problem solving. A contract must prove its worth in the short term or it will not usually get a chance to prove itself in the long term. Clients rarely refuse absolutely to negotiate about behaviour, but are more concerned to establish a reasonable *level* of behaviour, and to negotiate exchanges of positive behaviours at what they see as a reasonable 'price', measured by the effort involved.

Figure 6(5) gives an example of a contingency contract which meets most of the general criteria of good practice. Here is an example of one which does not *(Figure 6(6))*. The reader is invited to identify its many flaws. I am grateful to my friend and colleague Barbara Hudson for supplying the raw material for this example.

Jokes suffer badly from having to be explained, but could you count the following faults?
(a) General one-sidedness of the contract (all clauses).
(b) Vagueness of terminology (clauses 2 and 4).
(c) Rewards sometimes precede the performance of required task (clause 1).
(d) Reinforcement not contingent on specific performances (clause 1).

168 Behaviour Modification

Figure 6(6) Contract (Harris family)

Between fifteen-year-old Peter Harris and Mr and Mrs Harris, in order to improve the atmosphere in the home.

Conditions

1 Peter agrees that every weekday he will do three hours homework in order to make up for lost time.	In exchange for this, on Saturday he will receive enough pocket money for the whole week.
2 He further agrees to improve himself, will try to be good, and will be friendly to his parents at all times.	He will then receive the privilege of going out to the cinema once a week on a day to be determined by his parents.
3 Peter further agrees to help his mother with the housework and shopping when she wishes it.	In exchange, Peter will then receive the privilege of spending Saturday as he wishes – until 8 p.m., and subject to his father's approval of his plans.
4 Peter agrees that in weekly school tests he will get at least a B and will behave in such a way as to earn this grade.	Parents will encourage this in every way possible.

Failure to keep to this contract If Peter does not keep to his side of the bargain on one of these points he loses all his privileges for a week, and in severe cases he will also be punished in a way to be determined by his father.

(e) Hopelessly high levels for target behaviours (clauses 1 and 4).
(f) Parental vetoes available (clause 3).
(g) Some required behaviours are beyond the control of the signatories (clause 4).
(h) Neither positive nor negative consequences follow immediately and invariably upon given performances (clauses 1, 3 and 5).
(i) The contract has 'limited liability' clauses: 'when she wishes'; 'subject to father's approval'.
(j) The contract contains long-term punishment clauses likely to discourage positive responses ('failure' clause).

As if this were not enough, there are other kinds of errors associated with the use of contracts (see *Figure 6(7)*).

Figure 6(7) Contract (Parkinson family)

Between Mr and Mrs Parkinson and Billy (aged fourteen).	
Billy agrees to stay out only until 1 a.m. on weekdays and 3 a.m. on Saturdays and Sundays.	Providing Mr and Mrs Parkinson will give up asking the whereabouts of the cat.
Billy agrees to reduce his spending on alcohol to £5 per week.	Providing Mr and Mrs Parkinson supply a new sheath knife of Billy's choice for each complete week in which this target is met.
Billy agrees not to mug citizens above pensionable age unless strongly provoked.	In exchange, Mr and Mrs Parkinson agree to provide money for Billy's discussions with 'Aunty Lil' on Thursday nights.
Billy agrees to visit his social worker at least once per calendar month for ongoing discussions about his attitude.	Providing Mr and Mrs Parkinson refrain from telephoning about care proceedings and stop asking Billy to attend school.
Signed	Signed ....

Less exaggerated versions of the foregoing have, not without some justification, brought the idea of therapeutic contracts, and social workers in general, into considerable disrepute:

> 'Social workers have drawn up an amazing contract giving pretty 14-year-old Justine Carter freedom to stay out ALL NIGHT. . . . "I begged the social worker for assistance (said Mrs Carter) and a contract is what I got . . . I signed it to keep the peace but I certainly didn't agree with it."'
>
> (*Daily Mirror*, Headline: 'Let her stay out till dawn'; 21.10.78)

The technical principle of starting with small reductions in problematic behaviour and working gradually from there is a good one. After all, coming in at midnight is better than coming in at 3 a.m. However, by agreeing to an incremental change in dangerous, markedly deviant, or unlawful behaviour, the social worker can easily fall into the trap of appearing to condone it. The argument that the client would probably be doing something worse were it not for an agreement with the social worker does little to allay public consternation.

In less controversial cases of this general type, the best approach is to have the practical necessity for a policy of reducing problematic behaviour in stages, discussed by as many of those on whom it will impinge as possible. This may include the clients' families, other agency staff, or potential complainants such as school authorities or the police. Generally speaking, it is only in this way, with some kind of rough mandate from interested parties, that the social worker is justified in using contracts which give the appearance of licensing potentially harmful, or seriously anti-social behaviour.

NEGOTIATING CONTINGENCY CONTRACTS

To a considerable extent 'the medium is the message' so far as the actual process of negotiating contracts is concerned. The social worker, insofar as he has the ability to conduct open and honest negotiations and to reduce conflict by compromise, will serve as a model for the other participants. This will be so whether he is aware of the fact or not.

There is, therefore, an opportunity here to go beyond negotiated truces between clients, or *détente* between client and social worker. The process of drawing up a contract can itself serve as a device for teaching and demonstrating the skills of non-aggressive self-assertion, or the skills involved in repairing damaged relationships. Indeed, unless some kind of learning and generalization does occur, the contract has fulfilled only a limited function.

Here is a list of further points to keep in mind when trying to produce a workable contract:

(a) For a contract to be worthy of the name there must be some degree of equality between the parties to it. Legal contracts may be set aside where the relative powers held by the signatories are deemed to be grossly unequal – as in the case of a desperate tenant who signs an agreement which purports to exclude him 'consentingly' from his rights under the Rent Act.

There are similar ethical dangers with social work contracts, where an anticipation of coercion or loss of privilege can produce the same kind of sham voluntarism. This is a particular danger where the social worker has a 'captive' client population – as in many residential care establishments (see Chapter Eight).

(b) If a contract is to work well, then all parties must see clearly that they will get something out of it. The benefits of keeping to the contract must be worth the 'costs' of the change in behaviour that this requires. It is vital, therefore, that the negotiator checks out thoroughly the balance of value to the respective parties.
(c) The worker must not be afraid to offer to renegotiate contracts where they are not doing their job satisfactorily. In this way agreements can be adapted to changing circumstances, and clients can be given further practice at defending their points of view in a reasonable manner. There are, of course, dangers in constant renegotiation, but in general a series of definite if short-lived agreements is better than staggering on with one over-distended and complicated version of the original.
(d) Wherever possible the contract should be couched in positive terms. That is, it should be clearly stated that from now on *this* pleasant consequence can be relied upon to follow *that* particular behavioural sequence; rather than arranging for unpleasant consequences to operate *unless* X behaves in a particular way – this can mean that the non-performance of one sequence of behaviour results in the other party having to withhold adaptive behaviour (Jacobson and Margolin 1979). Where punishment and negative reinforcement have to form part of a contract, then these features should be well counter-balanced by regularly occurring positive consequences for desired behaviour.
(e) Once substantial agreement has been reached, a draft should be produced and used as a basis for further discussion. Ideally the final document should be typewritten, logically set out, and written in clear and unambiguous language. Each of the signatories should have his own copy.
(f) It is a good idea to fix in advance a regular series of meetings to review the operation of the contract. This makes it less likely that parties will withdraw unilaterally following a dispute.
(g) Contracts cover most of what we do in our daily lives outside the home – in employment, and in our commercial relations. However, when they are brought in to regulate aspects of family life, they have an artificial feel. We prefer the rules by which we govern ourselves in this setting to be implicit rather than explicit. To some extent this is also the case with social worker/client relationships, though there are fewer definite expectations here. Given the force of this cultural norm, it is very important that the

purely temporary nature of contracts should be regularly underlined. As soon as sufficient stability has been achieved, and the main contract terms are implicitly rather than explicitly observed, the social worker can begin to phase out the contract – clause by clause if necessary. A good indicator of when to do this is provided when the clients start to apply the principle of non-acrimonious negotiation about behaviour to aspects of functioning other than those covered by the original document.

(h) Contracts fail for three main reasons: (i) the terms are not specific enough and are interpreted differently by the various parties, leading to early disappointment; (ii) new behaviour is insufficiently reinforced and/or there is too great a time lag between performance and the counter-response supposedly guaranteed by the contract; (iii) there is insufficient supervision of the operation of the contract by the social worker in the early stages.

Contracts can also be used to define more clearly the relations between social worker and client (Sheldon 1980). They are not a panacea; neither are they always an end in themselves. Often their main function is to provide a dependable structure, within which long overdue consideration can be given to how problems work and have their effect, and to whether these problems can be eradicated by the development of a specific policy.

The biggest danger surrounding the use of contracts is that they may come to be overused and applied to cases indiscriminately. When they fail to meet inflated expectations, they are discarded like some disappointing toy. This has been the fate of many quite promising approaches, but in my view it would be particularly sad if it happened in this case.

Finally here are some data *(Figure 6(8))* drawn from a case in which marital problems were the main focus of work (see also Azrin, Nastor, and Jones 1973; and Linehan and Rosenthal 1979).

The contract used in this case was an extremely simple one. The couple concerned had identified two key problems, which were really two markedly different styles of handling conflict: 'clearing the air' by having a row was the preference of the husband, whereas complete social withdrawal was the reaction of the wife. Both disliked the other's behaviour in this regard and contracted (i) to limit their own response; (ii) to practise resolving conflicts through discussions

Figure 6(8) Handling marital conflict

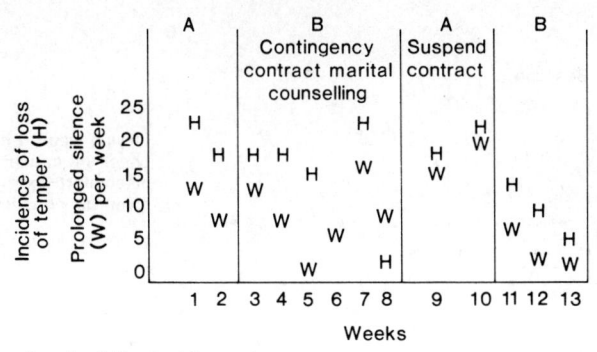

```
                          A        B         A        B
                                Contingency  Suspend
                                contract marital contract
                                counselling
                    25
                          H              H             H
                    20                                 W
Incidence of loss        H  H  H         H    H
of temper (H)       15      W     H  W   W    H
Prolonged silence   10   W  W                      H
(W) per week         5      W  W      W       W
                     0         W         H         W  H
                                                      W
                        1  2  3  4  5  6  7  8   9  10 11 12 13
                                    Weeks
```

[1] Operationally defined with couple.
Source: Sheldon and Baird (1978).

governed by pre-set rules (for example, wife would not refuse to discuss problems if husband agreed to do so calmly). The rise in the second A phase was probably due to therapist demand.

Operant extinction techniques

Extinction is a process most often used in combination with other contingency management techniques, but with simple unidimensional problems it can work well on its own. Here *(Figure 6(9))* is an example of its use in a common problem – excessive crying in children. Although infant crying is an everyday occurrence for most parents, where it occurs to excess, and on top of other problems and frustrations, it can be a powerful factor in child abuse (Gambrill 1981).

Approaches based on negative reinforcement

The therapeutic application of negative reinforcement principles (see page 53) is called avoidance training. Clients are taught to make responses which terminate pre-existing aversive influences. For example, in a social skills group of my experience, adolescents with a reputation for truancy and disruptiveness in the classroom were taught to reduce teacher disapproval by asking general questions, by admitting to not being able to understand a specific point, by apologizing for disruptive behaviour, and so on (Sheldon 1978b).

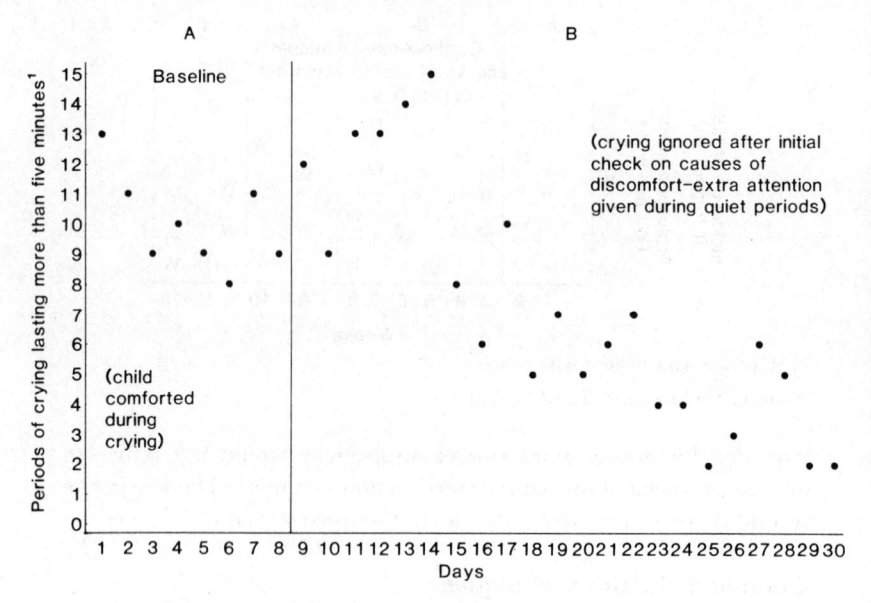

Figure 6(9) Excessive crying in a one-year-old child

Periods of crying lasting more than five minutes[1]

A — Baseline (child comforted during crying)

B — (crying ignored after initial check on causes of discomfort – extra attention given during quiet periods)

Days

[1] Medical examination showed no physical cause.

More rarely, aversive procedures are actually applied by the therapist as a means of generating avoidance responses – as when isolation is used at a community school for bad behaviour, but can be terminated if measures are taken to apologize and make restitution to those concerned. Adaptive responses are thereby reinforced and are more likely to occur in future – perhaps on the basis of a prompt.

Negative reinforcement is usually just one of a number of factors in contingency management programmes. The concept itself is useful in explaining why maladaptive behaviours are performed in the first place. Many are an easy means of escape from aversive circumstances – such as when a low achiever at school plays truant to escape criticism and the daily evidence of his ineptitude, or when a mother takes a tranquillizer to 'switch off' or at least 'turn down' what appear to be the constant demands of her children. In such cases the therapist has the option of trying to remove the cause of the negative reinforcement (by trying to obtain a more sympathetic approach from the teacher in the first case, or a behavioural scheme to change the behaviour of the children in the second).

Satiation

Satiation schemes are based on the simple principle that while certain consequences reinforce behaviour, a flood of the same objects, or constant exposure to the same series of events, will remove their reinforcement value. (Think of a laboratory rat who gets a cageful of food pellets every time he presses his bar!) Thus, it may be possible to eliminate ritualistic behaviour by having the client go through his ritual so many times that its reinforcement value is lost (Ayllon and Michael 1959), or by giving the obsessional hoarder so many items of junk that he loses interest.

Shaping, fading, chaining, prompting

These procedures are grouped together partly because they have been dealt with elsewhere in the book and partly because they are all really sub-techniques rather than full-blown strategies. This means that they are more likely to be used as features of a more comprehensive programme than in their own right.

Shaping (see page 59) was a feature of the two main contingency management case examples used in this chapter (page 131 and page 132), and involves the reinforcement of successive approximations of the finally desired performance. It is therefore a major feature of most contingency management programmes. In *Figure 5(5)* on page 120, better and better approximations of non-disruptive classroom behaviour and higher and higher reinforcement rates were required before reinforcement occurred.

Fading (see page 60) involves the standard shifting of control from stimuli occurring in one setting to those which occur in another. It is a vitally important dimension of behaviour modification in residential settings, where the recently acquired behaviours will eventually have to be performed under somewhat different circumstances. Bringing responses under the control of variables likely to be found in the outside world, by fading out 'artificial' reinforcers and introducing the more naturally occurring variety, is therefore likely to be a powerful factor in determining long-term results of the programme. In the case example on page 149, monetary support for the outings used to reinforce adaptive behaviour was reduced by stages, as parents began to think it worthwhile to budget for these themselves. Similarly, the daily report card was faded by being brought home at less frequent intervals, eventually to be replaced by a more generally phrased note of weekly progress.

Chaining occurs when complex performances are broken down into their component parts and each stage in the sequence positively reinforced. The reinforcer then becomes the discriminative stimulus that cues the next stage in the sequence. A variant of this approach, *backward chaining*, is widely used in teaching basic skills to mentally handicapped clients. For example, in the case of dressing, the procedure is to start with the garment already in place; one arm is removed from the sleeve, and then physically guided back into the sleeve. This prompt can eventually be faded and the next stage, putting on the coat from the 'two-sleeves empty' position, can be attempted, and so on until the person has learned the whole sequence. With backward chaining the positive reinforcement of having the coat on (together with any additional praise) is fairly immediate to start with, becoming conditional on a longer chain as progress is made with the task.

Prompting is a series of discriminative stimuli which indicate that a certain behaviour is now appropriate, or that if performed, it will be reinforced. The example of backward chaining above included prompting. Prompts were also used in the case of the socially unconfident client, described on page 108, and usually took the form of gestures and facial expressions to cue verbal responses and eye-to-eye contact. Prompts can be faded as soon as the behaviour is brought under control of other, naturally occurring, situational cues.

Over-learning and over-correction

This approach employs similar principles to satiation. The client is encouraged first to engage in a sequence of maladaptive behaviour – for instance fire lighting – and then to *over-correct* this behaviour – perhaps by dowsing the fire and cleaning up every particle of ash, while rehearsing to himself the dangers of lighting fires.

Enuretic clients who have made substantial improvements are sometimes given water to drink before bedtime for a period so that the association between a full-bladder feeling and an 'accident' is well learned; that is learned beyond normal everyday requirements, giving the client an extra capacity for control.

Attention to discriminative stimuli

Behaviour can also be changed by the therapist manipulating the naturally occurring discriminative stimuli which elicit it. In the case of the difficult foster child (see page 159), the foster mother eventually became very skilled in spotting situations that were likely to give rise to attention-seeking behaviour, and would do her best to remove these or distract the child's attention from them.

Table 6(2) *Summary of contingency management techniques*

technique	main features	application
contingency management	This is really a compendium approach using all appropriate reinforcement, extinction and punishment applications (see below). The environment is changed so as to support useful behaviours and ignore or discourage unwanted behaviour.	Used to increase the frequency, strength, and so on of adaptive behaviours by providing *contrasting* consequences for the two. Wide range of applications: child problems, mental handicap, or any setting where some control can be gained over the consequences of behaviour.
positive reinforcement	A consequence is provided which increases the likelihood that a given behaviour will be performed. Immediacy of reinforcement is an important factor.	Used to increase desirable behaviour. Behaviours incompatible with problematic behaviours can also be reinforced. The technique of choice in a wide range of social work programmes, it is important that the behaviour to be reinforced should occasionally occur at reasonable strength, since this is otherwise a rather labour-intensive approach.
token economy systems	Tokens (generalized reinforcers) are given for pro-social behaviours and are exchangeable for a variety	Used mainly in residential hospital settings – particularly chronic wards of psychiatric hospitals

continued

Table 6(2) *Summary of contingency management techniques* – continued

technique	main features	application
	of goods, privileges, access to activities, and so on.	(but increasing application in community schools).
use of Premack's principle	High probability behaviours are made conditional on some performance of low-probability behaviours.	Used where it is difficult to specify reinforcers in the usual way. Increasing levels of low-probability behaviours are usually sought in exchange for opportunities to perform high-probability behaviours. Particularly useful in the mental handicap field.
contingency contracts	An exchange of equally valued behaviours (which each party would like to see more of) is negotiated. The performance of one item is contingent upon the performance of an item from the other.	Used in interpersonal problems – marital work, and relationship problems between parents and children.
operant extinction	Removing available reinforcement from a response.	Used for attention-seeking behaviours, usually in combination with the positive reinforcement of incompatible behaviours.
negative reinforcement	Aversive stimulation is maintained *until* desired behaviour is performed and then terminated.	Mainly used as a feature of broader contingency management programmes.
punishment	A known aversive stimulus is presented on contingency and reduces the frequency or intensity with which a behaviour is performed.	Can be used as a suppressant of behaviours likely to interfere with programmes based on positive reinforcement. Punishment has the disadvantage that it strongly encourages escape and avoidance behaviours.

technique	main features	application
satiation	Such an excess of reinforcing stimuli is provided that their reinforcing power is lost.	Used for low-level addictions, hoarding, and so on.
shaping	Control of behaviour is shifted from one stimulus to another which resembles it fairly closely.	Used by the therapist to build on behaviours vaguely similar to those already in repertoire, and gradually change them, so that they more closely resemble the performance required.
fading	Therapist-supplied reinforcement is gradually withdrawn to bring new behaviour under the control of naturally occurring (non-artificial) sources of reinforcement.	An essential feature of all reinforcement programmes. Especially important in residential work prior to discharge.
over-learning and over-correction	This involves the intensive rehearsal of an adaptive behaviour well beyond the level normally required. Aids clear discrimination.	Used (for example) as a special feature in programmes with enuretics. On the attainment of complete dryness, the client is encouraged to drink before bedtime, so that inhibiting responses are well-learned.
attention to discriminative stimuli	The cues known to elicit behaviour are changed.	Should be a feature of all behavioural programmes. Particularly useful when problematic behaviour is known to occur regularly in similar settings.

7
Response control techniques

In the previous chapter our attention was concentrated on behavioural techniques that exert their main influence through specific alterations to the client's environment, such as changing the contingencies which surround him – producing new cues and consequences which affect his behaviour. Now we turn to a set of techniques which focus on the nature of the *responses* produced within a given set of contingencies, rather than to the stimuli themselves. These *response control* techniques (Bandura 1969) are directed towards the production, by direct-teaching methods, of new and more adaptive motor, verbal, emotional, and cognitive responses. In other words, they seek to change what a person does, feels, and thinks in response to his environment, since it may not be desirable, appropriate, or possible to change the environment.

Let us begin as before by locating ourselves on the assessment diagram, *Figure 5(1)* on page 104. Response control techniques are mainly used where the answer to the question: 'Are these behaviours already in repertoire at any significant level?' is 'no'. That is, when clients have either: (i) never learned to perform the types of responses which are needed to solve their problems; or (ii) where the responses have been learned in the past, but are now lost – as with certain psychiatric problems and associated institutional syndromes; or (iii) where the required behaviours occur very infrequently or at a low level, and operant shaping is likely to be too labour intensive an approach. There are also occasions where responses are in excess – as in the case of aggressiveness, where either the therapist is unable to gain sufficient control over the contingencies supporting this behaviour, or the problem stems from behavioural deficits (the client never having learned how else to respond). These *prepotent* responses can also be brought under control by the teaching of new behaviours which are incompatible with the old. Sometimes problematic behaviour is under the control of variables to which the therapist does not have ready access – for instance, when the client is influenced by his peer group, or when problems occur at work. Here, although ideally it is the contingencies supporting the problem which should be modified, work has to concentrate on helping the client to modify these conditions for himself. Although it makes sense to attack the problem of bullying at school, or exploitation at work, by trying to change the behaviour of the bullies and the exploiters, quite often this is impossible, and so we are left with the option of changing the client's own responses so that bullying and exploitation become less reinforcing for those who engage in it.

The theoretical backing for each of the techniques listed in *Table 7(4)* (page 219) has already been reviewed (see Chapter Three). Reference to this material will be made as necessary, but this chapter will concentrate mainly on the practical application of these theories.

Modelling techniques and social skill training

Modelling is a technique that could easily be included in the social worker's repertoire of helping methods. Arguments have already been put forward about the dangers of relying exclusively on the interpretation of problems and verbal descriptions of what needs to be done about them, and then expecting the client to come up with the new behaviours while his environment obligingly supports his new efforts. Modelling approaches are a way of bridging the gap between an understanding of what needs to be done and actually being able to do it.

Some authors draw a distinction between modelling and social skill training. While this is technically correct, because modelling theories attempt to explain how new responses are developed through observation alone, in most therapeutic programmes modelling is used in conjunction with rehearsal and selective feedback on performance. Also, since social workers are mainly concerned with deficits in the social performances of clients, the distinction between the two approaches virtually disappears.

182   Behaviour Modification

STAGES IN MODELLING

When modelling is used in this way, with feedback and appropriate reinforcement, the process normally passes through the following stages.

(a) Identifying specific problems resulting from gaps in the client's behavioural repertoire, and deciding what new behaviours could be developed to fill these.
(b) Dividing the target responses into their component parts (for example: coming into a room full of people; deciding who to stand next to and what to say; introducing oneself; getting in on the conversation; and so forth).
(c) Demonstrating to the client what a competent performance looks like; repeating any problematic parts of the performance or going through it slowly and deliberately; emphasizing options and decision points.
(d) Encouraging the client to perform simple sequences, with the worker shaping and correcting these as required.
(e) Developing more complex performances by chaining together different sequences.
(f) Paying attention to any problems of discrimination; that is, identifying any difficulties the client may have in knowing whether a certain piece of behaviour is appropriate for a given setting.
(g) Gradually introducing difficulties likely to be found in real-life situations as the client becomes more able to cope with these (for instance, not getting an immediate answer when trying to gain access to a group). Gradual fading of artificially strong or explicit reinforcements.
(h) Supervising practice, or practical assignments on which the client reports back (for example, getting the client to initiate three short conversations or to ask for clarification from an official).

MODELLING TO REDUCE FEARS

Modelling can also be used to reduce maladaptive fear reactions (as in the case of animal or insect phobias). These, though trivial-sounding, can be crippling to people who avoid all the places where – say – spiders or dogs *might* be found, that is, just about everywhere.

The aim here is to present the client with a clear picture of someone coping reasonably well with the circumstances they fear. The learning components of such an approach could include any of the following. (i) Through watching and experiencing the usual emotions, the client's fear eventually subsides since nothing terrible happens. This is known as vicarious extinction and is a kind of vicarious exposure therapy (see below). (ii) The client may learn new things about the feared objects or circumstances, or about how to handle them – in other words that dogs do not usually bite if approached confidently, that they usually respond to affection, and so on. Or in the case of fears about a social performance, the client can learn that there are 'tricks of the trade'. (iii) Through 'imagining-along' with the modelled performance, the client's expectations of himself may change; he may repeatedly imagine himself coping with such a situation, and so in future, thinking about the stimulus conditions may not trigger such powerful emotional reactions and thoughts of escape (see discussion of perceived self-efficacy on page 87). (iv) A further dimension concerns the reinforcement conspicuously available to the model as a result of his effective performance. This should make a tentative matching-response more likely (Bandura 1965; Kanfer 1965).

OPTIMUM CONDITIONS FOR MODELLING

From the foregoing discussion and the previous section on the theoretical basis of modelling, the reader will have seen that attention needs to be paid to three different components if new learning is to occur efficiently.
(a) Characteristics of the modelled performance.
(b) Characteristics of the matching response.
(c) Feedback and reinforcement characteristics.

Taking each of these in turn, the ideal model is someone who can easily capture the client's attention, and who has high status in his eyes. This last point has little to do with formal authority. To the members of an Intermediate Treatment group, the person with the highest status may be the toughest-sounding kid, and the worker will be wise to make use of this fact. The next point concerns credibility – a feature often overlooked in discussions of modelling. The rash of interest in role play by social workers and social work educators has often resulted in some bizarre requests being made of both clients and students. If it is just not possible to imagine Charlie as a headmaster, or Freda as a juvenile delinquent, then the whole episode becomes farcical and a little embarrassing (Sheldon 1979). This is probably the greatest threat to the success of home-based schemes in general, and programmes involving children and adolescents in particular. Without getting carried away with complicated coaching and 'stage direction', the worker can do much to improve on the situation described above. First, he can make sure that his own performances are not 'wooden', by practising beforehand. Next, and again without 'going over the top', he can make sure that his performances include appropriate emotional expression.

Particularly in the early stages of modelling, the therapist is trying to teach *coping skills*, not complete mastery. His performance must match this aim of relaxed competency. If he is embarrassed, then he will be modelling embarrassment; but at the same time a virtuoso performance may be written off by the client as quite beyond his reach.

Ideally speaking, new models should be introduced later on, so that the client is not left with stereotyped responses and can learn from a range of different styles. In this way learning is more likely to generalize. Where modelling takes places in a group-setting, its effects can be strengthened by making sure that appropriate performances result in the reinforcement of the modeller. Similarly, incentives for attention can be provided where necessary.

Where complex tasks are being demonstrated, it may be useful to 'talk through' the performance so that the observers can see what features the model is attending to, and what forms the basis of his decision about how to behave next. If clients do the same, this may help them to remember what sequence follows the last: 'Right, here I go, the door's open so I don't bother to knock, several people are looking at me, that's fine . . . smile . . . wave to the only person I know . . . now look expectant . . . someone's coming over . . . now for the introduction . . . is he going to shake hands?'

The performance characteristics of the client need only a brief comment, since the things to pay attention to here are much the same as with any type of behaviour modification programme. First, the performance must be broken down into manageable chunks. If the client feels more anxious as a result of participating in the programme, then a key element (lessening anxiety and engendering feelings of confidence) has been lost. Similarly, the worker must be ready to prompt new behaviour and then to reinforce approximations of it, *as* they are performed – not just at the end – because it may not be worth the wait.

The setting in which the programme is used is also important. No teenager is going to practise less aggressive behaviour (which he may initially regard as 'cissy') if he thinks that his mother may enter the room at any moment. Few mothers will care to practise handling their child differently, if their husbands (who may think such skills genetically endowed) can hear everything in the next room. They need to be fully involved or completely excluded. A feeling of security is important, so that cultural norms about pretending, and practising things which, by all accounts, should somehow have already been learned, are not too seriously violated.

Feedback on approximate performances should always be couched in positive terms. The concept of *shaping* covers what is necessary here. Clients who already associate certain kinds of social behaviour with fear and embarrassment will be very sensitive to criticism, even where this is just implicit. Elaborate explanations are best avoided. Showing the client what is meant, and prompting him by a re-enactment of the same, or a similar sequence, is much more effective.

The ultimate aim of any modelling programme is to bring newly acquired responses under the control of naturally-occurring reinforcers and of self-reinforcement. Attention and praise are often sufficient, if the client accepts the need to develop new skills as likely to make life easier. In other circumstances, material reinforcement may have to be supplied to start with.

Closed circuit television is an ideal medium for modelling new behaviours. Using portable equipment (which now costs about the same as six wasted visits by a social worker), it is possible to produce lively, believable performances, which are intrinsically interesting to observers. Sequences can be 'frozen', re-run, played without sound to concentrate attention on the non-verbal element, or run without the picture to achieve the opposite effect. This easy-to-use equipment promises to revolutionize certain aspects of social work training (Sheldon 1979), and it may well do the same for behaviour therapy.

CASE ILLUSTRATION DEMONSTRATING THE USE OF
MODELLING TECHNIQUES

Background

Paulette Douglas had spent five of her twenty-six years in mental hospitals and psychiatric clinics of various kinds. She was diagnosed as 'schizophrenic' and presented as a shy, withdrawn, self-preoccupied girl, intelligent, but somewhat bizarre in her behaviour. For example, she avoided the centre of rooms as if they were mined; constantly hung her head; shuffled around the house; neglected dress and personal hygiene; and spent whole days in her room reading, refusing to eat, or to speak to anyone. This case was referred to Social Services for 'after-care' following discharge from a psychiatric unit and the failure of a course of rehabilitation therapy.

Assessment

Initially grudging conversation between Paulette and the social worker revealed that Paulette knew that her behaviour 'put people off', but that she was too shy to do much about it alone. She felt very conspicuous when confronted with new people or situations, and was deeply ashamed of her psychiatric history.

It was decided not to delve further into the historical background of this problem, but to identify clearly one or two behavioural deficits, and try to remedy them.

Procedure

First, the view was put to Paulette that people could only think her mad if her behaviour put this idea into their heads. She found the notion that 'mad is as mad does' quite interesting, and a series of training sessions was set up with the explicit intention of showing her how to behave in the type of circumstances she found difficult.

Two basic items of behaviour capable of being built on later were selected: (i) walking confidently into a room and introducing herself to a visitor; (ii) giving non-verbal reinforcement to other people during a conversation, as a means of conveying interest and understanding, and so counteracting Paulette's usually rather vacant appearance.

These two classes of behaviour were broken into their component parts and repeatedly modelled by two students. The students played counter-roles and also offered constructive criticism on each other's performance. The sessions became increasingly friendly and lighthearted and always ended in a period of conversation about novels and various other cultural pursuits, known to interest the client. The length of this period (its overriding importance to Paulette was only discovered later and by accident) was varied in rough proportion to the amount of effort exerted by Paulette in the exercises – the more she tried, the lengthier the discussion afterwards.

After seven half-hour sessions Paulette had mastered walking into rooms, and her mother and younger brother were introduced into the programme. They were encouraged both to look for, and reinforce, behaviours of a similar kind throughout the rest of the day.

Believable, non-verbal signals of understanding were harder to establish. Paulette's performance approximated to that of the modellers only vaguely and mechanically, and the initial programme had to be slowed down and re-thought. Maintaining eye contact was discovered to be a primary problem and this was selectively reinforced with approval, and made a condition of the discussion at the end of each session. When low levels of eye contact had been established, Paulette's other non-verbal behaviour improved substantially.

By the end of the students' placement, Paulette had two new pieces of behaviour which she did not possess before, and her family showed increasing tolerance towards her, and an increasing interest in what else she might be capable of.

Before the students left the department a Community Service volunteer was introduced, who was familiar with the principles of the programme. Under supervision, he introduced a reinforcement programme to encourage personal hygiene and successfully worked with Paulette's mother to this end. Paulette later re-entered the employment training scheme and although she was unsuccessful in getting a job, afterwards she became increasingly involved with her parents in the work of a local self-help group for ex-psychiatric patients.

Conclusion

Modelling is a well-researched and effective technique for developing new behaviours and reducing the anxieties that often attach to inadequate social performance. One variant of it, social skill training, aims both to remedy particular deficits and to add other general-purpose skills to the client's repertoire. These techniques are being applied across a range of client groups, from psychiatric patients (Trower, Bryant, and Argyle 1978) to children (Van Hasselt *et al.* 1978) and can be used in combination with other approaches to help with a range of different problems.

Assertion training

Assertion training is a widely used behavioural technique, based on a combination of modelling, rehearsal, and operant reinforcement approaches. Its purpose is to teach people how to stand up for themselves without being aggressive. Since social workers, more than other professional groups, deal with the weak, the powerless, and the put-upon, this technique has particular relevance for us. However, it would be naive indeed if, as a result of our interest in behaviour therapy, we came to see these states as entirely due to behavioural or psychological deficiencies. In their extreme form they are structural in origin, a corollary of the way society works. Such factors are unlikely to yield before anything but a concentrated political effort – in which social workers, like any other citizens, are entitled to join. However, further down the scale there is much that can be done at an individual level. Not *all* oppression is due to the macro-effects of the political system; a broad range of everyday misery and oppression is psychological in origin, and to assign everything to the effects of capitalism is naive utopianism. To a considerable extent, exploitation depends on the expectations held by the exploiter (that he will be successful), and on the compliant behaviour of the 'exploitee'. Social psychology has much to tell us about the effects of these behaviourally-induced factors – as demonstrated by Milgram's (1974) dramatic experiments and by a legion of studies where the verbal content presented to an audience is held constant, but the style, expression, and appearance of the performers are varied to produce markedly different audience reactions (Hovland 1953; Cohen 1964).

Assertion training can be carried out with individuals and groups and is relevant to a wide range of interpersonal problems. It has also been used in a wide variety of settings, including: educational (Johnson *et al.* 1971); psychiatric (Schmidt and Patterson 1979); marital (Bach and Wyden 1968); in home-based and self-help programmes (Galassi and Galassi 1977). Other interesting applications include: women's groups (Jakubowski-Spector 1973; Meyers-Abell and Jansen 1980), and employment-interview training programmes (Alberti and Emmons 1970; Gambrill 1977). The approach has been well researched and a number of comparative and controlled studies exist, testifying to its effectiveness (McFall and Lillesand 1971; McFall and Marston 1970). It can be used both to *increase* assertive skills and to *reduce* aggressiveness in favour of assertiveness.

However, before we proceed further we need a definition of assertiveness:

> 'Assertion involves direct expression of one's feelings, preferences, needs, or opinions in a manner that is neither threatening nor punishing toward another person. In addition, assertion does not involve an excessive amount of anxiety or fear. Contrary to popular opinion, assertion is not primarily a way to get what one wants, nor is it a way of controlling or subtly manipulating others. Assertion is the direct communication of one's needs, wants, and opinions without punishing, threatening, or putting down the other person.'
>
> (Galassi and Galassi 1977:3)

I hope the foregoing has convinced the reader that assertiveness is a reasonable aim: that it enables others to know better where they stand with us; that it ensures clear messages about intentions, desires, and opinions; above all, that such a style of behaviour is likely to condition the behaviour of others towards us. An appropriately assertive style also produces important internal effects. That is, we are likely to think and feel differently about ourselves as a result of behaving assertively.[1] By letting other people see, through our behaviour, that we expect to be treated as a person of worth, we are also likely to affect our own evaluation of ourselves and what we are capable of. Here, then, is an example of a behavioural technique which follows research into the relationship between attitudes and behaviour (Cohen 1964), and suggests that the best way to improve self-esteem is to demonstrate and train clients in estimable behaviour.

Turning now to the training schemes themselves, assertion training programmes are likely to contain combinations of the following approaches.

(a) Assessment: often problems are confined to particular situations or settings (such as work or marriage) and no extra or special assessment is required. But in cases where there is a general inadequacy – as in the case of excessively shy or withdrawn clients – an assessment schedule such as the one reproduced in *Figure 7(1)* will give a better idea of the extent of the problem.

---

[1] False compliance may have its physical costs too. Several authors make the link between stress-induced illnesses, psychosomatic complaints, and so on, and link this to inassertiveness and an inability to express anger (Bach and Wyden 1968; Galassi and Galassi 1977).

(b) Discrimination training procedures: these can be used to teach the client to discriminate accurately between assertiveness, false compliance, and aggression.
(c) A modelling and rehearsal component: this is usually included so that the client is shown in a step-by-step fashion how to behave with different degrees of assertiveness, in different kinds of situation. The client will then rehearse and attempt to perform these behaviours himself, receiving guidance from the therapist.
(d) A reinforcement component: during training the therapist will try and positively reinforce useful approximations of the required behaviour. Attention needs also to be paid to the grading of tasks and assignments given, so that the client experiences success – rather than confirming his worst fears about himself.
(e) A desensitization component: as with other modelling techniques, a major aim of an assertion training scheme is progressively to remove the fear that is associated with certain behaviour. This is usually done through gradually exposing the client to such situations, but in some cases extra help with relaxation may be required (see page 218).
(f) Generalization: active steps must be taken to ensure that therapeutic gains generalize to the everyday experiences and problems of the client. The best way of achieving this is to vary the format of the programme and give the client experience in progressively more realistic settings.

Now let us look at each of these items in more detail.

ASSESSMENT

To start with, the client can be asked to complete a schedule (see *Figure 7(1)* and Rathus 1974). He does this as fully as he can, adapting the headings to his own particular circumstances, noting his feelings and anxieties at the time of each incident, and the practical effects of his behaviour. Also, when it would have been appropriate to behave as suggested in the chart, but he did not, he can be asked to note what the consequences were for him and for others.

DISCRIMINATION TRAINING

Some clients have difficulty in distinguishing between suitably assertive behaviour, aggressive behaviour, and falsely compliant behaviour. They may see all kinds of outspokenness as nasty, or as 'asking for

Figure 7(1) Assertion self-assessment checklist

	Friends of the same sex	Friends of the opposite sex	Intimate relations, that is, spouse, boyfriend, girlfriend	Parents, in-laws, and other family members	Children	Authority figures, such as bosses, doctors, teachers	Business contacts, sales-staff, or waiters	Workmates, colleagues, and subordinates
Expressing positive feelings								
Give compliments								
Receive compliments								
Make requests, for instance ask for favours or help								
Express liking, love and affection								
Start and maintain conversations								
Self-affirmation								
Stand up for your legitimate rights								
Refuse requests								
Express personal opinions including disagreement								
Expressing negative feelings								
Express justified annoyance and displeasure								
Express justified anger								

Behaviours / Persons

Source: Adapted from Galassi and Galassi (1977), by permission of The Human Sciences Press. Copyright © 1977.

trouble', and may rationalize compliancy into just a question of 'good manners'. Usually, however, people know what they would like to be able to say and do (as evidenced by the familiar internal dialogues and self-chidings that go on *after* the occasion has passed by). In these cases, discrimination training is used partly to clarify the different types of behaviours, and partly to provide opportunities for helpful candour. *Table 7(1)* outlines the main difference between the three kinds of behaviours.

Table 7(1) *Key differences between non-assertive, assertive, and aggressive behaviour*

Non-assertiveness	Complying with illegitimate requests.
	Agreeing with opinions you don't share.
	Avoiding people because they may ask you to do things and you find it difficult to say 'no'.
	Failing to express your own opinions.
	Failing to make requests or to ask favours of others.
	Avoiding forthright statements – giving mixed, vague, or confused messages.
Aggressiveness	Expressing strong feelings but for your own benefit.
	Dominating conversation with threats and demands, and adopting a behavioural style that is dominating, pushing, and demeaning to other people.
	Giving no consideration to the other person's rights, needs, or feelings.
	Possibly resorting to verbal abuse and often making an attempt to humiliate the other person.
	Failing to acknowledge, or act upon, the other person's point of view.
	Adopting a threatening bodily stance, with eye contact overlong and glaring, and gestures which appear to be the forerunners of physical attack.
Assertiveness	Expressing feelings directly, but without accompanying threats.
	Politely refusing unreasonable threats.
	Making reasonable requests.
	Expressing opinions while not automatically agreeing with those of others.
	Standing up for your own rights and needs, and making clear your wants, while making no attempt to infringe those of others.

Performing these behaviours without undue fear or anxiety. Being relaxed when asking for what is legitimately due to you.
Expressing anger and affection as appropriate.
Maintaining appropriate eye contact.
Matching body posture to mood.

To start with *Table 7(2)* gives a simple example of behaviours which the reader might like to categorize in line with *Table 7(1)* (answers are given below). Some excellent training manuals containing more complex examples are available. (See Alberti and Emmons 1970; Galassi and Galassi 1977.)

Table 7(2) *Simple assertiveness discrimination exercise*

Your spouse or friend arrives late and the meal you have prepared is spoiled. You feel annoyed. You say:

Response	Tick one
(1) Hello, have you been busy? You must be hungry, what can I get you to eat?	(a) assertive (b) non-assertive (c) aggressive
(2) I hope you have a good explanation, I've been waiting for an hour and the meal I made is spoiled now.	(a) assertive (b) non-assertive (c) aggressive
(3) I wonder you bothered to come home at all, where the hell have you been? This is the last time I ever cook for you. You're just too inconsiderate to bother with.	(a) assertive (b) non-assertive (c) aggressive

With a little practice it is easy to think up situations where an assertive response is required, and then to identify its aggressive and non-aggressive alternatives.

(1) (b) non-assertive: Feelings are being disguised and there is a pretence that nothing of importance has happened.
(2) (a) assertive: Feelings are duly expressed about the inconvenience caused and the consequences of it are spelled out (dinner is spoiled) but there is an opportunity to explain.
(3) (c) aggressive: Sarcasm, threats and denunciation are used and there is also a reference to general failings.

MODELLING ASSERTIVE BEHAVIOUR

The principles of modelling and the verbal component of assertive behaviour have already been covered (see page 73), and so here we shall concentrate on the non-verbal factors that make up a successful performance. Particular attention should be paid to the following.

(a) Stance and posture: it is difficult for the client to begin to make an assertive response unless he faces the person he is to address. If seated, leaning forward slightly demonstrates interest, concern, and lack of fear.

(b) Eye contact: if the client finds prolonged eye contact difficult, he should be persuaded to practise it at a distance and gradually move closer to the other person for increasingly long periods of time. Another way of beginning is to get the client to focus on some other part of the face and progress gradually towards eye-to-eye contact. Eye contact, conveying sincerity and lack of fear, is an important characteristic of assertive behaviour.

(c) Facial expression: the client can practise this alone in front of a mirror. Using this method (or closed circuit TV if available and appropriate) will teach clients the difference between what they feel like inside and *think* they are conveying and what it actually *looks* like. Sometimes the difference is marked.

(d) Use of gestures: confident but not exaggerated hand gestures do much for a social performance. These must not be aggressive – as striking the palm of the hand is, for instance – for the key point, as with facial expression, is that gestures should be congruous with other behaviour. This is a matter of practice and appropriately detailed feedback from the therapist.

(e) Voice level and tone: it is not uncommon to meet clients with loud voices who think it unlikely that they can be heard, and clients with squeaky little voices who think themselves perfectly audible to anyone *really* interested in listening. Tape recorders are a useful way of dealing with this problem, as the client can hear, and try to improve upon playbacks. In addition to an appropriate voice level, appropriate inflection adds conviction to a performance.

(f) Accent: many people are afraid to speak up because they are ashamed of their accents. This is particularly true in Britain, where accent and dialect carry strong social-class connotations. A little 'cognitive restructuring' is required here! Express the view

Response control techniques 195

that dialect adds richness and colour to the language, and that the important consideration is whether a person speaks clearly and can get his meaning across.

REINFORCEMENT PROCEDURES

As with the other techniques discussed in this chapter, the key principles involved in application are: simple tasks to begin with; a clearly modelled performance which is believable without being elaborate; reinforcement for usefully approximate matching-responses, together with helpful feedback to help the client improve. The programme then proceeds in step-by-step fashion to the point where real-life assignments are possible. Before the client undertakes complex assignments or tries out his new skills in situations which really matter, it may be useful to equip him with a range of responses for dealing with rebuffs and unexpected reactions.

DESENSITIZATION AS PART OF ASSERTION TRAINING

Another reason why people feel unable to assert themselves is that they fear the emotional and behavioural consequences of so doing. Therefore, to a limited extent it may be useful to try to analyse with the client exactly what he expects to happen as a result of self-assertion and to point out any inconsistencies or exaggerations in his beliefs. Often clients believe that their condition of shyness is inborn, or is an unalterably fixed part of their personality. While this is not so, a lifelong experience of kowtowing to other people is not easily set aside. Fear and anxiety will be partly conditioned through previous bad experiences, and any escape or avoidance responses which reduce this fear will have been negatively reinforced. Alternative ways of reducing anxiety must be employed.

This reduction of anxiety is partly handled through the therapist's arrangement of a gradual progression from simple to demanding tasks. Such a procedure not only aids the acquisition of new responses, but also acts as a kind of desensitization therapy – the client feeling increasingly relaxed as his performance improves, and a new, benign association gradually builds up. However, care must be taken to ensure that the client does not get out of his depth too quickly, with the result that the old vicious circle is reinstated.

Once the new assertive responses have been learned, they may be regularly reinforced in place of avoidance behaviour, since their deployment will reduce both anxiety and the often-reported sensation of having feelings 'bottled up'. These assignments are best pre-planned with the client and the likely sequence of events can be sorted out on paper, together with possible variations: for example how to cope with ridicule from an adolescent peer group when the client decides not to go along with them.

CASE ILLUSTRATION

Assertion training was used with Mr Thomas, the husband in the case outlined on page 108. He felt unable to do any of the following.
(a) Refuse unreasonable requests from his less conscientious workmates to do their work after finishing his own.
(b) Refuse overtime when he had other plans.
(c) Compliment his wife in any way.
(d) Initiate sexual intercourse.
(e) Speak up when it was his turn at the bar, in a meeting, or in a group of friends.
(f) Check his change in shops, or ask for clarification from shop assistants when buying something.

The problems that occurred at home were dealt with by a contract (see page 161), and the work-related items became the main focus of work since they caused frustration which the client was apt to take out on his wife.

Procedure

Progress was very halting to begin with, but when the scheme was transferred to the social service office, and an agreement made not to discuss the details of the programme with his wife, things improved dramatically. Typical problem-sequences were analysed and re-enacted with the aid of a student, with the emphasis on how to talk to the foreman when fixing which days in the week would be available for overtime. Key phrases were written up on charts and Mr Thomas made his own notes for later study. In the initial stages considerable praise was required for quite small gains. Mr Thomas's first assignment was to accompany the therapist to a local tobacconist, buy cigarettes, and check his change in front of the shopkeeper (not being able to do this, despite having previously been given short change, seemed of disproportionate, symbolic, importance to Mr Thomas). He achieved it first go, but with considerable blushing. Some help was given with relaxation to overcome this (see page 218), and after a while conversation about the weather and so forth was included in the assignment, without further difficulties. Mr Thomas tackled his foreman after five weeks (seven sessions), and on his own initiative mentioned to his workmates (who were apparently sitting around doing little or nothing) that he would not help them later if they got behind with their work. The main positive effect of this programme was on the marital relationship, since Mr Thomas came home on time, as planned, and was a much less frustrated person.

GROUP APPLICATIONS

There are many advantages to carrying out assertion training in groups (Lazarus 1968). For a start, the client realizes that his is not a unique or isolated problem. Group training also provides opportunities to practise new responses in front of an understanding audience of fellow sufferers – an audience, moreover, well aware of all the tricks of self-deception which excessivily shy people make use of. In addition, trainees at different stages can learn from each other, and may be encouraged by the progress of other group members. Additionally, the range of feedback the client is able to receive on his attempts to be assertive is much greater. Against this must be balanced the fact that having a number of clients together, each perhaps with subtly different problems, perhaps inclined to criticize rather than to facilitate, and perhaps inclined to reinforce each other's avoidance-behaviour, could lead to the sessions becoming a club for the socially disabled. Everything depends upon the selection of clients (see Bates and Zimmerman 1971), the clear establishment of rules for group behaviour, and the balance the leader is able to strike between the encouragement of individuals and the control of the group as a whole. Alberti and Emmons (1970) report on experiments suggestive of the following conclusions: two therapists (ideally of different sexes) are better than one; frequent sessions are best (they suggest twice-weekly sessions of one and a half hours each as an ideal). The enthusiasm of these authors is supported elsewhere by research into the effectiveness of this technique. Absenteeism and drop-out rates are generally very low, given the demands made by this method on concentration and personal effort.

DECISIONS ABOUT ASSERTIVENESS

I can think of few worse fates than being surrounded by people *constantly* asserting their needs, wants, and preferences – even if not directly at my expense. The important point to stress throughout training is that an assertive reaction is an *option*. Sometimes relationships can be improved by one party deliberately *refraining* from self-assertion in conditions where the other person knows full well that he or she has no right to expect an extra helping of tolerance or forbearance. Through assertion training we are really extending the client's choice of available responses, so that he knows he can assert himself when he chooses and when it matters – that is, when he is too often called upon to deny his true feelings or to bear more than his fair share of the emotional costs of living in harmony with other people.

Self-management and self-control techniques

The behaviour modification field has recently witnessed an upsurge of interest in self-help programmes of various kinds. In 1976 the prestigious Banff conference in Canada was devoted entirely to this topic (see Stuart 1977). Some of the theoretical reasons for this interest have already been reviewed: the development of social learning and other cognitive-mediational theories of behaviour, for example. In addition, as more people have begun to apply behavioural principles in their work, the field has opened up to include settings far removed from laboratory and clinic-based programmes. The practical problems posed by this are clearly identified in this quotation:

> 'How can you ensure that desired behaviours will occur at times and in places where you can neither prompt nor reinforce the behaviour? How can you get someone to do something – over there, in some other time or place – when you cannot intervene over there in that setting?' (Risley 1977:71)

An alternative to the use of mediators (for there are many settings inaccessible to them, too), and to reliance on generalization-effects to cover behaviour in natural settings, is to teach behavioural principles to the client and enlist *his* help in administering a suitable programme. Anything which promises to extend the range of behavioural methods is an attractive proposition, but, once again, caution is necessary. A principal ingredient of 'traditional' behaviour modification approaches has been the attempt to control contingencies in the client's environment directly. Might not the effect of leaving this complicated task to the client be that we are led down the primrose path towards ill-designed and sloppily monitored programmes – as other disciplines have been before us?

There are three possible safeguards against this possibility. The first is that behavioural self-control programmes tend to be monitored and evaluated rather more carefully than other kinds of self-help approaches. The second comes from a corresponding emphasis on the concreteness and specificity of the assignments given to the client, so that he is in no doubt as to how he should respond. The third stems from the level of training given to clients in the procedures they are to apply to themselves and the amount of time given to rehearsal. It follows, then, that these are likely to be demanding programmes for clients, and so they are probably best reserved for people who express a clear desire to change, but who perhaps do not know how best to go about it, or for people who have hitherto been unwilling to pay the price of change, but may make the effort if a stage-by-stage approach is adopted. Alternatively, in marginal cases, it may be possible to design small-scale pilot programmes designed to give an experience of success and opportunities for reinforcement and shaping.

The general aims of self-control programmes are to teach the client about the environmental factors that influence his behaviour, and to widen the range of appropriate responses which he can make in the face of these.

Here, in more detail, is the range of approaches that can be used in such programmes.

(a) The client can be taught about eliciting stimuli (S^ds) which may 'trigger off' unwanted behaviour. These may be identifiable if the client fills out an A.B.C. chart (see page 107), or if he is encouraged to keep a record of the thoughts occurring prior to the performance of unwanted behaviour.

(b) The client can be taught about the particular contingencies affecting him, with a view to changing these, or substituting more appropriate responses to them. For example, connections can be made between a client's excessive desire to please, his tendency to volunteer for extra work, and the hurtful criticism which he receives when he fails to meet his quota.

(c) New associations between activities and places, which provoke fear and avoidance in the client at present, can be built up by the selective use of positive images, which he learns to employ.
(d) Where external reinforcement for adaptive behaviour is weak or unavailable, clients can be taught how to reinforce themselves, following agreed or pre-rehearsed procedures.
(e) Cognitive techniques are available, which seek to change clients' expectations about the efficacy of their own behaviour and its likely outcome (see page 202).

Here is an example which relates particularly to items (a), (b), and (c) above. The instructions set out below were used with a group of chronic night-time worriers and insomniacs:

(1) Lie down, intending to go to sleep *only* when you are sleepy.
(2) Do not use your bed for anything except sleep, that is, do not read, watch television, eat, or worry in bed. Sexual activity is the only exception to this rule. On such occasions the instructions are to be followed afterwards when you intend to go to sleep.
(3) If you find yourself unable to go to sleep, get up and go into another room. Stay up as long as you wish and then return to the bedroom to sleep. Although we do not want you to watch the clock, we want you to get out of bed if you do not fall asleep *quickly*. Remember the goal is to associate your bed with falling asleep quickly! If you are in bed more than ten minutes without falling asleep and have not gotten up, you are not following this instruction.
(4) If you still cannot fall asleep, repeat step 3. Do this as often as necessary throughout the night.
(5) Set your alarm to get up at the same time every morning, irrespective of how much sleep you get during the night. This will help your body acquire a consistent sleep rhythm.
(6) Do not sleep during the day.

(Bootzin 1977:189)

Programmes of this type have also been used to control compulsive eating. In these cases the client may eat as often as he likes, but *only* at the table – which must be properly set. As soon as the meal or snack is finished, the table must be cleared and everything put away. Set meal times must be observed, however many snacks have been taken. This sort of scheme does away with absent-minded nibbling, and with any self-deception about how much food has actually been consumed. In time it introduces a new set of discriminative stimuli (table, knife and fork, set mealtimes, and so on), and eventually establishes a new set of associations – eating at particular times of day rather than at idle moments, and eating in particular places.

The principle used in both the previous examples is that of teaching the client how to re-programme his environment so that it gives maximum support for adaptive behaviours.

Another method of building up, or maintaining, a low-probability behaviour, is to train the client to reinforce himself (Kanfer 1971). In some cases this can be done with the aid of a contract or schedule which specifies certain rewards for the completion of approximate tasks. Later, self-administered material reinforcers are faded in favour of rewarding self-statements or mental images and associations. Here the client is given as much practice as possible in clearly visualizing himself obtaining mastery over certain behaviour, or situations – say, being introduced to someone attractive and holding her attention during the subsequent conversation. We all like to imagine ourselves performing well from time to time. In self-reinforcement this is brought under control, so that scenes are imagined contingent upon an adaptive sequence of behaviour. Walter Mitty-type fantasies are to be avoided: the aim is to get the client to visualize a pleasant but *believable* scene as a consequence of having performed the target behaviour. This also produces a new association between these behaviours and the pleasant sensation of congratulating himself. (Cognitive procedures of this kind are discussed more fully on page 202.)

Gambrill (1977) quotes the case of a depressed woman where the main treatment goals were discriminating occasions for self-reinforcement, and the self-reinforcement of behaviours incompatible with sitting around and worrying:

'Mrs M was first helped to lower her goals for self-reinforcement to more reasonable ones, so that it could occur more frequently. Each goal was written down, identifying the performance clearly before the task was attempted. After finishing a task, she was asked to assess her performance. If she decided that she had met or superseded her goals (her self-selected target behaviours were mainly household tasks), she was to do something pleasant immediately. This could consist of a positive self-statement or some event such as telephoning a friend or having a cigarette.'

(Jackson 1972:298)

A critical factor in self-control programmes is the level of monitoring by the therapist. There is little point in giving the client a list of instructions and leaving him to get on with it. Time limits should be set on all homework assignments and the client's levels of achievement noted, and appropriately reinforced by praise, references to progress, and to the new options open to the client as a result of his efforts. Clients also report that they visualize the social worker's likely reaction to their behaviour as they perform it, and the more cues to appropriate behaviour of this kind there are the better. This depends upon very clear instructions to the client from the worker, and on time spent rehearsing what the client's reactions to setbacks and obstacles should be.

Both the nature of the job, and the well-established concern of social workers to involve clients as fully as possible in decisions regarding their treatment, mean that they should quickly feel at home with this kind of approach.

In addition, there is a growing empirical literature suggestive of the fact that full participation by clients greatly affects outcome (Willer and Miller 1976).

Cognitive behaviour modification

This is behaviour modification's new frontier. Although there are few well-established rules and procedures yet, there has been a considerable amount of experimentation already, and there are emerging trends worth reporting (see Michenbaum 1974; 1977).

The aim of cognitive behaviour modification is to modify the following.
(a) Thoughts and thinking styles.
(b) Self-talk and 'internal dialogues'.
(c) Imagery associated with particular behaviours and settings.
(d) Maladaptive emotional reactions – to the extent that these are cued and maintained by thought patterns and thinking styles.

The main theoretical assumption here is that maladaptive cognitive events trigger maladaptive behaviour, and that it is possible to alter this by changing the cognitive events that mediate stimulus-reponse connections. A representation of this model is given in *Figure 7(2)*.

Figure 7(2) A cognitive-mediational view of behaviour

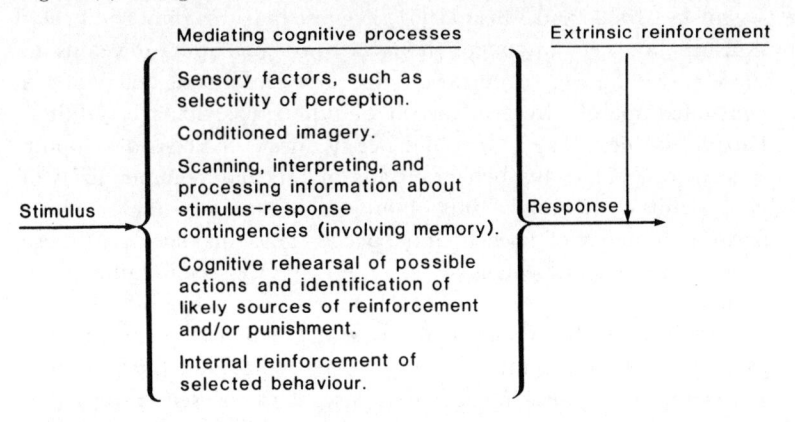

```
                    Mediating cognitive processes              Extrinsic reinforcement

              ⎧   Sensory factors, such as
              ⎪   selectivity of perception.
              ⎪   Conditioned imagery.
              ⎪   Scanning, interpreting, and
              ⎪   processing information about
  Stimulus  ⎨   stimulus-response                            Response
   ─────→    ⎪   contingencies (involving memory).              ─────→
              ⎪   Cognitive rehearsal of possible
              ⎪   actions and identification of
              ⎪   likely sources of reinforcement
              ⎪   and/or punishment.
              ⎪   Internal reinforcement of
              ⎩   selected behaviour.
```

There may be occasions when cognitive events themselves are the target of modification – as in the case of obsessive thoughts and ruminations, and accompanying images relating to future disasters; conditions found in 'psychotic' disorders, cases of clinical depression, and of obsessive-compulsive 'neurosis'. Also, and at a less intense level, cognitive events become the target of modification where thoughts and images about failure inhibit social performances which the client might otherwise carry out reasonably well. However, in most cases we are interested to hypothesize about relations between cognitive and motor behaviour because we want to influence the latter – to change what people do; and here it must be noted that directly changing what people do often changes the accompanying thoughts and feelings. Therefore, the sensible approach to cognitive behaviour modification, in its present state of development, is to experiment with it carefully, as an added dimension of conventional programmes.

The main cognitive techniques available to us at present are: (i) self-instructional training; (ii) stress inoculation training; (iii) cognitive restructuring (Michenbaum 1977); (iv) covert conditioning approaches; (v) thought-stopping procedures. Each of these methods is discussed in more detail below.

SELF-INSTRUCTIONAL TRAINING

A major premise of self-instructional training is that what we say to ourselves – that is, the content of our 'internal dialogues' – cues, shapes, and maintains our overt behaviour. The Soviet psychologists Vygotsky (1962) and Luria (1961) suggest that this important relationship between language, thought, and behaviour, develops in three stages during socialization. In early childhood, behaviour is controlled mainly by the speech of others (particularly adults). During the next stage, the child begins to use his own developing speech to regulate his behaviour (as in the play commentaries of young children). Finally, this function is assumed by the cognitive accompaniments of speech and speech 'goes inside'. It is these sequences of cognitive cues to behaviour that we seek to influence in adults.

In this view, behavioural excesses and deficits can result from inadequacies in cognitive controls over behaviour (lack of self-governing responses in the first case; lack of self-encouraging responses in the second). A second proposition is that it is possible to remedy these deficits by teaching the client to re-programme his responses with the aid of appropriate *self-statements*. Michenbaum (1977) refers humorously to this approach as 'teaching clients to talk to themselves'.

In problems resulting from impulsiveness, the client is instructed to interrupt the sequence of behavioural and cognitive events that leads to, say, an aggressive reaction, by deliberately thinking, or saying aloud to himself, a pre-rehearsed statement, and/or visualizing a series of images which are incompatible with the behaviour he is about to embark upon. The emphasis in self-instructional training is on *coping skills*, which the client brings into operation in situations which he finds difficult. These coping skills are maintained by cognitive cues, reinforcing images, and by covertly or overtly recited instructions, covering each step in the sequence. These techniques are, therefore, often combined with social skill training and modelling approaches (as in the case described below).

CASE ILLUSTRATION

Here is an example of self-instructional training from a programme designed to eliminate paranoid ideas in a thirty-four-year-old ex-psychiatric patient living in a hostel. The client (also under treatment for chronic mutism and social withdrawal) complained initially that noises coming from other rooms seemed excessively loud, that there was more laughter to be heard than before, and that she felt much of this was directed at her. She also listened intently to silences because she felt people had lowered their voices so that she could not hear. The hostel staff knew of nothing unusual in the behaviour of the other residents.

Procedure

The seemingly irrational beliefs were the first focus, and the inconsistencies in the client's account were discussed (partly by letter). These were that Laura felt people were talking about her *both* when they were behaving noisily *and* when they were quiet – she couldn't win with this belief. The idea that she was a person likely to excite this constant level of interest was discussed. The client was asked to think about her own interest in other individuals and whether this could ever be concentrated on one person for twenty-four hours. The client, grudgingly, thought not, and when pressed she laughed and admitted that it would be boring. What then was so especially interesting about her? Her answer was that she looked strange and didn't talk to anyone – which was true to some extent. The client was then shown videotapes of herself from early on in treatment, when she looked dishevelled and had a kind of 'Old English Sheepdog' haircut. These pictures were then compared with more up-to-date tapes, showing a considerable improvement. Next the client was reminded of the effort she was making (weekly sessions, homework assignment, letter writing, and exercises in reading aloud). Wasn't she trying very hard to overcome her difficulties and become more sociable? Did all this effort count for so little? The answer eventually given was 'no', and in future sessions the client was reminded of these points. The following self-instruction sequence was also agreed and the client was taught to review it, item by item, whenever she felt her ideas of reference returning.

(a) Steady now, deep breaths, it's only because I'm on my own and paying too much attention to what is going on outside my room that I am reading things into those noises that are not really there. Everyone does it from time to time, I do it too much.
(b) I think people are talking about me because I don't have much to do with them. This may happen occasionally but definitely not all the time and among so many different people.
(c) I am trying very hard to overcome my shyness but I am not ready to cope with talking to other people yet – one day I will be, that is my aim, and that is why I am working with Mr Sheldon.

(d) I look better now than I have ever looked, and I intend to go on looking after myself in future. This is one problem I am on top of.
(e) Right, I agree that this is all nonsense and not worth worrying about. I have better things to do – like one of my homework exercises ... (client instructed to repeat reading exercise).

Laura first read from these typewritten instructions, and eventually memorized parts of them for use in other settings.

Use of imagery

Laura found that relaxing, and deliberately engaging in a favourite fantasy (pony trekking, or grooming a horse meticulously stage by stage), were more effective than homework exercises as an activity to follow after going through her instructions. Two further images were made use of. First, a visualization based on videotape recordings was used, comparing her appearance of nine months ago with today. To this were added comments of my own about her improved standard of dress and hygiene. This image was used whenever she felt unduly conspicuous or had thoughts about derogatory comments by other people. Second, she was offered an image of the therapist praising her for the effort she was putting into her work, reminding her of the progress already made. In seven weeks the ideas of reference disappeared. In addition she had abandoned a grisly self-punishing ritual of repeatedly sticking pins into her arm as atonement for whatever her neighbours were supposed to be criticizing her for.

STRESS INOCULATION TRAINING AND SELF-INSTRUCTION

These techniques involve the therapist in rehearsing coping skills with the client, preparatory to his entering into a stressful situation. They are used mainly in programmes designed to combat maladaptive fear and phobias, where research is suggesting that rapid exposure to the threatening stimulus – with the client remaining in the stressful conditions using pre-rehearsed coping mechanisms – is a faster and more effective treatment approach with many clients than desensitization (Marks 1971; 1975; see also page 213). Orne (1965) makes use of the concept of *immunization* in his discussion of the importance of changing the beliefs of clients about their ability to cope with stress given appropriate rehearsal, an emphasis that should remind readers of Bandura's theories regarding the importance of modifying efficacy and outcome expectations (Bandura 1977; see also page 86). *Table 7(3)* shows a typical schedule of self-instruction, which came into operation after appropriate rehearsal with the therapist of the different elements in the process of confronting a particular stress.

A further consideration when using self-statements in this way is the voice clients use to talk to themselves. We are all familiar with the 'sound' of our parent's voice inside our heads admonishing us, and with the experience of 'hearing' ourselves praised and having our views supported by figures noted for their sanity and intelligence (I always use Lord Soper). At least I hope this is true, otherwise I probably need some professional help myself! I raise this point here because it may have therapeutic implications in cases such as the one described above, where it might have been useful to have the client respond to anxiety in the voice of another reassuring figure.

COGNITIVE RESTRUCTURING

The reader has already been shown an attempt to correct a disabling belief by confronting the client with arguments about its illogicality (see page 204). Techniques of this kind depend very much on the pioneering work of cognitive therapists, such as Beck (1970), and more particularly, on the Rational-Emotive approach of Albert Ellis (1977, 1979). The main theoretical assumption in this approach is that beliefs, apart from being situation-specific, cognitive, and emotional accompaniments to behaviour, are themselves organized into systems, which have a durable effect on behaviour across a *range* of settings. The logical corollary of this is that if we can correct these faulty beliefs, or faulty thinking styles, then we can change problematic behaviour. The cognitive notion of *thinking style* is quite close to the behavioural notion of *learning history*, that is, the sum total of learning experiences which the individual is known to have undergone. It is easy to see how a particularly disjointed learning history, resulting from perverse or depressing childhood and family experiences, educational failures, and so forth, can lead to a pervasively negative view of the world which, by the usual procedure of the self-fulfilling prophecy, is regularly confirmed. Ellis has noted several unnatural patterns of thinking, such as 'awfulizing' – believing that it is *awful* not always to meet targets – or the belief that surrounding circumstances are always part of a mischievous conspiracy

Table 7(3) *Self-statements*

Preparing for a stressor	What is it you have to do?
	You can develop a plan to deal with it.
	Just think about what you can do about it.
	That's better than getting anxious.
	No negative self-statements, just think rationally.
	Don't worry: worry won't help anything.
	Maybe what you think is anxiety is eagerness to confront the stressor.
Confronting and handling a stressor	Just psych yourself up – you can meet this challenge.
	You can convince yourself to do it. You can reason your fear away.
	One step at a time: you can handle the situation.
	Don't think about fear; just think about what you have to do. Stay relevant.
	This anxiety is what the doctor said you would feel. It's a reminder to use your coping exercises.
	Relax, you're in control. Take a slow deep breath.
Coping with the feeling of being overwhelmed	When fear comes, just pause.
	Keep the focus on the present; what is it you have to do?
	Label your fear from 0 to 10 and watch it change. You should expect your fear to rise.
	Don't try to eliminate fear totally; just keep it manageable.
Reinforcing self-statements	It worked; you did it.
	Wait until you tell your therapist (or group) about this.
	It wasn't as bad as you expected.
	Your damn ideas – that's the problem. When you control them, you control your fear.
	It's getting better each time you use the procedures.
	You can be pleased with the progress you're making.
	You did it!

Source: Michenbaum (1974).

against one's aims. Readers could probably add to such a list from their own experience. For purposes of illustration, I offer the 'Eeyore syndrome':

> 'Sometimes,' said Eeyore, 'when people have quite finished taking a person's house, there are one or two bits which they don't want and are rather glad for the person to take back, if you know what I mean. So I thought if we just went –'
> 'Come on,' said Christopher Robin, and off they hurried, and in a very little time they got to the corner of the field by the side of the pine-wood, where Eeyore's house wasn't any longer.
> 'There!' said Eeyore. 'Not a stick of it left! Of course, I've still got all this snow to do what I like with. One musn't complain.'[2]

A recent reviewer summarized the aims and methods of the cognitive therapies as follows:

> 'Thus both Beck and Ellis regard change in fundamental cognitive structures and beliefs as the ultimate goal of therapy. Beck et al. (1978) describe the aims of therapy as "to identify, reality-test and correct maladaptive, distorted conceptualizations and the dysfunctional beliefs (schemes) underlying these cognitions"; and Ellis (1977) sees therapy as needing to produce a "profound cognitive and philosphic change in clients' basic assumptions, especially their absolutistic, demanding, masturbatory, irrational ways of viewing themselves, others and the world".'
> (Marzillier 1980:251)

The main approach in attempts to change irrational belief systems is to clearly identify and exemplify such patterns for the client; to rehearse with him alternative views of reality, and alternatives to his negative self-statements. This can be augmented with practice in different styles of thinking (as discussed on page 138), cued by predecided self-statements, and maintained by self-instruction schedules and appropriate self-reinforcement. To this sequence must be added practice in alternative ways of behaving, since, as we have seen, extrinsic reinforcement for alternative behaviours is likely to affect

---

[2]Source: A. A. Milne (1928:11). Reprinted in the English language edition by permission of Eyre Methuen Ltd; E. P. Dutton (copyright 1928, by E. P. Dutton & Co Inc., renewal 1956 by A. A. Milne); McClelland and Stewart Ltd (the Canadian publishers). Reproduced in foreign language editions by permission of Curtis Brown Ltd.

thinking patterns – or at least to give weight to discussions about their effects. Similarly, the evaluation of such programmes should include a behavioural indicator (see page 110) if we are to avoid the old problem of working with purely subjective data.

One further word of caution. Certain well-established, and presumably highly functional, delusional patterns in psychiatric cases are unlikely to yield to anything; except, just possibly, to really intensive work of this kind. Nevertheless, with less extreme cases, good results are being recorded across a range of problems and client groups (Ellis 1979). Stern (1978), for example, combines cognitive re-structuring techniques with positive self-statements, social skill training, and a simple differential reinforcement programme managed by the husband of the client, in a case of mild depression. (But note that in unsupervised settings and in cases of any severity, safety is of paramount importance.)

COVERT CONDITIONING APPROACHES

Counter-conditioning techniques (the application of stronger, incompatible stimuli to weaken maladaptive conditioned responses) pre-date cognitive approaches, and their application is reviewed on page 110. Covert counter-conditioning (which relies upon the same principles but uses *images* rather than overt stimuli) is discussed here so that it can be seen for what it is – a cognitive technique (Kazdin and Smith 1979).

Covert conditioning techniques are of two kinds. First, there are the *positive* techniques, where the client is trained to visualize himself coping well with a particular fear-provoking circumstance and receiving reinforcement. Alternatively, he can be trained to imagine a pre-rehearsed scene which he finds pleasant, and to relax while under stress. Training usually takes the form of just clarifying the image, with practice at summoning this on cue, and then visualizing the circumstance that arouses the fear-reaction and countering this with the positive image. Practice *in vivo* usually follows mastery of this technique. An interesting development of this approach involves the training of problematically sexually deviant clients (for example, convicted sex-offenders) in image-switching during masturbation. At the point of no return, the deviant image – for instance of a child – is replaced by some other suitable, adaptively erotic scene, so that orgasm is paired repeatedly with this, and it eventually acquires reinforcing properties of its own (see Laws and O'Neill 1981).

Second, *covert sensitization* procedures may be employed (Cautela 1966). These techniques use punishing and negatively reinforcing images to develop avoidance responses. They are applied to maladaptive behaviours, such as dependence on alcohol or drugs, and over-eating. The client is trained first to summon punishing images to accompany visualization of the behaviour he wishes to remove: being sick over a friend after a drink in a bar, for example, or being caught engaging in some dubious practice by someone he regards highly. The next stage is for the client to terminate these aversive scenes by ceasing to perform the target behaviour. Adaptive and relief-providing responses can then be visualized and are negatively reinforced (Cautela 1970). Research evidence suggests that covert sensitization is more likely to be effective in changing very specific behaviours (Kazdin and Smith 1980), and, generally speaking, results are mixed. However, there are accounts of the successful application of such techniques in the literature (Barlow 1969).

THOUGHT STOPPING

Thought-stopping techniques have been employed by therapists of many different persuasions over the years. They may be used to control obsessive thoughts and ruminations, or as a method of controlling the self-presentation of images used in some of the cognitive approaches reviewed above. The usual procedure is to get the client to close his eyes and summon up a clear and detailed image of what it is that troubles or obsesses him, and then for the therapist to shout 'stop!' The client opens his eyes immediately. He then practises this for himself, first aloud and then sub-vocally. Alternatives reviewed by Tryan (1979) in her useful article include the use of thick elastic bands around the wrist, which can be stretched and released on cue, and deliberate counting backwards from ten followed by relaxation. The aim of these little devices is to interrupt the unwanted sequence of thoughts. Again, the research evidence on their effectiveness is mixed. Also, because thought-stopping techniques are usually employed in combination with other methods, it is difficult to obtain an independent measure of their potency. Positive results are, however, reported by Hays and Waddell (1976) and Yamagami (1971).

212 Behaviour Modification

Techniques for reducing anxiety and avoidance

Returning now to mainstream behavioural practice, behaviour modification is perhaps best known for the success of the work done on phobias, and on less severe, irrational fears and anxiety states. There are a number of techniques which can be used in the face of such difficulties, and each of these is now discussed in turn. (Notes on the theoretical origins of these approaches are contained in Chapter Three.)

POSITIVE COUNTER-CONDITIONING

The principle here is to 'break up' maladaptive conditioned associations (for example, fear of everyday events, objects, or animals) by introducing a new response which is incompatible with, and stronger than, the existing problematic response. This is Wolpe's principle of 'reciprocal inhibition' (Wolpe 1958), which states that if we pair a response capable of *inhibiting* anxiety with the anxiety-provoking stimulus, it can be used to weaken the conditional association between that stimulus and anxiety. This approach makes use of the simple fact that it is impossible to feel both anxious and relaxed at the same time, and by pairing the two responses, the client can, loosely speaking, 'unlearn' his fear reaction. It will also be seen that assertion training has a counter-conditioning component to it.

Jehu (1972) quotes the case of a young child who became very afraid of baths after slipping into the water on one occasion. To overcome this problem, toys were first placed in an empty bath, then into a sink partly filled with water, each time the child managed to go in and retrieve them. Finally, the child was washed in the water-filled bath – with much hugging and diversionary behaviour from parents. The response to the toys inhibited the anxiety reponse to the bath. I have used a similar procedure to reduce a powerful fear of hair-washing in an eight-year-old child in a children's home. Apparently her father had returned home the worse for drink one evening, to find the child grizzling over having her hair washed by her mother. He thrust her head into the sink, and held it there – an attack from which she took two years to recover. Favourite glove puppets were used in this programme: first they had their hair washed, then hers was wetted a little and then she was helped to wash her own hair in a small bowl, well away from the bathroom, and so on. (This technique, when used in step-by-step fashion, also has some of the features of *systematic desensitization* (see page 216) where carefully graded stages and accompanying relaxation are used in conjunction.) There may also be a positive reinforcement effect present in these two cases, with access to toys strengthening approach responses.

RAPID EXPOSURE TECHNIQUES

Rapid exposure (flooding) is used in the treatment of profound fears and is derived from respondent extinction research (see page 49). A phobia is a powerful, conditioned fear reaction to objects, animals, people, or just about any other environmental circumstance. The client experiences powerful physical reactions to particular stimuli, and, even if he knows that his fears are illogical, he is unable to control them. Phobias are *learned* reactions and obey the principles of classical conditioning. However, they are often partly maintained by negative reinforcement – maladaptive escape and avoidance responses being strengthened by the relief they bring. Phobias also generalize to circumstances which resemble the original stimulus conditions. The case described on page 46 is of a typical agoraphobia (fear of going out of doors); this, together with social phobias (fear of people and groups), is the type of reaction most often met with in social work.

For years the established treatment for these problems has been systematic desensitization: slow exposure to threatening stimuli accompanied by deep muscular relaxation, based on counter-conditioning principles (Wolpe 1958). This was the first of the behavioural approaches to establish itself in the therapeutic repertoire. However, recent research investigating the relative part played by each of the ingredients of systematic desensitization, plus the results of increasing experimentation in clinical settings with rapid exposure methods, has resulted in a considerable rationalization in this field (Marks 1975, 1978). In his highly recommendable book, Stern (1978) suggests that instead of viewing rapid exposure and systematic desensitization as two separate techniques they should be thought of as a continuum – from slow exposure to rapid exposure. Although it is now reasonable to suggest that rapid exposure to the feared stimulus is the treatment of choice in phobias, this is a little like suggesting that a large injection of money is the best approach to poverty. It may be a good idea but it is not always feasible. The client may be staunchly unwilling to confront his worst fears, however much encouragement and support is given to him. This leaves us having to work for an optimal solution. The problem remains: get the client to confront his worst fears *as quickly as possible* after due preparation and help him to stay there until his anxiety subsides. It is important to explain to clients that their fears *will* subside, however powerful the anxiety: if the client stays anxious for long enough in the same set of circumstances, the anxiety will eventually extinguish.

Where the client will not cooperate with a rapid exposure aproach, slow exposure is indicated, and to the extent that induced relaxation aids this process, we are left with a useful role for some form of systematic desensitization.

Procedure in rapid exposure therapy

(a) Preparation for rapid exposure is most important and may involve the therapist in using other techniques such as modelling and rehearsal. First the causes of phobias (see page 48) should be carefully reviewed with the client. I am not suggesting here that an academic discussion should be entered into, but that some basic principles arising out of the worker's investigation of the problem should be simply outlined. It is usually helpful for the client to grasp the ideas behind what is being proposed and to register that the method being employed is the result of considerable research and practical experimentation, not just a therapeutic whim. This is not just to impress him, but because (as when medical procedures are necessary) stress is easier to bear when we understand its origins, can estimate its likely duration, can assess the limits of its effects on us, and can have some actual control over it (Miller 1979).

(b) The next stage involves the mapping out of a treatment rationale which is acceptable to the client. Generally speaking, the fewer the number of steps before the client confronts the stimulus conditions which he most avoids the better. Against this must be weighed the risk of premature withdrawal from a session which he finds too overwhelming.

Clients do not usually experience difficulty in describing the various stages of fear-intensity and avoidance which given conditions produce, and a short hierarchy of these can be drawn up, as in *Figure 7(3)*.

Figure 7(3) Stages in the treatment of an excessive fear of dirt and germs

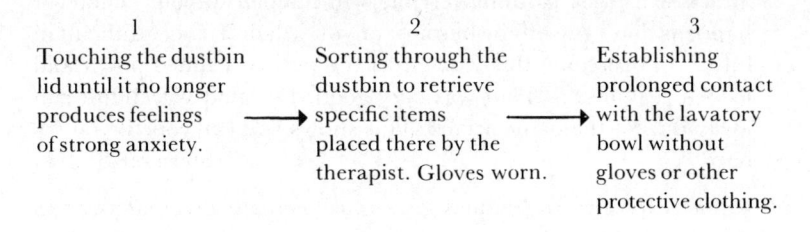

1	2	3
Touching the dustbin lid until it no longer produces feelings of strong anxiety.	Sorting through the dustbin to retrieve specific items placed there by the therapist. Gloves worn.	Establishing prolonged contact with the lavatory bowl without gloves or other protective clothing.

Ideally, the client should be presented with a written version of his programme (as above), and his definite agreement to it should be obtained. A simple contract, in which the client registers his commitment to the programme, may be helpful.

(c) There are many things that can be done to equip the client for coping with stress. Reassurances can be given about the relatively short-term nature of anxiety; worst fears and irrational expectations can be confronted and analysed. Reassurances can also be given that the therapist will stay with the client and help him to remain in contact with the feared circumstances as long as necessary. Alternatively, relatives can be trained as mediators and can help in this way. Rehearsal sessions can be started where the procedure is modelled by the therapist and then by the client. Cognitive techniques can be employed: for instance, getting the client to *imagine* his way through the programme with the therapist's help, and providing him with a repertoire of coping mechanisms and self-statements as discussed on page 204.

These methods aside, programmes of this type depend greatly on a relationship of trust between client and therapist; an approach characterized by supportive firmness in the face of fear, and by a clear commitment from the client that he will under no circumstances abandon the session before his anxiety has subsided. Homework assignments can be designed to cover the period between sessions, and Stern (1978) lays great stress on the importance of these behaviour-maintenance measures. Here is his description of a treatment session involving a man with a profound fear of travelling on public transport:

'During the first session of *in vivo* exposure to buses he had several short bursts of panic and grabbed the therapist's arm tightly. He also cried out "help", "help", to the surprise of fellow passengers.

The therapist told him: "Keep seated and eventually the panic attack will pass. Nothing terrible will happen to you. Whatever happens don't run off the bus now or you will find it very difficult in future to overcome this." Then as the patient calmed down and looked reassured: "That was very good. I'm glad you didn't run away during the panic attack. This shows you can cope if you try hard."' (Stern 1978:252)

Rapid exposure techniques necessarily create great anxiety in clients, and without being too dramatic about it, simple precautions are needed to ensure that people with heart ailments or respiratory problems do not attempt resolutions of this type. The best method of ensuring this is to discuss prospective cases with the GP or psychiatrist, and enlist medical cooperation at the assessment stage.

SLOW EXPOSURE AND SYSTEMATIC DESENSITIZATION

There are two kinds of systematic desensitization: *in vivo* (live practice); and imaginal, a cognitive approach using the same principles, but in imaginary form. Both forms have the same three main therapeutic ingredients: (i) a finely graded hierarchy of anxiety-producing stimuli; (ii) a relatively slow rate of progression through the stages of this hierarchy, the pace being dictated by a considerable lowering of anxiety before the next item is approached; (iii) a counter-conditioning element in the form of deep muscular relaxation. This was always an effective technique (Bandura 1969; Paul 1976), and rapid exposure methods are only coming to supersede it on the grounds that they are more efficient, more parsimonious, and produce even more reliable results (Marks 1971, 1978). Tests of the various elements of systematic desensitization, to see what components are the really potent ones and which could usefully be pruned away, suggest that the relaxation element, and the idea of a smooth progression through an incremental hierarchy, are much less important than was previously thought (Cooke 1968).

This recent research leaves us having to make three separate decisions about three essentially separate techniques.
(a) Will the client cooperate with the rapid exposure approach? (This decision should be based on a judgement of his *capabilities* as much as on his expressed intentions.)
(b) What is the optimum rate of progression towards the fear-

provoking stimulus in this client's case (remembering that he must remain in contact with it for some time)?
(c) Will deep muscular relaxation serve as a coping technique to help the client through the process of exposure?

The first point has already been covered. Turning to the second, it is important to emphasize that the rules of slow exposure are somewhat different to those of desensitization. In the latter approach, the idea was to *slide* gently along the hierarchy, keeping anxiety to a minimum and counteracting its effects in little steps. In slow exposure, the production of some anxiety is deliberate; it is the fact that the client remains in contact with the fear-provoking stimulus until its effects subside that is the active ingredient. An illustration may help to clarify this (see *Figure 7(4)*).

In the case of the agoraphobic housewife from Chapter Three an elaborate hierarchy was constructed.

Figure (7)4 Contact with fear-provoking stimuli

17	Stand alone on footbridge for ten minutes	*High anxiety and avoidance*
16	Stand alone on footbridge for three minutes	
15	Stand near footbridge for ten minutes	
14	Stand near footbridge for three minutes	
13	Stand 100 yards from footbridge	
12	Walk to town (unaccompanied)	
11	Walk to edge of town (accompanied)	
10	Walk to shops	
9	Cross the road	
8	Walk twenty yards down road	
7	Stand on pavement	
6	Stand at front gate	
5	Clean windows	
4	Put out washing	
3	Stand in garden	
2	Stand on front step	*Low anxiety and avoidance*
1	Stand in porch	

She was taught how to relax during these assignments (see page 218) and spent several sessions on each item — sometimes accompanied by the social worker, and sometimes — deliberately — not. If the next step looked too large, the progression from one to the other could be bridged by spending longer completing the task. The procedure was rather labour-intensive, and with hindsight could probably have been very foreshortened. In fact, this client never did make the footbridge during the course of the programme. She said firmly that she could easily go to town another way, so that it was not a real problem. However, she reported on follow-up that she had at last conquered this fear. Following a row with her husband, she had felt particularly determined about the issue and had marched to the bridge and stood trembling on it for ten minutes. She reported feeling very scared at first, but found that this diminished in time. A client well ahead of the established therapeutic practices of the period!

RELAXATION THERAPY

The reasons for considering this technique separately have already been given. It has specific uses for clients who have high background levels of anxiety, who suffer migraine attacks or frequent tension headaches. In addition it may be used as a technique to cope with temporary or situation-specific stress, and has a place as an adjunct to the cognitive procedures outlined above.

Procedure

(a) First the client is taught about the nature of anxiety, that it is a *bodily* phenomenon (see page 93), and that it can be brought under conscious control to a considerable extent.
(b) Next the client is taught to distinguish clearly between muscular contraction and relaxation. The procedure is that he first tenses then completly relaxes each muscle, working in sequence from toes upwards to the forehead muscle.
(c) Instruction is given in deep breathing, so that a slow, sighing respiration can be produced on cue.
(d) The client may also be encouraged to imagine pleasant or peaceful scenes and with practice should be able to use these images to induce relaxation.
(e) Relaxation training is usually given with the client lying down at first, or sitting in a comfortable chair; practice is necessary if the client is to learn to relax while going about his everyday business.
(f) In imaginal desensitization, items from a prepared hierarchy of threatening items are introduced one by one; while the client is in a relaxed state, he imagines himself coping with these in a step-by-step fashion (Wolpe and Lazarus 1966).

Relaxation tapes are widely available and clients can use these at home. It is quite important that anyone using relaxation techniques in therapy should have made use of them himself first. Several good texts are available (Madders 1978; Carkhuff 1969).

BIOFEEDBACK DEVICES

Biofeedback instruments amplify internal organic events and levels, such as heart rate, blood pressure, and skin resistance, so that to some extent they can be brought under conscious control. Behavioural management techniques exist for heart disorders such as tachycardia; also for hypertension and migraine. The device most relevant to social work is the Galvanic Skin Response (GSR) meter which gives an index of arousal (anxiety) by detecting small changes in the electrical resistance of the skin. Changes in skin resistance are part of a conditioned response, arising from the body's tendency to prepare to combat threat by rapid heat loss. This is a sort of pre-sweating response, and part of the fight/flight reaction described on page 46. Some of these machines are portable and can be worn like a hearing aid. They emit a tone, which the user attempts to reduce by whatever means he chooses – muscle relaxation, slower breathing, thinking of something else, or whatever. Such devices are cheap, costing about as much as two ineffective visits by a social worker.

Table 7(4) *Summary of main response control techniques*

technique	main features	application
modelling	Demonstration of key elements in behaviours likely to prove useful to client. Usually coupled with positive feedback on successive approximations from client.	Used for learning deficits of all kinds plus vicarious extinction of fears and phobias.
social skill training	As above, but with extra emphasis on rehearsing social and conversational skills and deciding on which occasions a given performance is appropriate.	Used for withdrawn and unconfident clients; the mentally handicapped; psychiatric patients; children, and in work with delinquents.

continued

Table 7(4) *Summary of main response control techniques* – continued

technique	main features	application
assertion training	As 'modelling' above, but with extra emphasis on fears associated with assertiveness, and on discriminating between assertive and aggressive responses.	Used with excessively shy or withdrawn individuals. Often used in groups.
self-management techniques	Designed to teach coping skills. Emphasis on helping clients to re-label their experiences and change expectations of personal efficacy and the likely outcome of their behaviours. Also teaches clients to obtain environmental support for new responses by changing contingencies.	Used in a wide range of personal problems, especially with deficits and avoidance behaviours resulting from these.
cognitive approaches	Means of identifying the personal constructs applied to self and to problems and making appropriate changes in these. Emphasis on use of positive self-statements and self-reinforcement to maintain new responses.	Useful for wide range of performance difficulties. Particularly applicable to relatively unstructured field settings. Can be used in conjunction with other programmes.
positive counter-conditioning	The introduction of a response capable of inhibiting anxiety to weaken conditioned anxiety reactions.	Used in the treatment of specific fears and anxieties.
rapid exposure	Controlled but rapid exposure to threatening stimuli maintained until anxiety extinguished.	Can be used to control excessive fears and phobias in actively cooperative clients.
slow exposure and systematic desensitization	Gradual exposure to hierarchy of threatening stimuli, initially to the accompaniment of muscular relaxation (systematic desensitization).	Used to control excessive fears and phobias where clients are unable to cooperate with rapid exposure.

technique	main features	application
		(Muscular relaxation component can be used independently to overcome stress reactions.)
biofeedback	Use of electronic instruments to amplify and display data from bodily processes such as heart rate, galvanic skin response, and blood pressure, with a view to bringing these under conscious control.	Can be used in desensitization therapy but more often employed in the treatment of stress reactions and stress-related illness.

8
Ethical considerations

Behaviour modification has a bad name in some quarters. Over the years it has attracted a lot of critical attention from philosophers, lawyers, and journalists – more than any other psychological therapy in the extensive present-day repertoire (Holland 1978; Epstein 1975). There are two main reasons for this interest: (i) behaviour modification is a visible process; what is done is uniquely open to inspection and criticism; (ii) behaviour modification works relatively well; it has practical, tangible effects, and anything that succeeds in changing people raises certain questions. Change for good or ill? Whose idea of change? By what right are people being changed? In this sense, the critical clamour that has greeted the development of the behaviour therapies, and which irritates many *aficionados*, is really a mark of respect. If it were not a potent method, no one would bother. Because it is potent, it has a potential for ill as well as good, and so merits scrutiny. But while the use of behavioural methods certainly does give rise to ethical questions, these are not, by and large, issues qualitatively different from those that could be raised about any type of therapeutic endeavour. It is the success of the approach that draws the fire of critics; the fact that the target is in full view is what makes it so tempting.

In this chapter I would like to try and categorize, and respond to, the commonly raised objections to the use of a behavioural approach by social workers, as well as discussing one or two worries of my own.

The question of control

It is above all the idea of the *control* of human behaviour that raises the ethical hackles of social workers. Partly this is a sentimental reaction, made on behalf of clients who have more than enough controls in their lives as it is, but in part it may just be what Leon Festinger (1957) has called 'dissonance reduction'. Let me begin with this point. The worst accusation that can be made about social workers, in their own book, is that they are 'agents of social control'. This view (advanced mainly by the salaried revolutionaries in our midst) usually produces a blanket denial, and social workers have tried hard to get the charge dropped altogether. A more constructive approach would be to set about discriminating between those types of social control which we might well be *pleased* to be identified with: the supervision of offenders as an alternative to prison, perhaps; protecting the rights of minorities; or protecting the relatively powerless by controlling those who threaten them.

There are two powerful fallacies at work here.
(a) The idea that social work intervention (or for that matter psychological intervention in general) is such a powerful medium of change that, even in the face of client resistance or disinterest, *great* moral restraint is required in its application.
(b) The idea that social workers and other therapists introduce controls and liberty-endangering influences, where none existed before.

In the light of much of the available research, point (a) could be seen as a case of advanced self-flattery, hence my point about dissonance-reduction. My own survey of the field of social influence (Sheldon 1978b) leads me to the conclusion that change of the kind that most therapists seek to produce is rather harder to come by than this view suggests. Furthermore, apart from certain important exceptions (cases where substantial amounts of material aid are, or might be thought to be, dependent upon compliance, or certain residential settings where clients are literally 'captive' and dependent on staff for the meeting of their basic needs), the scales are heavily loaded *against* the would-be influencer. (Alan Sillitoe's *The Loneliness of the Long-Distance Runner* shows this beautifully.) In reality, clients who are not persuaded of the need for social work help have very many ways of avoiding it. I shall return to the exceptions cited later.

First, I would like to argue a more general point, namely, that concern about the occasional unwanted side-effects of therapeutic good intent needs to be balanced by an equal concern that the 'goods' should be delivered to clients – as agreed, and within reasonable time limits. In my view this concern should replace self-aggrandizement and titillation of the 'dare we intervene' variety, as the major cause of heart-searching and hand-wringing in the profession. The following comment from Bandura, although addressed primarily to the faint-hearted among psychotherapists, has a wider relevance:

> 'Discussions of the moral implications of behavioural control almost always emphasize the Machiavellian role of change agents and the self-protective manoeuvres of controlees. The fact that most people enter treatment only as a last resort, hoping to modify patterns of behaviour that are seriously distressful to themselves or to others, is frequently overlooked. To the extent that therapists engage in moral agonizing, they should fret more about their own limited effectiveness in helping persons willing to undergo hardships to achieve desired changes, rather than in fantasizing about their potential powers. The tendency to exaggerate the power of behavioural control by psychological methods alone, irrespective of willing cooperation by the client, and the failure to recognize the reciprocal nature of interpersonal control, obscures both the ethical issues and the nature of social influence processes.'
>
> (Bandura 1969:85)

As for the second fallacy, about exercising control where none existed before, the standard behaviourist line is already familiar: that we are each bombarded daily by countless controlling influences and that to see control as a game of billiards, where only one influence at a time operates, is indeed to take a naive and mechanistic view of human behaviour. It is more sensible to see the therapist as entering, and *possibly* affecting, an already active field or a network of contingencies. Bandura again:

> 'All behaviour is inevitably controlled, and the operation of psychological laws cannot be suspended by romantic conceptions of human behaviour, any more than indignant rejection of the law of gravity as antihumanistic can stop people from falling.'
>
> (Bandura 1969:85)

In which case, given that lots of things are already happening, *not* intervening is an influential decision just as much as intervening is.

Ethical considerations 225

The decision not to intervene, or excessive procrastination about the issues raised by intervention, means that the behaviour of the individuals concerned is governed by forces which the therapist has decided *not* to try to control; not to replace with other, hopefully more benign influences; and which he has *not* taught the client how better to control for himself. Sometimes it is right, or judicious, or necessary, to stay out of a case, but this should be recognized as to some extent an abandonment of the client to *other* controls, and not as a simple decision not to seek control. There are no real vacuums in social life and some influence or other will prevail. Therapeutic 'sins of commission' must therefore be weighed carefully against equally damning 'sins of omission'.

CASE ILLUSTRATIONS

I can think of two cases which illustrate clearly some of the dilemmas mentioned above. In the first I was asked, as duty social worker, to interview a tearful fifteen-year-old schoolgirl and her Physical Education teacher. The teacher thought that her student, in writing rather mild-sounding love letters to her, was demonstrating 'lesbian tendencies', which needed to be nipped in the bud. The obvious thing to do here was nothing – at least nothing beyond telling the teacher not to be so silly. But the effect of this would undoubtedly have been to produce further embarrassment for the pupil and another referral to an agency more likely to view 'crushes' in fifteen-year-olds as evidence of psycho-pathology. Here is what was done.

– The teacher was visited at school and reassured about her worries. She had genuine doubts about possible allegations of sexual misconduct, and so had decided to pre-empt such a possibility by the referral. These worries were later put to the headmistress who in turn reassured her colleague.
– A female social worker was assigned to the student and did the following. She made it clear to the student as reassuringly as possible that the allegations were a gross over-reaction, but that they could, nonetheless, still have unwanted consequences for her. A series of appointments was made to discuss the student's sexual worries – she tended to avoid boys because of a fear of sexual entanglements (her mother, a widow, was unusually strict concerning dates).
– Some appointments were devoted to: the issue of contact with

boys; coping with unwanted advances; ways of discussing things with mother in an unacrimonious way; coping with affection for an older woman, and expressing this in ways likely to prove acceptable to her.

When the case came up for discussion at a case conference soon after referral, a number of colleagues favoured leaving it alone altogether, and taking a strong line with the school authorities. There were also considerable misgivings as to whether something called the girl's 'naturally developing sexual identity' was being messed about with by nasty, conformist, and probably male chauvinist behaviour therapists. My own view was that to do nothing would be to abandone the girl to her fears, and to the fears of the school staff. Something had to be done and to be seen to be done. The client kept every appointment, continued at the school, improved her relationship with her mother, and no further referrals occurred.

The next case illustrates the opposite point. Here it would have been better never to have used behaviour modification at all – except that it did clearly reveal the problem. The main facts of the case are as follows.

– Jane McDonald, aged twelve, was referred for social work help by a child guidance psychiatrist. Her problem (apparently) was soiling and smearing faeces on the walls of her bedroom. A physical examination had revealed no organic problems and a number of psychiatric outpatient interviews had been conducted – producing blank denials that anything was wrong. The psychiatrist suspected unspecified 'problems in the family'.

– An interview with the family, including a five-year-old sister, produced a series of shoulder-shrugging responses to questions about how they all got on together. Interviews with Jane produced similar expressions of polite surprise. Her story was that she just couldn't help soiling and 'didn't know what came over her' to make her smear. She was punished physically by parents, as well as by being sent to her room, having toys taken away, and being prevented from watching TV. She considered this 'fair'.

– Enquiries outside the home gave quite a different picture. Jane was apparently a model pupil at school, a keen member of various school clubs, a girl guide, and regular Sunday school attender. She was described by all as polite, helpful, keen, and mature beyond her years.

- Baseline recording revealed an average four times a week rate of soiling, but after that the case had to proceed very much on a 'hit and miss' basis. A behaviour modification scheme was devised – directed purely at the soiling and smearing. The main components of this scheme were: (i) A differential reinforcement scheme withdrawing attention from soiling, with clear periods being reinforced by trips out alone with father to the cinema, swimming baths, and so on. (This initially caused problems of jealousy with younger sister but a simple star chart, aimed at improving her reading performance, removed this completely.); (ii) A response-cost scheme. Jane was to clean up her own mess and remain in her room for thirty minutes following a soiling incident; (iii) Polite prompts about visiting the lavatory were given at the danger times identified in the baseline records.
- For two weeks the scheme worked extremely well and the soiling rate fell to one incident in the first week and two in the second. In the third it shot up to seven and stayed there for another three weeks.
- At the end of this time I was telephoned by a very secretive-sounding Mr McDonald, who asked to see me 'in strictest confidence'. He came into the office as if being pursued by secret policemen and told the following story. The couple had been having severe marital difficulties for the past few years – following an affair between Mr McDonald and a female employee at work, which his wife had found out about. He described a catalogue of rows, badgerings, and humiliations, the latter extended into the sexual sphere, his wife having developed an appetite for degrading him as a prelude to occasional sex. Mr McDonald described himself as a 'prisoner' – unable to leave because of what would happen to Jane. The child had always been close to him and was now being used to punish him. Mrs McDonald apparently took great pleasure in punishing her and deeply resented the time she spent alone with her father. Mrs McDonald had followed them on two occasions, and had made references to her husband's 'unfatherly and unmanly interest' in the child. It also transpired that Mrs McDonald had been using, and illicitly extending, the behaviour modification scheme to make her daughter's life a misery from the moment when she saw it begin to work. Furthermore, the beatings had continued alongside the scheme, as had depriving Jane of the things she valued most – her girl guide and youth club activities.

Everyone in the family had been sworn to secrecy, but Mr McDonald felt now that he had to tell someone. He then tried to swear me to secrecy with the warning: 'She'll kill me if she finds out I've been here.'

- I had already explained to Mr McDonald that while I could be discreet, I could not meet his request for complete confidentiality if this meant an infringement of the rights of his daughter. He returned to work in trepidation. A private interview with Jane was arranged at school where she repeated her father's stories of cruelty at the hands of her mother – amplified by the behaviour modification scheme, which mother had been using as an excuse to punish her further as part of the 'cure' for her problem. Jane then expressed the wish to live away from home as soon as possible. A lengthy and very stormy family interview followed where the whole story was uncovered.
- Jane was brought into care and sent to a residential school, which she enjoyed and did well at. Mr and Mrs McDonald were referred to the Marriage Guidance Council for help, but decided to split up after one interview. This they did with considerable acrimony. Mrs McDonald went to live with her mother, and took her younger daughter. Mr McDonald found a flat and lived alone. He saw Jane frequently and their good relationship was maintained, but Jane refused to go and live with him, preferring the security that was hers already.

The lessons in this case for me were as follows. (i) That any therapeutic device can be used for good or ill, but that behaviour modification, with its control over rewarding and punishing consequences, perhaps needs special care when it is being used to modify the behaviour of those in generally inferior power positions (this point is discussed in more detail below). (ii) Things are not always what they seem, nor are the people referred as 'the client' necessarily the right targets of change. (iii) It is possible to be fooled, as I certainly was here; clients do lie sometimes, despite our professional inclination to see them as misunderstood or defensive rather than wicked. Mr and Mrs McDonald certainly needed help. They were offered it, by the psychiatrist, by me, and by the National Marriage Guidance Council, but, except for a brief foray with the latter organization, they refused to take up the offers. Mrs McDonald's life goal was nothing less than the complete degradation of her husband, who had been unfaithful to her, and (in her eyes) held her up to ridicule. Her chosen means of achieving this was by exploiting her husband's rather weak character and tormenting the person closest to him – his daughter – while he was forced to watch. For a time the behaviour modification programme helped her to do this on a really 'scientific' basis – ostensibly for the child's own good. I could argue here that 'at least the scheme brought everything out into the open', had the reader not already been sternly cautioned against the dangers of *ex post facto* reinterpretation of goals in an earlier chapter.

Psychological techniques: their uses and abuses

Whenever therapeutic regimes go sour, the argument is put forward that the *techniques* are morally neutral, but are abused by the people who apply them. This argument can be used to justify all sorts of dubious practices – from indiscriminate arms sales, to the development of germ warfare facilities. As an argument it is technically correct (water can be used for drinking and for drowning people in), but it is morally unconvincing. A different ethical standard needs to be applied, that is, does a particular technology do anything to *encourage* wrongdoing – to make it easier, or more tempting? Our concern here is the degree to which problems are *structured into* a given approach. Are the contingencies which make up the system more likely to shape behaviour towards evil rather than good, in the range of settings where the system tends to be used?

If serious problems do arise from the use of a particular approach, then we need to examine the extent to which these problems are *regularly accompanying* factors; effects which cluster around this particular type of programme or setting. For example, if formal behaviour modification schemes were to be used in juvenile detention centres, were regularly abused across the range of such settings, and were held by the inmates to be a repressive tool rather than a therapeutic opportunity, then it would be pointless and naive just to argue that behaviour modification *need not* be so applied. The question would be, does it *lend* itself to abuse in such settings, for instance, by giving the seal of scientific respectability to what is really crude coercion and maltreatment? (See 'Community Care' 2 August 1980.) We also need to examine to what extent the approach concentrates power without safeguard, almost as a necessary condition of its effective operation. If it does, then it may be unsafe in any hands and a regularly recurring pattern of abuse in different settings would confirm this as a serious problem.

Let us try now to measure behaviour modification, as generally practised, against this little template of moral sufficiency. Showing up clearly on the plus side is the fact that behaviour modification contains its own inbuilt safeguards against hard-to-detect wrongdoing. Its techniques are action-based; they centre on the client *doing* things differently, or more or less often. It is therefore very hard to explain away either the aims or the results of behaviour therapy in obscure or euphemistic terminology. Both ends and means are open to inspection – which is certainly not true of many other therapeutic approaches. Thus, whether a particularly objectionable 'means' is a regularly accompanying feature of programmes directed to particular problems, or to a particular client group, is open to scrutiny. Similarly, since the 'ends' being pursued will be couched in behavioural terms, they are less equivocal and less likely to be interpreted differently by the clients, the therapist, and by other interested parties. It is possible therefore to have an open debate as to why, if it is such an effective procedure, electrical aversion therapy is used mainly with homosexuals. Why not more often with other groups wishing to lose parts of their behavioural repertoire, if the moral arguments against this practice are as weak as some authors would have us believe (Brewer and Lait 1980)?

Behaviour modification has a large and vigorously pursued literature testifying to its humane and tangibly effective application across a wide range of problems. The means by which these results are obtained are always an explicit part of any discussion. This allows us to see that the approach has occasionally been misused. However, with many of the reports of misuse, we are left with a strong impression that the manifest intention of those in charge was to punish and subjugate those in their power. The idea of behaviour modification is brought in later, as a weak justification for this ill-treatment.

Nevertheless, behaviour modification has gained a reputation from *somewhere* for overdetachment. Perhaps the – sometimes rather cool – reactions of professionally secure and legitimate therapists to such malpractices has helped to reinforce this image? Consider this example:

'Cotter (1967), in his report of the uses of operant conditioning techniques in a Vietnamese hospital, found that after twenty electro-convulsive shock treatments, delivered as negative reinforcement, there were still non-responders. He found that three days total starvation produced 100 per cent response rate. Perhaps even these patients wouldn't have responded if they had known that discharge to the community was, for them, work in an Army-defended farm, surrounded by the Viet-Cong!'

(Hall and Baker 1973:255)

In making a judgement about the extent to which behaviourism encourages this sort of thing, we have to begin by weighing the tremendous good achieved by the application of these procedures against the few cases of actual harm. From this total we must then subtract some constant based on the human propensity for wickedness – with or without behaviour modification to use as a justification for this. What remains is down to us, and requires the very closest consideration.

In arguing thus, I am aware that there are genuine problems in trying to decide what is contingency management, what legitimate control, and what illegitimate coercion. In fact, there is no clear line of demarcation separating response-cost programmes from coercion, which is why behaviour modification is regularly linked in the media with *Clockwork Orange* fantasies and with brainwashing. It is silly just to deny *any* connection. To take an extreme case again: certain of the techniques used by the Chinese and North Koreans on captured American prisoners in the early 1950s would be recognizable to most behaviourists. They were used, of course, in the context of dire threats, either explicitly made or implicitly ever-present, and the victims knew of – and in some cases had already experienced – serious maltreatment (Farber, Harlow, and West 1966). Nevertheless the theoretical root principles, so misused then, were greatly amplified versions of the ones described in this book.

A system for discouraging aggressive behaviour among the pupils at a community school by assigning 'costs' to this behaviour (no privileges, home visits, access to recreational facilities, and so forth) is a form of coercion, albeit for a desirable purpose. The decisions about such programmes have to be made on utilitarian lines. To what extent do the rights of other people not to be physically abused require this sort of protection?

Two further points can be added to those made above. First, critics should ask to what extent clients are expected to *learn* something from a programme. Our ethical concern should increase, the more the scheme is used just as a device for *controlling* behaviour. A good test of this issue is whether the main features of a programme are faded, for individuals or for groups, once unwanted behaviour is brought under control (see page 60). In addition, critics should ask to what extent the behaviour of clients is shaped, so that it is brought under the control of the usual, socially acceptable stimuli. If no attempt is made to do these things, then the workers in charge must have little confidence that their scheme is anything other than an artificial device, which will not generalize to natural, or even to less rigid settings – where different and less easily manipulated contingencies operate.

It *is* possible, however, to conceive of a behaviour modification programme being used to 'clear the ground' for another type of therapeutic or educational emphasis – for example by removing disruptive or interfering behaviour that is preventing new learning (Bucher and Lovaas 1968). But, once again, the acid test is whether problematic behaviours are eventually brought under the control of this second treatment approach, or whether behaviour generated by this treatment approach successfully displaces unwanted behaviour.

The second point to be made is that the greater the emphasis on punishment, response-cost, and negative reinforcement, the more closely we need to look at a programme with ethics as our main concern. At some stage, and ideally on a concurrent basis, new behaviours need to be taught, and potentially useful responses reinforced and shaped. If this stage is long delayed, or occupies only a minor role in the scheme, then, generally speaking, the scheme is more to do with control than therapy. Here is a case example which shows some of the difficulties of distinguishing between these two aims.

CASE ILLUSTRATION

– Mrs Brown, a seventy-four-year-old widow and resident of an old persons' home, kept coming into the Senior Care Assistant's office at awkward times and staying there for lengthy periods. Baseline recording showed this to occur on average eight times a day. (This surprised staff, who thought it was much more.) Her visits were disruptive of certain types of work, they interrupted meetings, report writing, interviews with other residents and relatives, and so on. Furthermore, Mrs Brown was getting herself a bad reputation. Other residents would sometimes shout and jeer when they saw her taking one of her trips to the office, and on one occasion a junior

staff member had to be formally reprimanded for returning her to the dayroom rather roughly.
- An investigation of what occurred when Mrs Brown came into the office revealed: (i) that she would repeatedly ask the same question about her relatives (there were none locally and she received no visits); (ii) that most staff would repeatedly discuss the position with her and then escort her back to the dayroom. Occasionally they would remonstrate with her for repeated interruptions.

The following programme was devised, on the assumption that it would be better for all concerned if Mrs Brown limited her visits to the office, and also that the behaviour was probably being reinforced with attention that was legitimately available to her in other forms. Staff were therefore advised to respond politely, but briefly, to Mrs Brown's interruptions on the first occasion before lunch, and on the first occasion after lunch. On every other occasion Mrs Brown was to be asked to return to the dayroom, and five minutes later a staff member would attend to her. So far the programme was designed mainly to *control* behaviour for the sake of hard-pressed staff. However, in addition to this part of the scheme, Mrs Brown was to be approached by staff in the dayroom at random intervals to talk about matters of concern to her – writing a letter to a friend living some distance away, for instance, or talking about old times. Eventually this regular contact was augmented with a schoolgirl volunteer, and the problem of interruptions disappeared.

This latter part of the programme was more directed to Mrs Brown's own needs and balanced the earlier concern to run the home with reasonable efficiency for the good of all the residents.

The issue of control is not easily resolved and the two aims can be much more jumbled up together than in the example cited above – as in probation work, or work in secure treatment units. For many of its recommended approaches behaviour modification requires a fair degree of control over events and mediation, to reinforce quickly or to apply consequences firmly. The way in which this tension between therapy and control is managed is at the crux of many of the ethical decisions we need to make about behaviour modification. Another version of the same problem is examined below.

Motivational issues

A frequently reported criticism of behavioural approaches is that they only work well with 'motivated clients'. When an opponent of this view gives examples from operant work with clinically institutionalized mental patients, then the charge is usually amended to one of repression of the helpless. What can be said about this issue of motivation and control, apart from the usual 'you can't win with some people' brand of petulancy seen in some behavioural textbooks?

Let us begin by analysing just what is meant by the statement: 'Behavioural approaches only work with the well motivated.' The implication here is that there are lots of other therapeutic strategies which work very well with 'the unmotivated' (that is to say with people who, through fear, habit, or reasoning, decide that they want little or nothing to do with therapy and therapists). This is nonsense. Whether people decide to cooperate or not depends in the last analysis on their weighing up the benefits and the costs of cooperating against the benefits and the costs of not cooperating. Or – remembering classical conditioning – it can depend on what they associate with the things on offer and the way they are being offered. Potential clients may lack information on, or may misunderstand, many things about what is being offered and the problems of the status quo. Attempts can be made to correct these misapprehensions, to persuade, entice, reinforce, shape, beg, or cajole the client into cooperation. But if at the end of this he still stands firmly within the ranks of the *un*motivated, then there is little that can or should be done on the therapeutic front. The idea that by some subtle and hard-to-write-down method of verbal hypnosis the client can be wooed out of his recalcitrance is hard to take seriously.

It is the business of social workers and others to lay down clear views and guidelines for clients, to enhance, within reason, the attractiveness of the solutions they are putting forward, and to work to modify the environmental contingencies which may be maintaining the status quo. When these approaches have been tried, but the attempt to build a working relationship has failed, then the social worker has probably done all that he can. If society through legislation, or the agency through regulation, insists on continuing contact – as it often does – then it is vitally important that no one should misunderstand, or be able to misconstrue, the nature and purpose of this enforced contact. In many cases of juvenile delinquency, where courts grant Supervision Orders attaching social workers to clients, what is done will be just that – the client and his living group will be *supervised*, looked over, watched; they will have their activities monitored and assessed. In many cases nothing else is possible, and the wider community has its rights too. The danger comes here from the distinctions between these two different kinds of social work becoming blurred, both in the thinking and doings of social workers and their clients, and in the view of a society only too willing to salve its conscience by seeing the need for inspection as an opportunity for something 'more constructive' – in other words, therapy. Sometimes, when people decide they have nothing to lose by cooperating, there is such an opportunity, and sometimes there is not. By pretending that there almost *always* is (reports to magistrates' courts are usually very optimistic on this point) social workers are making four different mistakes.

(a) They are giving to the community a greatly exaggerated view of their unaided powers of influence, and the expectations to match.

(b) They are putting the profession time and again in the position of having to excuse itself for things over which – were it not for the point made in (a) – it could not reasonably be expected to have control. (No one likes a moaner, still less a moaner who blames his patron for giving him the commissions he asked for.)

(c) By failing to discriminate accurately those occasions when *mainly* inspection rather than *mainly* therapy is required or is feasible, they are bringing about a considerable waste of resources. This means that social workers are tied up for longer periods of time than may be necessary, and that resources are channelled into provided quasi-therapeutic services when they could be better used to finance improvements in social policy.

(d) By blurring issues of therapy and control or even therapy and punishment, social workers are sometimes a party to the infliction of greater distress. There is a certain dignity in being punished for acknowledged wrong-doing, which is lacking in regimes that are an unholy mixture of therapy and punishment. In other words, sometimes the things done in the name of 'helping' are more painful and degrading than the things done in the name of simple retribution, where the individual is held to be responsible for his actions. This is different from 'entirely to blame for his actions', hence the concept of mitigation. Szasz (1971) has done much to force these issues into public view in the field of psychiatry, but his views have a much wider relevance.

The effect of all this is not to decry therapeutic endeavour – quite the reverse – ideally it should be seen as a special benefit. It is, after all, difficult to do, taxing on both parties, something that demands time, energy, skill, and scarce resources, and therefore something that has to be done *with* people not *to* them. It is therefore, perhaps, something that would benefit from a little isolation from our other activities. I am not arguing here for a return to the bad old days of preciousness about therapy, when it was practised by an élite who did little else, and who regarded fuel bills and bad housing as epiphenomena. I am arguing for greater discrimination about who gets therapy (in other words, those who want it and can use it) and for equal, if different, energies to be spent on other worthwhile activities. People have a right not to be 'helped' and this important principle has always had a distinguished body of advocates:

> 'The only purpose for which power can be rightfully exercised over any member of a civilised community, against his will, is to prevent harm to others. His own good, either physical or moral, is not a sufficient warrant. He cannot rightfully be compelled to do or forbear because it will be better for him to do so, because it will make him happier, because, in the opinions of others, to do so would be wise, or even right. There are good reasons for remonstrating with him, or persuading him, or entreating him, but not for compelling him, or visiting him with any evil in case he do otherwise. To justify that, the conduct from which it is desired to deter him must be calculated to produce evil to someone else. The only part of the conduct of any one, for which he is answerable to society, is that which concerns others. In the part which merely concerns himself, his independence is, of right, absolute.'
>
> (John Stuart Mill 1859: 73)

This is a much tougher view to hold now than in 1859. In complex industrialized societies, people are much more inter-connected and inter-dependent, and the line between 'evil to oneself' and 'evil to others' is much harder to draw. Is the contemporary glue sniffer harming only himself by his habit, or do his actions contaminate others? In any case, Mill put forward many exceptions to his rule – for instance children, the insane, and the mentally infirm – and some of these categories demand, but at times defy, close definition. However, although this principle of not doing things to people to 'help' them if they do not themselves wish it is hedged around by all sorts of marginal cases, and has been nibbled away at the edges by bevies of philosophers, it stands nevertheless as a profound truth, a clearly

Ethical considerations 237

visible light to steer ourselves by. There may be all sorts of short-term justifications for changing course from it, but in the long term we do so at our peril.

Therapy should always be on offer where we have some knowledge and experience to back up our expectations of a positive result, or where, with the client's consent, we are conducting a genuine experiment. But it should be something for which clients have to 'sign up'. There should always be a contractual phase to it, a period of explicit negotiation about purposes and desired outcome. Where this is not possible (as in extremes of psychological infirmity, or in the case of very young children), we must be guided by those who care for the individual, make the best judgements we can, and try to render ourselves as publicly accountable for these decisions as possible. Outside this category, where no contract can be agreed either explicitly or implicitly, then the persons concerned are not clients in the strict sense of the word (the very notion of a compulsory *client* is paradoxical). They may still be people we need to see, even that we have been put 'in charge of' and they may still (we would hope) be treated with an exemplary and distinctive kindliness and concern. But we must not delude ourselves that we can help everyone, either with behaviour modification or with any other approach.

This once said, it is a dangerous thing to see freedom and ethical purity as virtues that flourish only when there is an apparent absence of control. An absence of proper control in the case discussed on page 226 simply allowed Mrs McDonald free rein to persecute her daughter.

The special case of institutional and residential treatment

Any ethical concerns we have about the use of behaviour modification techniques in general are likely to be multiplied when we consider their use in residential settings – particularly in closed or secure units. Much excellent work has been in these fields, but together with the penal field in the US, they have also been the setting for one or two of the more disturbing examples of misuse. Here is one critic's summary of the distorting factors which can affect programmes in such settings:

> 'Guards reinforce prisoners; nurses reinforce patients; and teachers reinforce students. The fear of manipulative control is well founded

when a professional-client relationship is lacking. Subjects of these behaviour control systems are not clients. Behaviour modifiers in prisons are fundamentally and inescapably responsible to the warden or Bureau of Correction, not the prisoner; in the classroom, they are responsible to the principal or Board of Education, not to the students. Put simply, today's token economies support established power structures.' (Holland 1975)

But it can be argued that because of the public nature of behaviour modification, we know of even these extreme cases from closed settings, and can do something to discourage similar excesses elsewhere. My own view is that the field of residential social work offers special opportunities for the application of behavioural techniques, but that, alongside these, special safeguards are required. First the opportunities, which derive from the following features.

(a) Behaviour modification is a labour-intensive method, particularly at the outset. Therefore, to have staff and clients together in the same locale is a distinct advantage. The residential social worker does not have to wait until the next visit to see that things are not going according to plan and that some adjustment is necessary.

(b) The arrangement of consequences is a key part of the behaviour therapist's function – either as part of an operant programme, or to provide back-up encouragement for modelling and other response control activities. Many field-based programmes fail because reinforcement or 'consequation' do not follow immediately on the performance of particular behaviour. In residential work – despite the many pressures on staff – having clients in close proximity ensures that this can be done more easily. Therefore more detailed and complex programmes can be mounted in these settings.

(c) Special facilities are required for certain types of programmes – 'time-out' rooms, playrooms where the client can be observed, 'mock-ups' of different situations in which the client experiences problems, and so on. Generally, these are more readily available in residential settings.

(d) Given that the necessary expertise exists, *in-situ* supervision is easier to arrange. Staff can more readily gain access to the person in charge of the project. This is a major problem in field settings where access is limited and often delayed. Now that basic courses

Ethical considerations 239

are more readily available, the next urgent priority – if we take our own theories about the importance of support for new behaviours seriously – is the setting up of supervision facilities for relative newcomers to the discipline. Residential social work is by no means immune to the administrative problems this poses, but the excellent record of certain residential programmes in providing supervision for junior staff makes the situation look rather more hopeful.

Now for some of the problems.

(a) Residential settings provide opportunities for considerably greater *control* over the behaviour of clients than elsewhere in social work. As indicated above, such opportunities can be used for good or ill. However, in line with our previous discussion about 'structured-in' problems, we need to decide whether these exist to any great extent in the application of behavioural techniques in this type of setting. My own view is that a number of built-in problems do exist, and that – while they are not insurmountable – they always need to be guarded against. The first of these is the tendency of large institutions in particular to try and take short cuts with residents, to try and rub the awkward corners off them, and to socialize them into the ways of the institution. This process of *institutionalization* is not usually any individual's specific intention; it happens because of the problems thrown up by having a large group of individuals living in the same space. Individuality has to be sacrificed sometimes, just to keep the place ticking over. To this problem can be added our experience of what happens when the real therapeutic goals of a residential agency get subverted by the interests of administrative neatness, order, 'discipline', and so on – described so well by Goffman (1968). Add to this the social work phenomenon which I call 'risk management' (making sure above all things that the Department's name stays out of the newspapers), and we have a well prepared seedbed for therapeutic tyranny. It need not occur; it usually doesn't; but the conditions are just right.

When behavioural techniques are used in settings which show a tendency to have these problems, they can very easily come to be misused – particularly at the face-to-face staff levels. We must expect this: it has happened with psychotropic drugs and ECT in mental hospitals, and with the 'remission for good behaviour' system in prisons. Misuse in this context has three main effects. (i) It provides a really detailed, scientific means of ensuring conformity for conformity's sake. Unless care is taken clients can be systematically shaped into institutional behaviour, rather than into behaviours likely to be of use in the outside world. (ii) Institutional control is dressed up as harsh therapeutic necessity. (iii) Where residents can see no distinction between behavioural control for internal, institutional reasons, and behavioural control for good, individual, therapeutic reasons, the system is brought readily into disrepute. Although its main requirements may be met so as to obtain rewards and privileges, these behaviours will not become a permanent part of the individual's repertoire (see Festinger 1964). Token economy schemes in residential centres for delinquents are often paid lip-service to by youngsters, but any influence such schemes might have is more than countermanded by the contingencies which apply in the under-life of the institution. It is just possible that new habits may be acquired and reinforced under such circumstances – but rather unlikely. More powerful controls lie with the peer group and, unless the treatment scheme has gained respect or toleration at this level, it has little chance of success in the long term.

(b) The way out of some of these difficulties is not so straightforward as it sometimes is in fieldwork settings. The obvious solution of obtaining the 'free consent' of clients who are on the receiving end of a regime needs a second look. First, what is 'free consent'? For any semblance of a contractual relationship between parties to exist, there has to be some semblance of equality between them. The danger is that, given the considerable disparity in actual taken-for-granted power that exists between staff and clients in certain types of residential institution, compliance can easily be mistaken for consent. Where cooperation with a therapeutic regime is – or could be thought by the client to be – linked to his standing or security, to the meeting of his need for food, shelter, human contact, affection, approval, and stimulation, then a 'free choice' is virtually impossible. An *unconstrained* choice probably does not exist in nature anyway, and we would be fools not to make our therapeutic programmes attractive just in case anyone joined in for the wrong reasons. Perhaps the best we can do here is to argue for an absence of deliberate sanctions surrounding the decision whether to participate or not. But the problem remains to some extent. Here are my own suggestions. (i) Where tangible rewards and inducement are used they must always be over and above the basic civilized provision. (ii) Where possible, behavioural programmes should be *modular* rather than all-embracing (schemes which embrace every aspect of the client's life and which rob him of any 'breathing space' are a temptation in residential settings because of the 'captive audience effect', referred to above). (iii) Clients should have to commit themselves formally to behaviour change programmes in some way, knowing clearly that they need not do so, and that basic residential and/or educational facilities are theirs by right anyway. This point needs to be explained carefully – it may on occasions make programmes more attractive if they are difficult to get into! (iv) Time should be spent in explaining the purposes behind the scheme and, where feasible, residents should have a hand in managing it themselves. Where clients take part in setting targets for themselves and their peers, these are more likely to be met. Many residential settings have regular meetings and councils, made up of staff and clients, to discuss the running of the place they are in. There is no reason why, given appropriate technical advice, these bodies should not be encouraged to play a part in designing therapeutic programmes too. Where this happens there is less likelihood that schemes become identified solely with staff interests and complied with for the wrong reasons.

(c) Large-scale operant schemes in residential work, where a wide array of contingencies is managed solely by staff, can easily come to reinforce feelings of 'them and us' in the recipients. Discipline which is *imposed* as an external force is not necessarily learnt from. Understanding is vitally important, not only at an ethical level, but at a technical level too. Some behaviour therapists have in the past been guilty of using their subjects for what looks more like advanced human puppetry than therapy. Where clients understand in detail what they are being encouraged to do and why, then results tend to be superior, both at the acquisition and the generalization stage (Ayllon and Azrin 1964).

The present trend discernible in residential work, away from the use of operant schemes in isolation towards combinations of methods, including social skill training and modelling, is to be warmly welcomed. There is far less chance that schemes of this type, which have an educational rather than a controlling emphasis, will become distorted by the pressures of communal life.

But what of those clients and patients who are ill equipped to make choices about participating in therapy? It may be that we sometimes underestimate the decision-making ability of our clients, whether they are children or long-stay psychiatric patients, and could try harder to win genuine consent. But having said that, we are still faced with a large group of potential clients who for one reason or another cannot be fully involved. The only possible answer here is that someone has to decide for them. The only possible criteria for evaluating such decisions are: whether they are reasonable; whether they are publicly made, with due consultation with other interested parties; whether the therapist would be happy if in similar circumstances similar decisions were made about a member of his own family (an acid test); whether they have the effect of trying to promote independence, self-sufficiency, the ability of the client to be in better control of himself and his environment; and whether they result in an enhancement of the range of responses he is capable of making. Of these criteria the most important are that decisions should be clear, unambiguous, and open to inspection and criticism. All the rest flow from these and are dependent upon them.

Deciding who is likely to benefit from behaviour modification

If the advocates of therapeutic and clinical approaches in social work are guilty of anything, then it is of giving insufficient thought to their choice of targets. The tendency of social workers to respond unthinkingly to someone else's administrative categories – that is, to *cases* rather than to problems – has rightly come under attack lately (Pincus and Minahan 1973). The 'integrated' or 'unitary' approach to social work and social work training is very valuable indeed, and a much needed corrective to the old reflex of attempting to change the person who happens to get referred – as if this were always a rational and uncritical process. In this way, children with educational problems, chronic truants, hospital patients, debtors, and the physically handicapped have all been the recipients of therapeutic social work services, when in many cases the solution to their problems lay elsewhere – with the school, the hospital, the social security office, or wherever. A key element in the recent literature is the need

Ethical considerations 243

for a clearer definition of 'client' and 'target'. The client is the beneficiary of what is done, the targets the person or persons who need to change if the benefits are to be forthcoming.

The criticism that behaviour modification is usually undertaken with the poor and the weak – people in reality suffering at the hands of *others* – is only partly justified. In fact it is a criticism of clinical social work as a whole rather than of any specific methods employed. The clinical model has tended to suggest that whoever comes forward should be helped, regardless of class, race, or creed, and it has thought of itself as democratic in this respect. A genuinely democratic approach would place much greater emphasis on deciding with the client what is the just, the appropriate, and the propitious point for intervention. In its concentration on environmental factors (usually the behaviour of other people), behaviour modification already does this, and this approach actively counteracts the tendency to see the problem as belonging entirely to the person complaining of it.

Feelings about the imposition of techniques

There is a certain arrogance about intervening in the life of another person, never better expounded than by Barbara Wootton (1959), who argued that if social workers could really do the things claimed for them in various definitions of their role, then their skills were wasted on the poor and troubled, and, for the good of all, should be applied immediately to politicians and world leaders! Social work has always been well aware of this sort of thing – arguably too well aware of it – and the literature positively oozes with cautionary phrases about 'starting where the client is', noting carefully his version of events, not offering advice except as a last resort (Hollis 1964). As discussed in Chapter One, this over-reaction and hedging round what social workers are supposed to actually *do* about someone's problem can leave us with the impression that social work is meant to serve the same function as a warm bath – good for all sorts of aches and pains, so long as they amount to nothing very serious or specific (see Sheldon 1978b).

To social workers raised in this way, behaviour modification can seem a bit brash and 'pushy'. However, if this book has a central theme, then it is to advocate a soft-hearted, but not necessarily soft-headed approach to helping. This is not just a call for a simple shift in attitude; developing such an approach as part of mainstream practice will call for some difficult decisions, and quite a lot of work. Behavioural research often recommends markedly different styles and approaches to those with which we are most familiar, but we must not hang on to styles of practice just because they suit *us* and because *we* feel comfortable with them.

Conclusions

There is nothing in the nature of the procedures discussed in this book to suggest that they need be applied in an excessively clinical or mechanical way. Indeed, the principles themselves suggest that this would be self-defeating. Behaviour modification does suggest specific remedies for specifically defined problems, but *how* these remedies are applied is also very important. Social workers, with their traditional (but by no means unique) concern for the individual, are temperamentally well equipped to apply these techniques in a sensitive and humane fashion.

Knowledge of the application of the procedures themselves has been available for some time, but has produced only a very patchy response from the profession. Other preoccupations aside, one reason for this may be that to use behavioural techniques effectively requires a detailed and a specific knowledge of the various procedures – ideally of the underlying theory and the procedures together. This discipline cannot be approached in the same way as so much else in social work, as general, background, or contextual knowledge, where the method of application is left almost entirely to the worker. If these techniques are to amount to anything more than just another interesting sideline, then a reappraisal of the rather 'woolly' therapeutic stance developed in social work over the last fifty odd years will be necessary.

In addition, a reassessment of certain outmoded views on how people come to have behavioural problems in the first place will be required. It makes little sense to seal off different theories and beliefs about such things into different 'mental compartments' and ignore their many points of incompatibility – a sort of mindless eclecticism, fostered – I fear – by some training courses. Some sort of synthesis of 'most plausible' explanations should at least be attempted (Sheldon 1978a). Using the language of this book, there has always been too little positive reinforcement for this kind of thing, and now we are more likely to see a shift towards negative reinforcement – supplied

Ethical considerations 245

by our critics. It is important that we do not respond to this merely by jumping onto a new bandwagon. Instead we should set about fostering a greater respect for empiricism in social work. We can do this first, by adopting an active and critical approach to the research literature relevant to our field, and second, by evaluating our own work in an exemplary way.

Appendix: Checking baseline/outcome differences by simple statistical measurement (after Bloom)

Bloom (1975) has produced an admirably clear, step-by-step guide for the evaluation of marginal results from single-case designs. A version of this is reproduced below, together with a case example *(Figure A1)*, and the appropriate statistical table for calculating results *(Table A1)*.

Figure A1 Problem behaviours (Alan)

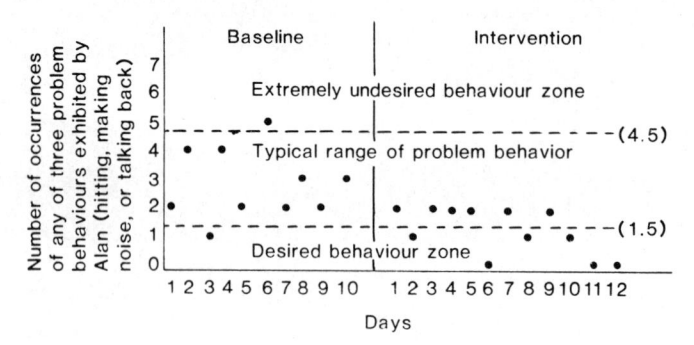

```
                              Baseline          Intervention
Number of occurrences    7
of any of three problem  6      Extremely undesired behaviour zone
behaviours exhibited by  5   — — — — — — | — — — — — — — — — (4.5)
Alan (hitting, making    4   •  •  Typical range of problem behavior
noise, or talking back)  3         •  •
                         2   •        •  •       •  •  •  •
                         1   — — — — •— — — | — — •— — — •— — (1.5)
                         0         Desired behaviour zone  •    • •
                             1 2 3 4 5 6 7 8 9 10  1 2 3 4 5 6 7 8 9 10 11 12
                                              Days
```

Source: Adapted from Bloom (1975). Reproduced by permission of the author and publishers.

(a) Count the *number of time units* on the horizontal line of the baseline period. (This is ten in Alan's case.) Do *not* count the number of individual acts (two the first day, four the next . . .).

Appendix 247

(b) Next identify the typical range of problem events. 'Typical range' refers to a statistical pattern like the middle two-thirds of a normal curve. To find the middle two-thirds, divide the number of time units by three and multiply the result by two. (For Alan, this would be 10 divided by 3, which is 3.3; and then 3.3 times 2, which is 6.6.)

(c) Draw lines enclosing the nearest approximation to this middle range of problem behaviours. The nearest whole number to 6.6 is 7, but as is often the case there is no way to enclose seven events representing a typical middle range in Alan's case. We *must* leave at least one event above and below the typical range in order to calculate the proportions needed.

(d) The middle range of problem behaviours is represented by the nearest approximation to two-thirds of the stable baseline distribution of problem occurrences; this is what the teacher expects as typical problem behaviour from Alan. The desired behaviour zone includes at least one event from the preintervention period and represents the zone in which the goals of intervention appear. In Alan's case, this zone includes one and zero occurrences. Even if the teacher's goal is to have zero occurences of problem behaviour, we must include the entire zone in our calculations because we must start from where the client is in evaluation as well as in practice. The extremely undesired behaviour zone includes those behaviours worse than typical. Because it is possible that the intervention may be harmful, we must be able to indicate when matters have become significantly worse. When there is a choice in approximating the middle range of behaviours, as in Alan's case where we might include either the six occurrences of 2s and 3s or the eight occurrences of 2s, 3s, and 4s – both being one unit away from the approximate middle range of seven occurrences – we must let the nature of the problem determine our choice.

Comparison of preintervention and intervention period events

Now the question arises: how statistically likely is a set of events that occurred during the intervention period to have occurred by chance alone? This question is one form of the statistician's null hypothesis, comparing what might have happened by chance with an alternative hypothesis, that is, that the worker's intervention affected the events in a planned way. (This is a one-directional hypothesis, assuming a positive outcome; we must be prepared to test for a negative outcome, using a two-directional test, as will be discussed below.) The question is answered by the following procedure.

(a) On how many occasions during the preintervention period was the client's behaviour in the desired zone? (For Alan it was 1 time out of 10, or a proportion of .10 which is the number of desired instances divided by the total number of occurrences during the preintervention period.) Look at *Table A1* and locate the left-hand column labelled *Proportion*, which stands for the proportion of observations of the type considered during the preintervention period. The proportion listed in steps of .05, with several common fractions also included for convenience.

(b) How many time units are in the intervention under consideration? Locate *Number* which stands for the total number of observational units during the intervention period. The numbers run by 2s up to 20 and 4s up to 100. *Figure A1* shows twelve time units in the intervention period with Alan. Note that the intervention period begins at day one, not at day eleven continuing from the preintervention period.

(c) Enter the body of *Table A1* at the intersection of the proportion of occurrences during preintervention and the total number of time units in the intervention period. (In Alan's case these numbers are .10 and 12, respectively, and the cell entry is 4.) The table shows the number of occurrences of a specific type – in this case, the number of desired occurrences of fewer-than-typical acting-out behaviours, during the intervention period, that are necessary to represent a significant increase at the .05 level over the proportion of such occurrences during the preintervention period. Actually the cell entry means 4 or more – 5, 6, 7, 8, 9, 10, 11, or 12 – any one of which would be a significant increase beyond the .05 level of significance. *Figure A1* reports six out of twelve occurrences of acting out behaviours were below Alan's typical pattern and thus the pattern of events showed a statistically significant improvement.

Evaluation of results

The intervention plan in this example was designed to reduce acting

Table A1 Showing the number of observations of a specified type (for example, a desired behaviour) during the intervention period that are necessary to represent a significant increase at the .05 level over the proportion during the preintervention period[1]

Proportion	Number																										
	4	6	8	10	12	14	16	18	20	24	28	32	36	40	44	48	52	56	60	64	68	72	76	80	84	88	92	96	100
.05	2	2	3	3	3	3	3	4	4	4	4	5	5	5	6	6	6	7	7	7	8	8	8	8	9	9	9	10	10
.10	3	3	3	4	4	4	5	5	5	6	7	7	8	8	9	9	10	10	11	12	12	13	13	14	14	15	15	16	16
1/8	3	3	4	4	5	5	5	6	6	7	8	8	9	10	10	11	12	12	13	14	14	15	15	16	17	17	18	19	19
.15	3	3	4	4	5	5	6	6	7	8	8	9	10	11	12	12	13	14	15	15	16	17	18	18	19	20	21	21	22
1/6	3	4	4	5	5	6	6	7	7	8	9	10	11	12	13	13	14	15	16	17	18	18	19	20	21	22	23	23	24
.20	3	4	5	5	6	6	7	8	8	9	10	11	12	13	14	15	16	17	18	19	20	21	22	23	24	25	26	27	28
.25	4	4	5	6	7	7	8	9	9	11	12	13	14	16	17	18	19	20	22	23	24	25	26	27	29	30	31	32	33
.30	4	5	6	6	7	8	9	10	10	12	13	15	16	18	19	21	22	24	25	26	28	29	30	32	33	35	36	37	39
1/3	4	5	6	7	8	9	9	10	11	13	15	16	18	19	21	22	24	26	27	29	30	32	33	35	36	38	39	41	42
.35	4	5	6	7	8	9	10	11	12	13	15	17	18	20	22	23	25	27	28	30	31	33	35	36	38	39	41	42	44
3/8	4	5	6	7	8	9	10	11	12	14	16	18	19	21	23	25	26	28	30	31	33	35	36	38	40	42	43	45	47
.40	4	5	6	8	9	10	11	12	13	15	16	18	20	22	24	26	28	29	31	33	35	37	38	40	42	44	46	47	49
.45	4	6	7	8	9	10	11	13	14	16	18	20	22	24	26	28	30	32	34	36	38	40	42	44	46	48	50	52	54
.50	—	6	7	9	10	11	12	13	15	17	19	21	24	26	28	31	33	35	37	40	42	44	46	48	51	53	55	57	59
.55	—	6	8	9	10	12	13	14	16	18	21	23	26	28	31	33	35	38	40	43	45	48	50	52	55	57	59	62	64
.60	—	6	8	9	11	12	14	15	17	19	22	25	27	30	33	35	38	41	43	46	48	51	54	56	59	61	64	66	69
5/8	—	—	8	10	11	13	14	16	17	20	23	25	28	31	34	36	39	42	45	47	50	53	55	58	61	63	66	69	71
.65	—	—	8	10	11	13	14	16	17	20	23	26	29	32	35	38	41	43	46	49	52	54	57	60	63	65	68	71	74
2/3	—	—	8	10	12	13	15	16	18	21	24	27	30	32	35	38	41	44	47	50	53	55	58	61	64	67	70	72	75
.70	—	—	—	10	12	13	15	17	18	21	24	28	31	34	37	40	43	46	49	52	55	58	61	64	67	70	73	75	78
.75	—	—	—	—	12	14	16	17	19	22	26	29	32	35	39	42	45	48	51	55	58	61	64	67	70	74	77	80	83
.80	—	—	—	—	12	14	16	18	20	23	27	30	34	37	40	44	47	51	54	57	61	64	67	71	74	77	81	84	87
5/6	—	—	—	—	—	—	16	18	20	24	27	31	34	38	42	45	49	52	56	59	63	66	69	73	76	80	83	87	90
.85	—	—	—	—	—	—	—	18	20	24	28	31	34	38	42	46	49	53	56	60*	63	67	70	74	78	81	85	88	92
7/8	—	—	—	—	—	—	—	—	—	24	28	32	36	39	43	47	50	54	57	61	65	68	72	76	79	83	86	90	94
.90	—	—	—	—	—	—	—	—	—	—	—	32	36	40	44	47	51	54	58	62	66	69	73	77	80	84	88	91	95
.95	—	—	—	—	—	—	—	—	—	—	—	—	—	—	—	—	52	56	60	64	69	72	76	79	83	87	91	95	99

[1]Tables of the Cumulative Binomial Probability Distribution – By the staff of the Harvard Computational Laboratory, Harvard University Press, 1955. Tables constructed under the direction of Dr. James Norton, Jr, Indiana University–Purdue University at Indianapolis, 1973. Reprinted by permission of Harvard University Press.

out behaviours by systematic use of positive reinforcements. This pattern of reduced acting out behaviours did occur after the initiation of the intervention plan, and, by using the statistical procedure in connection with *Table A1* we are able to say that such an event could have occurred by chance less than five times in one hundred. Evaluation of results involves an *inference* that, within the context of the client-worker situation and the conceptualized network of events that constitute the individualized plan of intervention, the occurrence of the desired pattern of events leads to support for the *hypothesis* that the worker's efforts were the likely *cause*. There is no necessary connection between a statistically significant event and causation, but it is by inference, within the context of a theory, that we can entertain such a hypothesis. We continue to use this causal inference in the development of other hypotheses to be tested in practice.

References

Alberti, R. E. and Emmons, M. L. (1970) *Your Perfect Right.* California: Impact.

Ayllon, T. and Azrin, N. H. (1964) Reinforcement and Instructions with Mental Patients. *Journal of the Experimental Analysis of Behaviour* **7**.

—— (1965) The Measurement and Reinforcement of Behaviour of Psychotics. *Journal of the Experimental Analysis of Behaviour* **8**.

Ayllon, T. and Michael, J. (1959) The Psychiatric Nurse as Behavioural Engineer. *Journal of the Experimental Analysis of Behaviour* **2**.

—— (1968) *The Token Economy: A Motivational System for Therapy and Rehabilitation.* New York: Appleton-Century Crofts.

Azrin, N. H., Nastor, J., and Jones, R. (1973) Reciprocity Counselling: A Rapid Learning Based Procedure for Marital Counselling. *Behaviour Research and Therapy* **11**.

Bach, G. and Wyden, P. (1968) *The Intimate Enemy: How to Fight a Fair Fight in Love and Marriage.* New York: Morrow & Co.

Baird, P. (1981) Last Word. *Social Work Today* **12**(8).

Bandura, A. (1965) Influence of Models' Reinforcement Contingencies on the Acquisition of Imitative Responses. *Journal of Personality and Social Psychology* **1**.

—— (1969) *Principles of Behaviour Modification.* New York: Holt, Rinehart & Winston.

—— (1977) *Social Learning Theory.* Englewood Cliffs, NJ: Prentice-Hall.

—— (1978) Perceived Self-Efficacy. *Advances in Behaviour Research and Therapy* **1**(4).

Bandura, A. and Rosenthal, T. L. (1966) Vicarious Classical Conditioning as a Function of Arousal Level. *Journal of Personality and Social Psychology* **3**.

Barlow, D. H. (1969) The Experimental Control of Sexual Deviation through Manipulation of a Noxious Scene in Covert Sensitization. *Journal of Abnormal Psychology* **74**.

Bateman, H. M., in Jensen, J. (ed) (1977) *The Man Who . . . and Other Drawings*. London: Eyre Methuen.

Bates, H. D. and Zimmerman, S. F. (1971) Toward the Development of a Screening Scale for Assertive Training. *Psychological Reports* **28**.

Beck, A. (1970) Cognitive Therapy: Nature of Relationship to Behaviour Therapy. *Behaviour Therapy* **1**.

Birch, R. A. (1976) *Manpower and Training in the Social Services*. London: HMSO.

Blakemore, C. (1977) *Mechanics of the Mind*. Cambridge: Cambridge University Press.

Bloom, M. (1975) *The Paradox of Helping*. New York: Wiley.

Bootzin, R. R. (1977) Effects of Self-control Procedures for Insomnia. In R. B. Stuart (ed) *Behavioural Self Control*. New York: Brunner/Mazel.

Boswell, J. (1740: 1980 edn) *Life of Johnson*. Oxford: Oxford University Press.

Brewer, C. and Lait, J. (1980) *Can Social Work Survive?* London: Maurice Temple Smith.

Brown, G. D. and Tyler, V. O. (1968) Time Out from Reinforcement: A Technique for Dethroning the 'Duke' of an Institutionalized Delinquent Group. *Journal of Child Psychology and Psychiatry* **9**.

BSWG (Behavioural Social Work Group) Details from the author at The University of Birmingham, PO Box 363, Birmingham B15 2TT.

Bucher, B. and Lovaas, O. I. (1968) Use of Aversive Stimulation in Behaviour Modification. In M. R. Jones (ed) *Miami Symposium on the Prediction of Behaviour: Aversive Stimulation*. Miami: University of Miami Press.

Cannon, W. B. (1927) The James-Lange Theory of Emotions: An Analytical Examination and an Alternative Theory. *American Journal of Psychology* **39**.

References 253

Carkhuff, R. (1969) *Helping and Human Relations*, Vol 1, Appendix B. New York: Holt, Rinehart & Winston.

Cautela, J. R. (1966) Treatment of Compulsive Behaviour by Covert Sensitization. *Psychological Record* **16**.

—— (1970) Covert Negative Reinforcement. *Journal of Behaviour Therapy and Experimental Psychiatry* **1**.

Clare, A. (1976, 2nd edn 1980) *Psychiatry in Dissent*. London: Tavistock.

Cohen, A. R. (1964) *Attitude Change and Social Influence*. New York: Basic Books.

Community Care (1980) 'Brutal Home May Stay Open'. 2 October: 3.

Cooke, G. (1968) Evaluation of the Efficacy of the Components of Reciprocal Inhibition Psychotherapy. *Journal of Abnormal Psychology* **73**.

Cooper, B., Harwin, C. B. G., Depla, C., and Shepherd, M. (1975) Mental Health Care in the Community: An Evaluative Study. *Psychological Medicine* **5**(4).

Corrigan, P. and Leonard, P. (1978) *Social Work Practice under Capitalism*. London: Macmillan.

Cotter, L. M. (1967) Operant Conditioning in a Vietnamese Mental Hospital. *American Journal of Psychiatry* **124**(1).

Daily Mirror (UK) (1978) Front page story recounting critical reactions on the use of a contract with a wayward adolescent girl. 21 October.

Davey, G. (ed) (1981) *Applications of Conditioning Theory*. London: Methuen.

Davies, M. (1979) Improving the Quality of Assessment. *Community Care* 20 October and 27 October.

Davison, G. C. (1968) Elimination of a Sadistic Fantasy by a Client-Controlled Counter-Conditioning Technique. *Journal of Abnormal Psychology* **73**.

Descartes, R. (1664: 1972 edn) *Traite de Homme plus Translation and Commentary* (Holt, T. S.). Cambridge: Cambridge University Press.

Ellis, A. (1977) Rational Emotive Therapy: Research Data that Supports the Clinical and Personality Hypotheses of RET. *Journal of Counselling Psychology* **1**.

—— (1979) The Basic Clinical Theory of Rational Emotive Therapy. In R. Grieger and J. Boyd (eds) *Clinical Applications of Rational Emotive Therapy*. New York: Van Nostrand Reinhold.

Epstein, I. (1975) Behaviour Modification, The New Cool Out Casework. In H. Jones (ed) *Towards a New Social Work*. London: Routledge & Kegan Paul.

Eysenck, H. J. (1964) *Crime and Personality*. London: Routledge & Kegan Paul.

—— (1976) *Experimental Studies of Freudian Theories*. London: Methuen.

—— (1978) Expectations as Control Elements in Behavioural Change. *Advances in Behaviour Research and Therapy* **1**(4).

Farber, I. E., Harlow, H. F., and West, L. J. (1966) Brainwashing, Conditioning and DDD (Debility, Dependency, and Dread). In R. Ulrich, T. Stachnic, and J. Mabry (eds) *Control of Human Behaviour*, Vol 1. Glenview, IL: Scott Foresman.

Ferster, C. B. and Skinner, B. F. (1957) *Schedules of Reinforcement*. New York: Appleton-Century Crofts.

Festinger, L. (1957) *A Theory of Cognitive Dissonance*. Evanston, IL: Row Peterson.

—— (1964) Behavioural Support for Opinion Change. *Public Opinion Quarterly* **28**.

Fischer, J. (1973) Is Casework Effective: A Review. *Social Work* **1**.

—— (ed) (1976) *The Effectiveness of Social Casework*. Springfield, IL: Charles C. Thomas.

Folkard, M. S. (1975 and 1976) IMPACT, *Home Office Research Studies*, Numbers 24 and 36. London: HMSO.

—— (1980) Second Thoughts About IMPACT. *Paper given at Hawkeswood College Symposium on Social Work Effectiveness, Gloucestershire, UK*. Reprinted in Goldberg and Connolly (1981).

Galassi, M. D. and Galassi, J. P. (1977) *Assert Yourself!* New York: Human Sciences Press.

Gambrill, E. (1977) *Behaviour Modification: A Handbook of Assessment, Intervention and Evaluation*. San Francisco, CA: Jossey-Bass.

—— (1981) The Use of Behavioural Practices in Cases of Child Abuse and Neglect. *International Journal of Behavioural Social Work* **1**(1).

Garber, J. and Seligman, M. (eds) (1980) *Human Helplessness: Theory and Application.* London: Academic Press.

Goffman, I. (1968) *Asylums.* Harmondsworth: Penguin Books.

Goldberg, E. M. and Connolly, J. (eds) (1981) *Evaluative Research and Social Care.* London: Heinemann Educational.

Gray, J. A. (1975) *Elements in a Two Process Theory of Learning.* London: Academic Press.

Grossberg, J. M. (1964) Behaviour Therapy: A Review. *Psychological Bulletin* **62**.

Hall, J. and Baker, R. (1973) Token Economy Systems: Breakdown and Control. *Behaviour Research and Therapy* **11**(3).

Hays, V. and Waddell, K. J. (1976) A Self-Reinforcing Procedure for Thought Stopping. *Behaviour Therapy* **1**.

Hebb, D. O. (1972) *Textbook of Psychology.* Philadelphia, PA: W. B. Saunders.

Heine, R. W. (1953) A Comparison of Patient Reports on Psycho-Analytic, Non-Directive and Adlerian Therapists. *American Journal of Psychotherapy* **7**.

Herbert, M. (1979) Why Not Behavioural Social Work?. *Paper given to First Annual Conference of the Behavioural Social Work Group, Leicester, UK.* (Available from the author at the University of Leicester.)

Heron, W. (1957) The Pathology of Boredom. In S. Coopersmith (ed) (1964) *Frontiers of Psychological Research.* San Francisco, CA: W. H. L. Freeman.

Hersen, M. and Barlow, D. (1976) *Single Case Experimental Designs.* Oxford: Pergamon.

Hilgard, E. R. (1948) *Theories of Learning.* New York: Appleton-Century Crofts.

Hilgard, E. R. and Atkinson, R. L. (1967) *An Introduction to Psychology*, 4th edn. New York: Harcourt Brace World.

Hilgard, E. R., Atkinson, R. C., and Atkinson, R. L. (1979) *An Introduction to Psychology*, 7th edn. New York: Harcourt Brace Jovanovich.

Hillner, K. P. (1979) *Conditioning in Contemporary Perspective.* New York: Springer.

Holland, J. G. (1975) Behaviour Modification for Prisoners, Patients and Other People as a Prescription for the Planned Society. *Mexican Journal of Behaviour Analysis* **1**.

—— (1978) Behaviourism: Part of the Problem or Part of the Solution? *Journal of Applied Behaviour Analysis* **11**.
Hollis, F. (1964) *Casework: A Psychosocial Therapy*. New York: Random House.
Homme, L. E. (1965) Perspectives in Psychology, 24. Control of Coverants, the Operants of the Mind. *Psychological Record* **15**.
Homme, L. E. and Tosti, D. T. (1965) Contingency Management and Motivation. *Journal of the National Society for Programmed Instruction* **4**.
Hovland, C. (1953) *Communication and Persuasion*. New Haven, CT: Yale University Press.

International Journal of Behavioural Social Work & Abstracts (eds Hudson, B. L. and Sheldon, B.). Oxford: Pergamon.
Isaacs, W., Thomas, J., and Goldiamond, I. (1966) Application of Operant Conditioning to Reinstate Verbal Behaviour in Psychotics. In R. Ulrich, T. Stachnic, and J. Mabry (eds) *Control of Human Behaviour*, Vol 1. Glenview, IL: Scott Foresman.

Jackson, B. (1972) Treatment of Depression by Self Reinforcement. *Behaviour Therapy* **3**.
Jacobson, N. S. and Margolin, G. (1979) *Marital Therapy: Strategies Based on Social Learning and Behaviour Exchange Principles*. New York: Brunner/Mazel.
Jakubowski-Spector, P. (1973) Facilitating the Growth of Women Through Assertive Training. *The Counselling Psychologist* **4**(1).
James, W. (1890) *The Principles of Psychology*. New York: Dorer.
Jehu, D. (1967) *Learning Theory and Social Work*. London: Routledge & Kegan Paul.
—— (ed) (1972) *Behaviour Modification in Social Work*. New York: John Wiley.
Johnson, T., Tyler, V., Thompson, R., and Jones, S. (1971) Systematic Desensitization and Assertive Training in the Treatment of Speech and Anxiety in Middle School Students. *Psychology in the Schools* (US) **8**(3).

Kanfer, F. H. (1965) Vicarious Human Reinforcement: A Glimpse into the Black Box. In L. Krasner and L. P. Ullman (eds) *Research in Behaviour Modification*. New York: Holt, Rinehart & Winston.
—— (1971) The Maintenance of Behaviour by Self-Gener-

ated Stimuli and Reinforcement. In A. Jacobs and L. B. Sachs (eds) *The Psychology of Private Events*. London: Academic Press.

Kazdin, A. E. and Smith, G. A. (1979) Covert Conditioning: A Review and Evaluation. *Advances in Behaviour Research and Therapy* **2**(2).

Kelly, G. A. (1955) *The Theory of Personal Constructs*, Vols 1 and 2. New York: Norton.

Krasner, L. (1968) Assessment of Token Economy Programmes in Psychiatric Hospitals. In R. Porter (ed) *CIBA Symposium on the Role of Learning in Psychotherapy*. London: Churchill Livingstone.

Laws, D. R. and O'Neill, J. A. (1981) Variations on Masturbatory Conditioning. *Behavioural Psychotherapy* **9**(2).

Lazarus, A. A. (1968) Behaviour Therapy in Groups. In G. M. Gazda (ed) *Basic Approaches to Group Psychotherapy and Group Counselling*. Springfield, IL: Charles C. Thomas.

—— (1971) *Behaviour Therapy and Beyond*. New York: McGraw Hill.

Levy, C. S. (1974) Inputs versus Outputs as Criteria of Competence. *Social Casework* **55**.

Lick, J. and Bootzin, R. R. (1975) Expectancy Factors in the Treatment of Fear: Methodological and Theoretical Issues. *Psychological Bulletin* **82**.

Linehan, K. S. and Rosenthal, T. L. (1979) Current Behavioural Approaches to Marital and Family Therapy. *Advances in Behaviour Research and Therapy* **3**.

Lovaas, O. I. (1967) A Programme for the Establishment of Speech in Psychotic Children. In J. K. Wing (ed) *Early Childhood Autism*. Oxford: Pergamon.

Luria, A. (1961) *The Role of Speech in the Regulation of Normal and Abnormal Behaviour*. New York: Liveright.

Luthans, F. and Kreitner, R. (1975) *Organizational Behaviour Modification*. Glenview, IL: Scott Foresman.

McFall, R. M. and Lillesand, D. B. (1971) Behaviour Rehearsal with Modelling and Coaching in Assertive Training. *Journal of Abnormal Psychology* **77**.

McFall, R. M. and Marston, A. R. (1970) An Experimental Investigation of Behavioural Rehearsal in Assertive Training. *Journal of Abnormal Psychology* **76**.

McGlynne, F. P. and Mapp, R. H. (1970) Systematic Desensitization of Snake Avoidance Following Three Types of Suggestion. *Behaviour Research and Therapy* **8**.

Madders, J. (1978) *Stress and Relaxation*. London: Martin Dunitz.

Marks, I. M. (1971) Flooding versus Desensitization in the Treatment of Phobic Patients. *British Journal of Psychiatry* **118**.

—— (1975) Behavioural Treatments of Phobic and Obsessive Compulsive Disorders: A Critical Appraisal. In R. Hersen *et al*. (eds) *Progress in Behaviour Therapy*. Academic Press.

—— (1978) Behavioural Psychotherapy of Neurotic Disorders. In S. Garfield and A. E. Bergin (eds) *Handbook of Psychotherapy and Behaviour Change*. New York: John Wiley.

Marmor, J. (1962) Psychoanalytic Therapy as an Educational Process. In J. H. Masserman (ed) *Science and Psychoanalysis*, Vol 5. New York: Grune & Stratton.

Marzillier, J. S. (1980) Cognitive Therapy and Behavioural Practice. *Behaviour Research and Therapy* **18**(4).

Masserman, J. H. (1943) *Behaviour and Neurosis*. Chicago: University of Chicago Press.

Mayer, J. E. and Timms, N. (1970) *The Client Speaks*. London: Routledge & Kegan Paul.

Meyer, H., Borgatta, E., and Jones, W. (1965) *Girls at Vocational High*. New York: Russell Sage Foundation.

Meyers-Abell, J. E. and Jansen, M. A. (1980) Assertive Therapy for Battered Women: A Case Illustration. *Journal of Behaviour Therapy and Experimental Psychiatry* **2**(4).

Michenbaum, D. (1974) *Cognitive Behaviour Modification*. Morristown, NJ: General Learning Press.

—— (1977) *Cognitive Behaviour Modification: An Integrative Approach*. New York: Plenum.

Milgram, S. (1974) *Obedience to Authority*. London: Tavistock.

Mill, J. S. (1859: 1971 edn) *On Liberty*. London: Dent.

Miller, S. M. (1979) Controllability and Human Stress: Method, Evidence and Theory. *Behaviour Research and Therapy* **17**(4).

Milne, A. A. (1978 edn) *The House at Pooh Corner*. London: Eyre Methuen.

Miron, N. B. (1966) Behaviour Shaping and Group Nursing with Severely Retarded Patients. In J. Fischer and R. E. Harris (eds) *Reinforcement Therapy in Psychological Treatment – A Symposium*.

References 259

Research Monograph Number 8, Department of Mental Hygiene, California.

Montgomery, J. and McBurney, R. D. (1970) Problems and Pitfalls of Establishing an Operant Conditioning Token Economy Programme. *Mental Hygiene* **54**.

Mullen, E. J. and Dumpson, J. R. (eds) (1972) *The Evaluation of Social Intervention*. San Francisco, CA: Jossey Bass.

National Association for the Care and Rehabilitation of Offenders (1981) (in Press) *Intermediate Treatment: The Hammersmith Teenage Project*. London: NACRO.

Olds, J. (1956) Pleasure Center in the Brain, *Scientific American* **195**: 105–16.

—— (1977) *Drives and Reinforcements: Behavioural Studies of Hypothalamic Functions*. New York: Raven Press.

Orne, M. (1965) Psychological Factors Maximizing Resistance to Stress with Special Reference to Hypnosis. In S. Klanser (ed) *The Quest for Self Control*. New York: Free Press.

Paul, G. L. (1966) *Insight versus Desensitization in Psychotherapy: An Experiment in Anxiety Reduction*. Stanford, CA: Stanford University Press.

Pavlov, I. P. (1897: trans W. H. Gannt, 1928) *Lectures on Conditioned Reflexes*. New York: International. See also: Anrep, G. V. (trans) (1927) *Conditioned Reflexes*. London: Oxford University Press.

Phillips, E. L. (1968) 'Achievement Place': Token Reinforcement Procedures in a Home Style Rehabilitation Setting for Pre-Delinquent Boys. *Journal of Applied Behaviour Analysis* **1**(3).

Pincus, A. and Minahan, A. (1973) *Social Work Practice – Model and Method*. Itason, IL: Peacock.

Popper, K. R. (1963) *Conjectures and Refutations*. London: Routledge & Kegan Paul.

Popper, K. R. and Eccles, J. C. (1977) *The Self and its Brain*. New York: Springer International.

Premack, D. (1959) Towards Empirical Behaviour Laws; 1. Positive Reinforcement. *Psychological Review* **66**.

Rachman, S. (1972) Clinical Applications of Observational Learning; Imitation and Modelling. *Behaviour Therapy* **3**.

Rathus, S. A. (1974) A Thirty Item Schedule for Assessing Assertive Behaviour. In E. J. Thomas (ed) *Behaviour Modification Procedure.* Chicago, IL: Aldine.
Reid, W. J. (1980) Paper: Recent Trends in Effectiveness Research, given at *Hawkeswood College Symposium on Social Work Effectiveness, Gloucestershire, UK.* Reprinted in Goldberg and Connolly (1981).
Reid, W. J. and Shyne, A. (1968) *Brief and Extended Casework.* New York: Columbia University Press.
Reiner, B. S. and Kaufman, M. D. (1969) *Character Disorders in the Parents of Delinquents.* New York: FSAA.
Risley, T. R. (1977) The Social Context of Self Control. In R. B. Stuart (ed) *Behavioural Self Control.* New York: Brunner/Mazel.
Rogers, C. R. (1951) *Client-Centred Therapy: Its Current Practice, Implications and Theory.* Boston: Houghton Mifflin.
Rose, G. and Marshall, T. M. (1975) *Counselling and School Social Work: An Experimental Study.* New York: John Wiley.
Rosenhan, D. L. (1973) On Being Sane in Insane Places. *Science* **179**.
Russell, E. W. (1974) The Power of Behaviour Control: A Critique of Behaviour Modification Methods. *Journal of Clinical Psychology, Special Monograph Supplement.*
Ryle, G. (1949) *The Concept of Mind.* London: Hutchinson.
—— (1979) *On Thinking.* London: Basil Blackwell.

Sandifer, M. G., Pettus, L., and Quale, D. (1964) A Study of Psychiatric Diagnosis. *Journal of Nervous and Mental Disease* **139**.
Sandifer, M. G., Hordern, A., Timbury, G. C., and Green, L. M. (1968) Psychiatric Diagnosis, a Comparative Study in North Carolina, London and Glasgow. *British Journal of Psychology* **114**.
Schacter, S. and Singer, J. E. (1962) Cognitive, Social and Physiological Determinants of Emotional States. *Psychological Review* **69**.
Schmidt, J. P. and Patterson, T. E. (1979) Issues in the Implementation of Assertion Training in Applied Settings. *Journal of Behaviour Therapy and Experimental Psychiatry* **10**(1).
Seebohm Report (1968) (CMND 3703) *Report of the Community on Local Authority and Allied Personal Social Services.* London: HMSO.
Seligman, M. E. P. (1971) Phobias and Preparedness. *Behaviour Therapy* **2**.
—— (1975) *Helplessness.* San Francisco, CA: Freeman.
Shaw, M. (1974) *Social Work in Prison* (Home Office Research Unit). London: HMSO.

References

Sheldon, B. (1977) Goal Analysis: Do You Know Where You Are Going? *Community Care* 6 August.
—— (1978a) Theory and Practice in Social Work: A Re-Examination of a Tenuous Relationship. *British Journal of Social Work* **8**(1).
—— (1978b) Social Influence: Social Work's Missing Link. In M. R. Olsen (ed) *The Unitary Model*. Birmingham: BASW Publications.
—— (1978c) Contingency Contracts: Making Contracts to Please. *Community Care* 24 May.
—— (1979a) Putting Realism into Televised Simulations. *Social Work Today*, **11**(8).
—— (1979b) Not Proven: The Case of Social Work Effectiveness. *Community Care* 14 June.
—— (1980) *The Use of Contracts in Social Work*. Birmingham: BASW Publications.
Sheldon, B. and Baird, P. (1978) Evaluating Student Performance. *Social Work Today* **10**(16).
Shenger-Krestovnika, N. R. (1921) Contributions to the Question of Differentiation of Visual Stimuli and the Limits of Differentiation by the Visual Analyser of the Dog. *Bulletin of the Institute of Science – Leshaft* **3**.
Skinner, B. F. (1953) *Science and Human Behaviour*. London: Collier-Macmillan.
—— (1957) *Verbal Behaviour*. New York: Appleton-Century Crofts.
—— (1971) *Beyond Freedom and Dignity*. Harmondsworth: Penguin.
—— (1974) *About Behaviourism*. London: Jonathan Cape.
Sloane, R., Staples, F., Yorkston, N., and Whipple, K. (1975) *Psychotherapy versus Behaviour Therapy*. Cambridge, MA: Harvard University Press.
Smale, G. G. (1977) *Prophecy, Behaviour and Change*. London: Routledge & Kegan Paul.
Smith, K. (1969) *Behaviour and Conscious Experience, a Conceptual Analysis*. Athens, OH: Ohio University Press.
Stein, T. J. and Gambrill, E. D. (1976) Behavioural Techniques in Foster Care. *Social Work* **21**(1).
Stern, R. (1978) *Behavioural Techniques*. London: Academic Press.
Stevenson, O. and Parsloe, P. (1978) *Social Service Teams: The Practitioner's View*. London: HMSO.
Stuart, R. B. (1975) Behavioural Remedies for Marital Ills: A Guide to the Use of Operant Interpersonal Techniques. In T. Thompson

and W. S. Dockens (eds) *Applications of Behaviour Therapy*. New York: Academic Press.
—— (1977) *Behavioural Self Management*. New York: Brunner/Mazel.
Szasz, T. (1971) *The Myth of Mental Illness*. London: Paladin.

Teasdale, J. D. (1978) Self Efficacy: Towards a Unifying Theory of Behavioural Change. *Advances in Behaviour Research and Therapy* **1**(4).
Temerlin, M. K. (1968) Suggestion Effects in Psychiatric Diagnosis. *Journal of Nervous and Mental Disease* **147**(4).
Tharp, R. G. and Wetzel, R. J. (1969) *Behaviour Modification in the Natural Environment*. London: Academic Press.
Thomas, A., Chess, S., and Birch, H. G. (1968) *Temperament and Behaviour Disorder in Children*. New York: New York University Press.
Thomas, E. J. (ed) (1974) *Behaviour Modification Procedure: A Sourcebook*. Chicago, IL: Aldine.
Thorndike, E. L. (1898) Animal Intelligence: An Experimental Study of the Associative Processes in Animals. *Psychological Review Monograph* **2**.
—— (1931) *Human Learning*. New York: Appleton-Century Crofts.
Trower, P., Bryant, B., and Argyle, M. (1977) *Social Skills and Mental Health*. London: Methuen.
Truax, C. and Carkhuff, R. (1967) *Towards Effective Counselling and Psychotherapy*. Chicago, IL: Aldine.
Tryan, G. S. (1979) A Review and Critique of Thought Stopping Research. *Journal of Behaviour Therapy and Experimental Psychiatry* **10**(3).
Tsuang, M. T. and Vandermey, R. (1980) *Genes and the Mind*. Oxford: Oxford University Press.

Ullman, L. P. and Krasner, L. (1969) *A Psychological Approach to Abnormal Behaviour*. Englewood Cliffs, NJ: Prentice Hall International.

Van Hasselt, U. B., Hersen, M., Whitehill, M. B., and Bellack, A. S. (1978) Social Skill Assessment and Training for Children: An Evaluative Review. *Behaviour Research and Therapy* **17**.
Verworn, M. (1916) *Irritability*. New Haven, CT: Yale University Press.
Vygotsky, L. (1962) *Thought and Language*. New York: John Wiley.

Watson, J. B. and Raynor, R. (1920) Conditioned Emotional Reactions. *Journal of Experimental Psychology* **3**.
Willer, B. and Miller, G. H. (1976) Client Involvement in Goal Setting and its Relation to Therapeutic Outcome. *Journal of Clinical Psychology* **32**(3).
Williams, D. R. and Williams, H. (1969) Auto-Maintenance in the Pigeon: Sustained Pecking Despite Contingent Non-Reinforcement. *Journal of the Experimental Analysis of Behaviour* **12**.
Wolpe, J. (1958) *Psychotherapy by Reciprocal Inhibition*. Stanford, CA: Stanford University Press.
Wolpe, J. and Lazarus, A. A. (1966) *Behaviour Therapy Techniques*. Oxford: Pergamon.
Wootton, B. (1959) *Social Science and Social Pathology*. London: Allen & Unwin.

Yamagami, T. (1971) The Treatment of an Obsession by Thought Stopping. *Journal of Behaviour Therapy and Experimental Psychiatry* **2**.
Yates, A. J. (1958) Symptoms and Symptom Substitution. *Psychological Review* **63**.

Name index

Alberti, R. E. 188, 193, 197, *251*
Argyle, M. 187, *262*
Atkinson, R. C. 40, 95, 96, *255*
Atkinson, R. L. 40, 42, 95, 96, *255*
Ayllon, T. 156, 158, 175, 241, *251*
Azrin, N. H. 156, 158, 172, 241, *251*

Bach, G. 188, 189, *251*
Bacon, Francis 103
Baird, P. 9, 12, 105, 131, 173, *251, 261*
Baker, R. 157, 230–31, *255*
Bandura, A. 11, 16, 32, 33, 37, 38, 74, 75, 76–7, 78, 79, 80, 86–7, 88–9, 121, 142, 180, 183, 206–07, 216, 217, *251–52*
Barlow, D. H. 129, 135, 211, *252, 255*
Bateman, H. M. 61, *252*
Bates, H. D. 197, *252*
Beck, A. 207, 209, *252*
Bellack, A. S. 187, *262*
Bergin, A. E. *258*
Birch, H. G. 39, *262*
Birch, R. A. 4, *252*
Blakemore, C. 27, 85, *252*
Bloom, M. 9, 246, *252*
Bootzin, R. R. 88, 200, *252*
Borgatta, E. 9, *258*
Boswell, J. 29, *252*
Boyd, J. *254*
Brewer, C. 6, 31, 230, *252*
Brown, G. D. 154, *252*
Bryant, B. 187, *262*
BSWG 3, *252*
Bucher, B. 232, *252*

Cannon, W. B. 85, *252*
Carkhuff, R. 8, 15, 16, 17, 219, *253, 262*

Cautela, J. R. 211, *253*
Chess, S. 39, *262*
Clare, A. 21, *253*
Cohen, A. R. 188, 189, *253*
Connolly, J. *254, 255, 260*
Cooke, G. 216, *253*
Cooper, B. 13, 14, *253*
Coopersmith, S. *255*
Corrigan, P. 15, *253*
Cotter, L. M. 230–31, *253*

Davey, G. 43, *253*
Davies, M. 15, *253*
Depla. C. 13, 14, *253*
Descartes, R. 24–6, *253*
Dockens, W. S. *261*
Dumpson, J. R. 7, *259*

Eccles, J. C. 27, *259*
Ellis, A. 89, 207–09, 210, *253–54*
Emmons, M. L. 188, 193, 197, *251*
Epstein, I. 222, *254*
Eysenck, H. J. 10, 36, 88, *254*

Farber, I. E. 231, *254*
Ferster, C. E. 62, *254*
Festinger, L. 12, 16, 70, 164, 223, 240, *254*
Fischer, J. 6–7, 11, *254, 258–59*
Folkard, M. S. 14, *254*
Freud, Sigmund 43

Galassi, J. P. 188, 189, 191, 193, *254*
Galassi, M. D. 188, 189, 191, 193, *254*
Gambrill, E. 5, 14, 164, 173, 188, 201, *254, 261*
Garber, J. *255*

Name index

Garfield, S. *258*
Gazda, G. M. *257*
Goffman, I. 239, *255*
Goldberg, E. M. *254*, *255*, *260*
Goldiamond, I. 59, *256*
Gray, J. A. 43, *255*
Green, L. M. *260*
Grieger, R. *254*
Grossberg, J. M. 37, *255*

Hall, J. 157, 230–31, *255*
Harlow, H. F. 231, *254*
Harris, R. E. *258–59*
Harwin, C. B. G., 13, 14, *253*
Hays, V. 211, *255*
Hebb, D. O. 80, *255*
Heine, R. W. 16, 37, 105, *255*
Herbert, M. 3, *255*
Heron, W. 85, *255*
Hersen, M. 129, 135, 187, *255*, *262*
Hersen, R. *258*
Hilgard, E. R. 40, 41, 42, 95, 96, *255*
Hillner, K. P. 40, *255*
Holland, J. G. 222, 237–38, *255–56*
Hollis, F. 17, 243, *256*
Homme, L. E. 81, 142, *256*
Hordern, A. *260*
Hovland, C. 188, *256*
Hudson, B. L. 167, *256*

Isaacs, W. 58, *256*

Jackson, B. 201–02, *256*
Jacobs, P. *256–57*
Jacobson, N. S. 171, *256*
Jakubowski-Spector, P. 188, *256*
James, W. 94, *256*
Jansen, M. A. 188, *258*
Jehu, D. 3, 154, 155, 212, *256*
Jensen, J. *252*
Johnson, Dr 29
Johnson, T. 188, *256*
Jones, H. *254*
Jones, M. R. *252*
Jones, R. 172, *251*
Jones, S. 188, *256*
Jones, W. 9, *258*

Kanfer, F. H. 183, 201, *256–57*
Kasdin, A. E. 210, 211, *257*
Kelly, G. A. 89, 138, *257*
Klanser, S. *259*
Klein, Melanie 66

Krasner, L. 33, 37, 39, 156, 157, *256*, *257*, *262*
Kreitner, R. 5, *257*

Lait, J. 6, 31, 230, *252*
Laws, D. R. 211, *257*
Lazarus, A. A. 44, 80, 197, 218, *257*, *263*
Leonard, P. 15, *253*
Levy, C. S. 15, *257*
Lick, J. 88, *257*
Lillesand, D. B. 188, *257*
Linehan, K. S. 163, 172, *257*
Lovaas, O. I. 70, 232, *252*, *257*
Luria, A. 204, *257*
Luthans, F. 5, *257*

Mabry, J. *254*, *256*
McBurney, R. D. *156*, *259*
McFall, R. M. 188, *257*
McGlynne, F. P. 88, 91, *258*
Madders, J. 219, *258*
Mapp, R. H. 88, 91, *258*
Margolin, G. 171, *256*
Marks, I. M. 206, 213, 216, *258*
Marmor, J. 11, *258*
Marshall, T. M. 5, 13, *260*
Marston, A. R. 188, *257*
Marzillier, J. S. 91, 209, *258*
Masserman, J. H. 50, *258*
Mayer, J. E. 9–10, 12, 106, *258*
Meyer, H. 9, *258*
Meyers-Abell, J. E. 188, *258*
Michael, J. 175, *251*
Michenbaum, D. 28, 80, 157, 202, 203, 204, 208, *258*
Milgram, S. 188, *258*
Mill, J. S. 236–37, *258*
Miller, G. H. 202, *262–63*
Miller, S. M. 214, *258*
Milne, A. A. 209, *258*
Minahan, A. 4, 242, *259*
Miron, N. B. *258–59*
Montgomery, J. 156, *259*
Mullen, E. J. 7, *259*

Nastor, J. 172, *251*
National Association for the Care and Rehabilitation of Offenders 13, 14, *259*

Olds, J. 94, *259*
Olsen, M. R. *261*
O'Neill, J. A. 211, *257*

Orne, M. 206, *259*

Parsloe, P. 10, *261*
Patterson, T. E. 188, *260*
Paul, G. L. 216, *259*
Pavlov, I. P. 39, 41–2, 43, 44, 49, 90, *259*
Pettus, L. 34, *260*
Phillips, E. L. 157, *259*
Pincus, A. 4, 242, *259*
Popper, K. R. 2, 27, 32–3, 37, 102, *259*
Porter, R. *257*
Premack, D. 146–47, 160, 178, *259*

Quale, D. 34, *260*

Rachman, S. 80, *259*
Rathus, S. A. 190, *260*
Raynor, R. 43, 44, *262*
Reid, W. J. 11, 14, *260*
Risley, T. R. 198, *260*
Rogers, C. R. 16, *260*
Rose, G. 5, 13, *260*
Rosenhan, D. L. 34, *260*
Rosenthal, A. 76, *252*
Rosenthal, T. L. 163, 172, *257*
Russell, E. W. 91, *260*
Ryle, G. 26, 85, *260*

Sachs, L. B. *256–57*
Sandifer, M. G. 34, *260*
Schacter, S. 96, *260*
Schmidt, J. P. 188, *260*
Seebohm Report 2, *260*
Seligman, M. E. P. 44, 50, *255, 260*
Shaw, M. 13, *260*
Sheldon, B. 2, 4, 5, 6, 9, 13, 22, 37, 82, 88, 104, 105, 122, 131, 161, 165–66, 172, 173, 184, 185, 223, 243, 244, *256, 260–61*
Shenger-Krestovnika, N. R. 49–50, *261*
Shepherd, M. 13, 14, *253*
Shyne, A. 11, *260*
Singer, J. E. 96, *260*
Skinner, B. F. 26, 29, 39, 51–2, 55, 56–7, 59, 60, 62, 65, 74, 76, 81, 82, 145, 162, *254, 261*
Sloane, R. 10, 18, *261*
Smale, G. G. 32, *261*
Smith, K. 40, *261*
Stachnie, T. *254, 256*
Staples, F. 10, 18, *261*

Stein, T. J. 14, *261*
Stern, R. 210, 213, 215–16, *261*
Stevenson, O. 10,. *261*
Stuart, R. B. 163, 198, *252, 260, 261*
Szasz, T. 235, *262*

Teasdale, J. D. 89, *262*
Temerlin, M. K. 35, *262*
Tharp, R. G. 20–1, 144, 147, *262*
Thomas, A. 39, *262*
Thomas, E. J. 147, *260, 262*
Thomas, J. 58, *256*
Thompson, R. 188, *256*
Thompson, T. *261*
Thorndike, E. L. 39, 51, *262*
Timbury, G. C. *260*
Timms, N. 9–10, 12, 106, *258*
Tosti, D. T. 142, *256*
Trower, P. 187, *262*
Truax, C. 8, 15, 16, 17, *262*
Tryan, G. S. 211, *262*
Tsuang, M. T. 39, *262*
Tyler, U. 154, 188, *252, 256*

Ullman, L. P. 33, 37, 39, *256, 262*
Ulrich, R. *254, 256*

Vandermey, R. 39, *262*
Van Hasselt, U. B. 187, *262*
Verworn, M. 30, *262*
Vygotsky, L. 204, *262*

Waddell, K. J. 211, *255*
Waller, Fats 15
Watson, J. B. 43, 44, *262*
West, L. J. 231, *254*
Wetzel, R. J. 20–1, 144, 147, *262*
Whipple, K. 10, 18, *261*
Whitehill, M. B. 187, *262*
Willer, B. 202, *262–63*
Williams, D. R. 43, *263*
Williams, H. 43, *263*
Wing, J. K. *257*
Wolpe, J. 212, 213, 218, *263*
Wootton, B. 31, 243, *263*
Wyden, P. 188, 189, *251*

Yamagami, T. 211, *263*
Yates, A. J. 33, 37, *263*
Yorkston, N. 10, 18, *261*

Zimmerman, S. F. 197, *252*

Subject index

A.B.C. chart 107, 199
abuse, likelihood of 229
abuse of behaviour modification 226–27, 230, 239–40
accent 194–95
achievements of clients 88, 144–45
affection problems 225–26
aggression 75, 154, 180–81, 188, 192, 193, 194, 231
agoraphobia 46–9, 105, 217–18
ambiguity in environment 49–50
American findings 9–13
animal phobias 182–83
anticipation 28, 75
anxiety 46, 47–8, 54, 80, 97, 187, 193, 195–96
anxiety reduction techniques 212–19, 220–21: and children's fears 212–13; and dirt phobias 215; and public transport phobias 215–16; biofeedback in 219, 221; counter-conditioning in 210, 212–13, 220; rapid exposure in 206, 213–16, 220; relaxation in 206, 211, 213, 216–19; slow exposure in 217, 220; systematic desensitization in 80, 88, 190, 206, 213, 216–18, 220–21
apathy 50, 68
approval, need for 16–17, 57, 59, 145, 147
arousal, states of 46, 50, 76, 85, 96, 140
artificiality in therapy 17–18, 145, 146, 171–72
assertion training 188–98, 220: and attitude change 189; and communication 189; and origins of compliance 188; and withdrawn

clients 125; assertion as an option 198; assessment in 189, 190–91; definition of assertiveness 189, 192–93; desensitization in 190, 195–96; discrimination in 190–93; generalization of 190; modelling in 190, 194–95; reinforcement in 190, 195
assessment 98–140: and analysing problems 106–10; and behavioural indicators 110–12; and contemporary behaviour 100; and problem hierarchies 112–15; in assertion training 189, 190–91; of cognitive and emotional factors 100, 137–41; of problematic behaviour 37, 99; qualitative 137; quantitative measurement in 115; stages in 103–06
assets of clients 105, 114–15
associations 39, 46, 80, 83, 200, 201
assumptions: of orthodox behaviourism 39; of psychoanalytic social work 31
attention, need for 57, 72, 111, 144, 146, 147, 159–60, 177, 184, 185
attitude change 12, 87, 90, 91, 97, 189
authoritarianism 36
autistic children 70
avertion therapy 36, 230
'awfulizing' 207–09

baseline data 115, 118–20, 123, 126–30, 133–36, 227, 246–50
bed-wetting 101, 176
behaviour: and thinking styles 140; as symptomatic 24–6, 30–2, 36–7; causes of maladaptive 174; cognitive

controls in 204; deficits in 99, 143, 181, 182, 186; demonstrating 182; descriptions of 35–6, 164; excesses in 99; experimentation in 51, 74, 138; flow of 29–30; general suppression of 50, 68, 70; high-probability *v.* low-probability 146–47, 159–60; incompatible with unwanted responses 143, 150; long-term change in 60, 64, 123–25, 126, 128; medical model of 30–6; operant 51, 52; origins of 23–8, 30–2; patterns of 28–9, 118; practising 11, 80, 94–5, 121, 182, 184–85, 186–87; predictors of 62, 101, 107, 144, 199; qualitative change in 98–9, 137; rates of 63, 65, 118–19, 149; reductions in unacceptable 169–70; shaping of *see* shaping; short-term change in 64; specificity of 199; spontaneity of 24, 162; stable measures of 119; target levels of 120–21, 153; withholding of 99; *see also under descriptive headings, e.g., deviant, helpful, etc.*
behaviour modification: abuse of 226–27, 230, 239–40; and coercion 231; and conformity 240; and control of behaviour 223–25, 231–35, 239–40; and manipulation 237–38; and motivation 233–37; cognitive 202–11; criticisms of 222–25, 243; in institutions 237–42; interruptions in programmes of 128, 130, 133; learning *v.* control in 230–33; long-term effects of 60, 64, 123–25, 126, 128; openness to inspection of 230; overdetachment of 230–31; power of 224; prevalence of punishment in 232; response control techniques in 180–221; stimulus control (contingency management) techniques in 143–79; tangibility of 3; targets of 242–43; techniques for 143–44; with groups 156
behavioural assessment interview 106
behavioural indicators 110–12, 209–10
behaviourism: definition of 26–7; interest in 3; philosophical implications of 23–37; theoretical basis of 38–9
beliefs 138, 139, 204–05, 209
biofeedback 88, 219, 221
'black box' 24, 76, 77, 81
boredom 72
brain 27, 85, 95

British research 13–14
bullying 181

Cannon-Bard theory 95, 96
case records 108–09
caseloads 18–19
case-sharing 19
casework 10–11, 14
chaining 176, 182
change 16, 130, 222: desire for 199; in attitude 12, 87, 90, 91, 97, 189; long-term 60, 64, 123–25, 126, 128; potential for 17
children 20, 75, 110, 127, 134, 147, 157, 159–61, 174, 184, 212–13
circumstances of behaviour 101
clients: achievements of 88, 144–45; and reinforcement 'packages' 144–45; and self-control programmes 199–202; and therapist variables 16–18; assets of 105, 114–15; consent to therapeutic programmes 237, 240–41; cooperation by 118, 234, 237; discussing conclusions with 106; explaining behaviour modification programmes to 146; manipulation of 16, 145, 146, 237–38; need for understanding by 100; own view of problems 18, 113; resistance to social work 223; response to reinforcement 148; right not to be 'helped' 237; selection of reinforcers by 147; talking with 9–10, 11–12; time spent with 18–19
clinging 160–61
closed circuit TV 185, 194
coercion 70, 164, 170, 231, 237–38
cognitive behaviour modification 202–11: aims of 207; and paranoia 204–06; and sexual deviance 210–11; behavioural indicators in 209–10; cognitive restructuring in 207–10; covert conditioning in 210–11; procedures in 205–06; reasons for 202–03; self-instructional training in 203–06; stress innoculation training in 206–07, 208; thought stopping in 211; use of imagery in 206
cognitive controls 204
cognitive factors, assessment of 137–41
cognitive learning 76, 80–6
cognitive-mediational theories 89, 90, 198, 203
cognitive restructuring 207–10

Subject index 269

cognitive structures 81–3
commonsense 28
communication 68, 102–03, 189
community 69, 169–79, 234–35
community schools 159, 174
compliance 188, 189, 192, 193, 195, 198, 223
compulsive eating 200–01
conclusions, discussion with client 106
conditionability 44–5
conditioning: classical 39, 41–51; coverant 81–2; covert 210–11; operant 39, 51–73, 74
confidentiality 228
consciousness 27–8, 30
consent to therapeutic programmes 237, 240–41
consequences of actions 99
consistency in approach 20
contemporary behaviour 100
contingencies: behaviour as influence on 86–7; new 143; possibilities for changing 143–44; rearrangement of 142; uncontrollable 181
contingency management 143–79: chaining in 176; contracts in 161–73, 178; differential reinforcement in 148–53; discriminative stimuli in 179; fading in 175–76, 179; in institutions 238; in self-control programmes 199–200; naturalness in 145–46; negative reinforcement in 173–74, 178; operant extinction in 173, 178; over-learning in 176, 179; positive reinforcement in 177–78; Premack's principle in 178; prompting in 176; punishment in 178; response cost schemes in 153–55; selection of reinforcers for 144–48; shaping in 175, 179; summary of 177–79; token economies in 155–59, 177–78
contracts 161–73, 178: bad practice in 167–69, 172; between parents and children 164–69; between social workers and clients 172; between spouses 172–73; controversial 169–70; design of 164–70; equality in 164, 167–69, 170–71; general points about 167, 170–72; negotiating 170–73; specificity of 164; temporary nature of 171–72
control 223–25, 231–32, 239–40
conversation 98, 186–87

cooperation from clients 118, 234, 237
coping skills 184, 204, 206–07, 208, 215
counter-conditioning techniques 210, 212–213, 220
covert conditioning 210–11
craving 53–4
creative responses 81–2, 84
criticism: of behaviour modification 222–25, 243; sensitivity to 185
cruelty 227–28, 229, 231
crying, excessive 174

Daily Mirror 169
data gathering 116–18
daydreaming 85
decision-making 84
delusional talk 128, 132, 133
demand effects 98
demonstration: of behaviour 182; of efficacy of behaviour modification 130, 133
depression 110, 112, 123, 201–02, 203
deprivation 56, 68, 147, 153, 154–55, 226
desensitization 80, 88, 190, 195–96, 206, 213, 216–18, 220–21
designs: A.B. 21–5, 119–20; A.B.A. 127–9; A.B.A.B. 129–33; B.A. 126–27; B.A.B. 133–34; multiple baseline 134–35, 136
despecialization 20–1
deviant behaviour 36, 39, 68, 69
diagnosis of problems 30–2, 33–5, 105, 186
diary schemes 153
differential reinforcement 63, 73, 143, 148–53, 160, 227
direct observation 116
dirt phobia 215
disciplinary problems 71, 136
discrimination 60–2, 70, 107, 149, 156, 159, 182, 190–93
discriminative stimuli 60–2, 84, 140, 144, 176, 177, 179
disruptive behaviour 71–2, 120, 149–53, 173
dissonance reduction 223
drinking problems 53–4
dualism 24–6
durability of reinforcement 148

effectiveness of social work 6–10, 12–13, 14, 15

270 Behaviour Modification

eliciting stimuli 62, 101, 107, 144, 199
emotions 92–7: analysis of 92–3; and compliance 195; and images of future events 28; and spinal cord lesions 96; cognitive factors in 96–7, 139; emotional reactions 45–6, 83; physiological components of 93–6; role of brain in 95; theories of 94–7; vicarious experiencing of 76
empathic learning 76–7, 183
empathy, accurate 18
encoding of information 77
environment: ambiguity of 49–50; and behaviour 86–7; dangers of 74; environmental control 28–30; environmental problems 5, 10, 36; punishing 68, 70, 72; unsupportive 50, 68; variability of 44–6, 66
escape behaviour 47, 48, 68, 69, 97, 162, 174
ethical considerations 222–45: and abuse of behaviour modification techniques 226–27, 230, 239–40; and change 222; and coercion 231; and contracts 170; and control of behaviour 223–25, 231–32, 239–40; and effectiveness of therapy 133; and family problems 226–29; and handicapped clients 242; and imposition of techniques 243–44; and learning *v.* control 230–33; and motivational issues 233–37; and punishment 232; and sexual fears 225–26; and targets of behaviour modification 242–43; and uses and abuses of psychological techniques 229–33; ethical requirements in institutions 241; in institutional settings 237–42
evaluation 248–50: and A.B. designs 121–25; and A.B.A. designs 127–29; and A.B.A.B. designs 129–33; and B.A. designs 126–27; and B.A.B. designs 133–34; and baseline data 115, 118–20; and multiple baseline designs 134–35, 136; and setting target levels 120–21; criteria for social work 7–8; data gathering for 116–18; in self-control programmes 199, 202; qualitative 98–9; quantitative 115; records for 115–16
expectations 86–9
experimentation in behaviour 51, 74, 138: cognitive 81–2
explanatory power of theories 33
exploitation 181, 188
extinction 49, 55, 63–5, 143, 144, 148–49, 151–54, 173, 178
eye contact 187, 192, 193, 194

facial expression 194
fading 59–60, 146, 167, 175–76, 179, 182, 232
family problems 110, 112, 130, 133, 161, 226–29
fantasies 201, 206
fashions in social work 1
fear 43–4, 46–8, 88, 91, 140, 182–83, 206–07, 212–18; *see also* phobias
feasibility of programmes 114
feedback 195: sensory 56–7, 76–7; *see also* biofeedback
'fight/flight mechanism' 46, 93–4
financial problems 126–27
fire obsession 111–12, 131, 153, 154–55
flexibility of approach 102, 103
follow-up visits 98, 123–25
formulations of problems 102
foster parents 159–61
free will 28–30
Freudian principles 9

Galvanic Skin Response meter 219
generalization 44–6, 190, 198
generalized reinforcers 56–7, 84, 147
genetic factors 39, 44
genuineness 17–18
gestures 194
goals 7–8, 9, 12–13, 21, 91, 102–03, 229
graphs 115–16
groups, work with 156
guidance for adaptive behaviours 70

helpful behaviour 161–62
'helping' 235, 236–37
helplessness, conditioned 50
history of social work 1, 3–4, 6
holistic approach to social work 3–4
homosexuals, treatment of 230
hostilities, reduction in 163, 166–67
hypotheses, testability of 33, 102

ignoring bad behaviour 150, 153, 154, 174
images 83, 90, 139, 201, 202, 203, 206
imitation 73–4, 75; *see also* modelling

Subject index 271

imposition of techniques 243–44
impulsiveness 204
inappropriate behaviour 99
inborn responses 93
individual *v.* group results 8–9
individuals, work with 10–11, 16–18
influences: control by 224–25; in learning 40–1
information, organization of 77–8
inner events 39, 100, 137–41, 189, 202–03; *see also* cognitive behaviour modification; emotions
inner sources of behaviour 23–7
inner speech 78, 83–4, 90, 139, 192, 201–08
insights into problems 11–12, 84
institutionalization 239
institutions 155–59, 223, 237–42
intentions 106–07
internal predispositions 69
interpreting 83–5, 86
intimidation 154
intrusiveness of approaches 137
isolation rooms 152, 154, 174

James-Lange theory 94–5, 96
judgement, reliance on 23, 154–55
juvenile delinquency 234–35

labelling 32, 34, 35, 36, 101–02
learning 38–91: accompaniments of 77–8; and contracts 170; and modelling 73–80; 181–87; and reinforcement 52–8; and shaping of behaviour 59–60; classical conditioning in 41–4; cognitive 77–86; cognitive mediation in 76, 77–8; definition of 40; empathetic 76–7; in behaviour modification programmes 126, 128, 130; influences in 40–1; insight 84; intention in 40; of coping skills 204, 206–07, 208, 215; of discrimination 156; operant conditioning in 51–73; preparedness for 44; social 86–9; stimuli in 41–6; stimulus generalization in 44–6; vicarious 75, 76, 86
learning history 100–01
long-term effects of behaviour modification 60, 64, 123–25, 126, 128

machine, man as 24–7

maladaptive behaviour 65–6
'man from Mars' technique 106
manipulation of clients 16, 145, 146, 237–38
manipulation of environment, successful 56–7
marital problems 172–73, 227–29
Marriage Guidance Council 228
matched-control studies 7–9, 14
mechanical aids to observation 117
mechanical approaches 17–18, 145, 244
mediators 19–21, 114: acceptability of 20; agreement among 159; and reinforcement 148; demands on 158; observation by 117; tasks of 19–20
medical model of behaviour 30–6, 105
medical profession 5, 34–5, 46
memory 81
mental handicap 142, 147
mind, concept of 23–7
mind-body relationship 24–8
misunderstandings between clients and social workers 106
modelling 73–80, 181–87, 219: and anxiety 80; and closed circuit TV 185; and coping skills 184; and empathetic learning 76–7, 183; and imitation 73–4, 75; and response range 75; and shaping 185; and vicarious learning 75, 76, 86; cognitively mediated 76, 77–8; credibility in 183–84; in assertion training 190, 194–95; optimum conditions for 183–85; settings for 185; stages in 182; to reduce fears 182–83; uses of 78–80, 181; verbal labelling in 184
'moral neutrality' 229
motivation 105, 113, 233–37
'muddling through' 68
multi-problem families 90, 135
mutual control in relationships 161–62

naturalness in therapy 145–46
needs, asserting 192
negotiation 170–73
nervous system 45, 93
neurosis, conditioned 49–50
non-material reinforcers 146
non-verbal behaviour 186, 187

observations, number of 119
obsessive thoughts 203, 211

obstacles for social workers 22
old people's homes 232–33
opinions, asserting 192
opportunities for behaviour modification 238–39
oppression 188, 230
outspokenness 190–92
overdetachment 230–31
overgeneralized behaviour 62
over-learning 176, 179

paranoia 204–06
participant observation 117
patients, condescending attitudes towards 34–5
Pavlovian concepts 41–4, 49
peer approval 111, 183
perceived self-efficacy 87–9, 90, 183
perception 139
personal constructs 138, 139
personal hygiene 187
philosophical implications of behaviourism 23–29
phobias 46–9, 105, 182–83, 213–18, 225–26
physiological components of emotion 93–6
placebo effects 88, 91, 122
pleasure centres 94
points system 157
posture 194
power structures 237–38
practising new behaviours 11, 80, 94–5, 121, 182, 184–85, 186–87
praise, need for 145, 185, 202
predictors of behaviour 62, 101, 107, 144, 199
Premack's principle 146–47, 159–69, 178
preparedness for learning 44
priorities: in intervention 113–15; of social work 4–5
Private Eye 162
problems: affection 225–26; behavioural components in 110; causes of 100; drinking 53–4; emotional 93; environmental 5, 10, 36; family 110, 112, 130, 133, 161, 226–29; financial 126–27; hierarchies of 112–15; in institutions 239–41; insights into 11–12, 84; interconnected 108, 110–11, 114; interpersonal 161–73; marital 172, 227–29; natural course of 122–23; psychological 12; social 8, 31
problem-solving attempts 50, 68, 84, 167: creative 81–2, 84
process *v.* outcome 14–15
prognosis of problems 35
progress cards 150–51
prompting 176
prophesies, self-fulfilling 31–3, 36, 37, 207
pro-social behaviour 56
proximity of clients to therapists 238
psychiatrists, poor diagnostic ability of 34–5
psychoanalysis in social work 30–3
psychological problems 12
psychological techniques, uses and abuses of 229
psychotic patients 147, 203
public transport phobia 215–16
punishment 66–70, 178: advantages of 69, 70; and response cost schemes 143–44, 153–55; as oppression 230; as part of environment 68, 70, 72; by deprivation 68, 147, 153, 154–55, 226; definition of 66–8; disadvantages of 69–70; in cognitive behaviour modification 211; in contracts 171; in interpersonal relationships 162, 227–29

qualitative change 98–9, 137

rapid exposure techniques 206, 213–16, 220
rare behaviour, reinforcing 64, 69, 80, 121, 143
Rational-Emotive approach 207
'reciprocal inhibition' 212
reciprocal reinforcement 161
reconciliation 162–63, 170
recording data 115–16
reinforcement: and conditioned reinforcers 54–6, 60, 138, 156; and generalized reinforcers 56–7, 84, 147; and personal constructs 138; and primary reinforcers 55–6; and satiation schemes 175; and selection of reinforcers 144–48; and self-reinforcement 200, 201, 205–06; and token economy schemes 56, 146, 147, 155–59, 177, 240; anticipated 75, 81–2; as process 145; checklists for

Subject index 273

147; clients' response to 148; delays in 55–6; differential 63, 73, 143, 148–53, 160, 227; fading of 59–60; feasibility of 147–48; in assertion training 190, 195; naturalness of 145–46; negative 53–4, 66, 72, 84, 143, 173–74, 178; positive 52–3, 72, 143, 177; Premack's principle in 146–47, 159–60, 178; schedules of 62–6; specificity of 146; unpredictability of 65
relapse, behavioural 60
relationships: and assertion training 188; balance in 161, 163; maintenance of 17; mutual control in 161–62; negotiation in 167; problems in 161–73; punishment in 162, 227–29; reciprocal reinforcement in 161, 163; reconciliation in 162–63, 170; reduction of hostilities in 163, 166–67
relaxation 206, 211, 213, 216–19
reliability checks 118
remedial reading schemes 151
report cards 175–76
requests, making 192
research:
 into diagnosis 34–5;
 into social work 7–9, 13–14
residential settings *see* institutions
resources of social work 18–19, 235
responding, levels of 63, 65, 118–19, 149
response control techniques 180–221: and anxiety reduction 212–19, 220–21; and assertion training 188–98, 220; and cognitive behaviour 202–11, 220; and modelling 181–87, 219; and self-control techniques 198–202, 220; and social skill training 184–85, 186–87, 219; reasons for 180–81; summary of 219–21
response cost schemes 143–44, 153–55, 231
responses: trimming of 63; wide range of 75, 198
responsibilities of social workers 3
retribution 235
revenge motives 69
rewards *see* reinforcement
right to independence 236–37
ritualistic behaviour 175, 206
rules, learning of 84–5
rumination 85

safety considerations 130

salivation, conditioned 41–2, 44–5
satiation 148, 175, 179
schedules of reinforcement 62–6:
 continuous 63–4; differential
 reinforcement 64; fixed ratio 63;
 intermittent 64–5; variable ratio 65–6
schizophrenia 59, 186
school attendance 124
scientific standards 2
security, need for 185
Seebohm reorganization 3
selection of reinforcers 144–48
self-care 110
self-control techniques 89, 198–202, 220: and compulsive eating 200–01; and depression 201–02; and discriminative stimuli 61; and insomnia 200; approaches in 199–200; monitoring of 202; necessity for 198; precautions in 199
self-determination 28–9
self-image 84, 90, 183, 189, 205–06
self-instructional training 203–06
self-observation 117–18
self-reinforcement 200, 201, 205–06
sensory:
 deprivation 85;
 feedback 56–7, 76–7
settings of behaviour modification programmes 148
sexual: counselling 127, 129; deviance 210–11; exhibitionism 141; fears 225–26
shaping: and ethical considerations 232; and learning 59–60, 93, 182; and modelling 80, 185; in contingency management 175, 179; in dangerous environments 74; in response cost schemes 144; in variable ration schedules 65; unintentional 16
short-term changes in behaviour 64
shyness 186, 195
'sickness' 31
signals for behaviour 62, 101, 107, 144, 199
single case experimental designs (SCEDs) 115–37
Skinner box 52, 54
sleep problems 127, 200
slow exposure 217, 220
social: confidence 124; gaffs 61; problems 8, 31; rules 59
Social Learning Theory 86–9

social skills: deficits in 69; training in 184–85, 186–87, 219
social work: and 'helping' v. retribution 235; as last resort 224; despecialization of 20–1; diversity of 4–5; effectiveness of 6–10, 12–13, 14, 15, 224; evaluation criteria for 7–8; fashions in 1; goals of 7–8, 9, 12–13, 21, 91, 102–03, 229; history of 1, 3–4, 6; holistic approach to 3–4; limitations of 223; priorities of 4–5; problems of 22; process v. outcome in 14–15; psychoanalysis in 30–3; qualitative effects of 8; research into 7–9, 13–14; resources of 18–19, 235; teamwork in 19; therapeutic ability of 235–37; with individuals 10–11, 16–18
social workers: and control 223; and controversial contracts 169–70; and making judgements 23; and modelling 183–84; and public expectations 235; and supervision 234–35; as models 170; caseloads of 18–19; obstacles for 22; responsibilities of 3
socialization 59, 73–4
soiling 226–28
spinal cord lesions 96
spontaneity 24, 162
spontaneous remission 123
stable measures of behaviour 135
statistical analysis of marginal results 247–50
status 20, 183
stimuli: ambiguous 49–50; and stimulus-response connections 44–6, 47–8, 82, 202; aversive 53–4, 66–8, 70, 143; 'bundles' of 48–9; context of 83; discriminative 60–2, 84, 140, 144, 176, 177, 179; eliciting 62, 101, 107, 144, 199; generalization of 44–6; in learning 41–6
stimulus control 143–79; see also contingency management
stimulus-response connections 44–6, 47–8, 82, 202
stress 206–07, 208, 214, 215
stress innoculation training 206–07, 208
subtlety in rule breaking 154, 155
superstitious behaviour 65
supervision 182, 234–35, 238–39
support: for clients 17; for staff 158–59
symptoms 30, 31, 34–5, 36–7
symptom-substitution 31, 33, 36–7
syndromes 31, 34

talking with clients 9–10, 11–12
tangible rewards 144–45; see also token economies
tantrums 66, 119, 159, 160
target levels of behaviour 120–21, 153
tautologies 28, 30, 31
teachers 151, 152–53, 173, 225–26
teamwork 19
testability of theories 1–3, 33, 37
theoretical approaches 10, 32–3, 105
therapeutic: methods 2; relationships 11, 17; strategies and motivation 234
therapist variables 15–18
therapy: discrimination in providing 236, 237, 242–43; limitations of 235–37
thinking 25–6
thinking styles 84, 138, 139, 140, 202, 207–10
thought control 141, 153, 203, 210–11
thought experiments 81–2
threats 192
'time out' 152, 160
time sampling 116–17
time spent with clients 18–19
token economies 56, 146, 147, 155–59, 177, 240
treatment, specificity of 35
trust between client and therapist 215

unconditional acceptance 16–17
unpredictability, behavioural results of 50
unpredictability of reinforcement 65
urgency of problems 113

variables in intervention 122
verbal approaches 88, 181
verbal labelling 77, 184
vicarious: experience 88; extinction 80, 183; learning 75, 76, 86; suppression 69
visceral feedback 94–5, 96
visits: follow-up 98, 123–25; supervisory 19
voice 194–95

warmth, non-possessive 16–17
warnings after bad behaviour 152, 154, 155
withdrawn behaviour 134